D1520721

MARK FERGUSON

# Build a Rental Property Empire

*The no-nonsense book on finding deals, financing the right way, and managing wisely.*

Fifth edition

Editing by Greg Helmerick
Typesetting by Justin Gesso
Cover art by Pixel Studio

This book was professionally typeset on Reedsy.
Find out more at reedsy.com

# Contents

# Praise for Build a Rental Property Empire

I have been following Mark Ferguson for a while now. Reading his information on InvestFourMore, getting his emails, and learning about how to run a business in rentals is great. I have a couple properties, but I am still in the brand-new phase, so looking at this book and all it has to offer is wonderful.

If you have questions about starting or working in the rental field, working as a real estate agent, and all the things in between, you should pick up a copy for yourself. Working at a regular job is great, but having something that you are building yourself is even better.

I am retiring from the military soon, and having another career to start is wonderful, and one of those careers is running a rental business. I am learning more so I can do well for my family, and being able to pass this on to others is very rewarding. Enjoy! - *Mack Shaffer*

This is a terrific and practical guide on how to work on your real estate business (not in it). Mark knows exactly what it is like to work in the Real Estate trenches as an agent, investor, flipper, and owner of rental properties. I have implemented many of Mark's concepts in my business and am already seeing a difference (offers on bank-owned properties now being accepted!). I appreciated Mark's insights on financing and managing my business. This book is useful for both novices and experts in Real Estate. - *Kim Martin*

I have been following Mark online for over a year now. I have learned many things through his blog, podcast, etc. that have helped me in building my rental portfolio. If you are looking for some straight-to-the-point, no nonsense approaches to learning about real estate investing, Mark is the guy. He is well-versed in many areas of real estate. You should definitely get this book. - *Corey Paszkeiwicz*

A truly insightful resource for anyone looking to get into purchasing rental properties. The book goes over, in-depth, all aspects related to the topic and even touches on many other aspects of rental properties that you would never think of originally. I highly recommend this well-written and easy-to-read book as a foundation for yourself before going out into the investing world. - *Jeremiah Dalton*

This book is filled with real-life examples and information from someone who's fully engaged in real estate investing. It's not HGTV, and it's not a book of theory from a real estate training corporation. It's a real guy doing "real" real estate.

Mark has great ideas on deciding whether you want rental properties or not, how to determine what to buy, how to finance, and when to keep or sell. I've been investing for many years, and Mark's book has given me many ideas on how to deal with the challenges investors face. This is one of the more practical books on real estate investing that I've read, and I read a lot of them. - *Eric Snell*

# Dedication

Thank you to my real estate team, who make all of this possible.

# Special Bonus and Investing Tools

I try to include as much information in my books as I possibly can. This book isn't meant to get you to sign up for a high-dollar coaching program. This is a step-by-step guide to investing in rental properties.

Some people both want and would like more information about me and real estate. If that's you or you just want updates on my investments, check out Investfourmore.com.

I have many free resources, an awesome podcast, and much more on my website.

I have written multiple books, created video coaching programs, and created coaching programs taught personally by me. A couple of my coaching programs include personal coaching calls and emails. If you are looking for more, check out the link below, which includes a special discount for those who buy my books.

Either way, enjoy the book!

https://investfourmore.com/bonus

# How to Use This Book

This book is all about rental properties and what I have learned about them over the years. Not only have I learned about rentals from buying, financing, managing, and selling them, but I have also learned so much from other investors and from research I have done for my blog.

This book is an encyclopedia of sorts, but it is written to be read from front to back. Before I started my blog, I thought I knew everything about real estate investing. Boy was I wrong! We can always learn new tips, tricks, and techniques. I tried to include everything I could in this book, and the table of contents lists the main topics by chapter to make navigation simpler.

I also discuss many different strategies in this book. There is no one-size-fits-all concept for real estate investing. We all have different goals and incomes, live in different areas, and have varying amounts of time we can spend on investing. Some strategies may be perfect for you, while you may not be ready for others.

Why should you listen to me? Below are a few of my career highlights (I am 39 now). I am not someone who just writes about hypothetical success—I have experienced it, and I am still actively pursuing it. As of this book's 2018 publication/update:

I own 20 rentals that generate about $12,000 in monthly income. I bought each rental with 20 or 25% down and for at least 25% below market value. Much of this book was written when I had 16 rentals. I have bought commercial rental since it was published.

My 20 rentals, which I started buying in 2010, have over $2 million in equity, and I invested about $300,000 to buy and renovate.

I have been a Realtor/broker for over 15 years and own my own brokerage: Blue Steel Real Estate.

I flip 20 to 30 houses yearly. I flipped 26 houses in 2017.

I started InvestFourMore.com in 2013, and it has since become one of the most popular real estate blogs around, with over 300,000 views each month.

I have been featured on the Washington Post, MSN, Yahoo, Zillow, Realtor.com, The Street, Forbes, The Huffington Post, and many other large media outlets.

I am a member of the Forbes Real Estate Council

In this book, you'll find a lot of information and many techniques that can become overwhelming. Do not try to do everything at once! If you only learn one thing on your first read, it will help you. The next time you read it, you might implement a few other things and slowly start building a solid foundation for success. If you focus on mastering one thing, you will be much more successful than if you halfway do 10 things at once.

If you like this book, please let me know: Mark@investfourmore.com. I personally respond to all emails and love hearing from my readers. I also would really appreciate any reviews you're willing to leave me on Amazon. If you are looking for a little more help or even more details, I offer additional resources on my blog: https://investfourmore.com/resources/.

# 1

# Introduction

Although I am successful now, I wasn't always. No, I never lived in my car or was down to $6 in my bank account. However, in my younger years, I did struggle as a real estate agent and investor. In 2006, I decided to fix up a flip myself. I replaced the windows, kitchen, baths, flooring, paint, doors, fixtures, and much more all on my own. I thought I would save so much money by doing the manual labor. I was wrong!

Fixing that house myself was the biggest mistake I ever made, but it was also a great learning experience. I made less than $30,000 that year, was stressed out beyond belief, and knew I had to change things. I started setting goals, taking responsibility for my actions, and working smarter. I became a better agent, flipped more houses, and knew I had to invest my money more wisely. The best investment I could find was rental properties.

I bought my first rental property in December 2010. I wanted to invest in rentals well before 2010, but things took a lot longer than I had hoped they would. Life always seemed to get in the way, whether it was buying a personal house, getting married, trying to have kids, or something else. In 2010, I decided enough was enough—I was going to buy a rental. I would figure out the money situation and the life situation, and I would start creating a better future for me and my family.

Even though my wife was pregnant with twins in the fall of 2010, I was able to get my first rental under contract. I used conventional financing

1

because I did not know any better. The process was a nightmare! Getting the loan took almost two months, even though my lender said it would take one. They wanted an incredible number of personal financial details. They wanted an explanation for every deposit exceeding $1,000 in my personal accounts for the past two years. I would give the lender all the information they requested, and then they would request more!

I managed to buy that house, and it has been a great investment. I bought my next rental property less than one year later, and then I really started to ramp things up. I bought three more the next year. As of September 2015, I own 16 rental properties, and I plan to buy many more.

My goal is to make cash flow with every rental property I purchase. My 16 rentals bring in over $8,000 in monthly income. That is not the full rent but rather money in my pocket after accounting for all expenses, including mortgage payments, taxes, insurance, maintenance, and vacancies. Not only do my rentals generate $8,000 each month, but they have also increased my net worth by over one million dollars. Through a mix of buying below market value, increasing value through repairs, and appreciation, my properties have done very well. Making that kind of money from rentals isn't easy, and it doesn't happen overnight. However, it isn't rocket science, and almost anyone can buy rentals. The trick is making sure you buy the right properties, knowing how to manage them, and developing a strategy that allows you to keep buying rentals until you reach financial freedom.

I wrote this book to show people what I have learned over the years as a real estate agent, real estate investor, and blogger. When I started my blog—*InvestFourMore.com*—in 2013, I thought I knew most everything about real estate, but boy was I wrong! There are so many strategies and techniques out there that beginners can find it very intimidating. In these pages, I discuss the most feasible and achievable techniques to help people realize the awesome power of real estate and how to start investing in real estate the right way.

# 2

# Why Rental Properties Will Help You Retire Faster than Investing in the Stock Market

I received a degree in business finance from the University of Colorado in 2001. While at college—and even in high school—I took many financial and business classes. I thought I learned a lot about the finance world, but what I realize now is they taught me almost nothing about real estate, alternative ways to invest, or how to make money.

We were told to go to college, get a good job, invest money in the stock market, and retire at 65. They say the stock market is the best way to accumulate retirement income because of steady returns over time. If you have seen those retirement calculators that tell you how much to save based on how long you want to live, you know the amount they recommend is staggering! For most, to make your money last in retirement, you must be frugal while spending less than you did before you retired.

Whether by accident or by luck, I managed to get into the real estate industry. I discovered it's an incredible way to invest money and set myself up to retire early. The key to achieving early retirement is investing in rental properties that produce cash flow month after month.

When I graduated from college, I could not find a finance-industry job that

I loved. I decided to work part-time for my father, who had been a real estate agent since 1978. He loved the business and had always made decent money, but I never wanted to be in the industry. I was constantly around real estate (when I was a toddler, I slept under his desk in the office), and I wanted to make my own path. Over time, I realized how much I liked real estate while noticing my friends hated their jobs. I ended up getting my real estate license, becoming an agent, and learning how to invest in fix-and-flips.

## Who wants to retire at 65?

In the beginning of my real estate career, I never earned more than $50,000, and some years, I earned much less. I was trying to save money, and thinking it was what I was supposed to do, I invested in the stock market. However, I began to realize I was not living my life to its full potential.

I have loved exotic cars since I was a kid. As a young adult, my dream of owning exotic cars had all but vanished thanks to society telling me how to live and me not pushing back and realizing how much more there was to life. As an agent, I was fairly happy and loved flipping houses, but I couldn't afford any exotic cars with the money I was making. I knew I had to change the way I did things to have a better life.

Instead of following in my father's footsteps (he was a traditional agent), I started to make my own career in real estate. I listed HUD homes and REO properties, which allowed me to break away from the traditional real estate model. When I started to make more and more money, I realized that my stock-market investments were not growing very fast. I had no control over my investments, and the retirement calculators were depressing. I would have to wait too long to retire, and I would not have a very enjoyable life in retirement either. I seriously started to wonder why everyone was so set on investing in the stock market and waiting 30 to 40 years before they could retire.

I decided retiring at 65 was not the choice I would make. I am not saying I do not like work, but I do not want to work that long. If you make a modest salary and invest in the stock market or mutual funds, you may not even be able to retire at 65 unless you make huge sacrifices. Those sacrifices might mean living an extremely frugal life before and after retirement. To retire early without living frugally, you need to change the way you invest or get a much higher-paying job. I like the idea of having a high-paying job and investing more money, but this book is about investing your money better—not earning higher income.

## There is a better way to save for retirement than investing in the stock market

The biggest problem I have with conventional wisdom regarding retirement plans is we must guess when we are going to die. We use a retirement calculator to find out how much money we will need and put an age in the equation to make sure we do not run out of money. If you get lucky and live too long, guess what: you run out of money and must work at Walmart handing shopping carts to people! How depressing is trying to guess when you are going to die and hoping you do not live too long. This is a horrible thought, feeling, and way to live. One reason I love investing in rental properties is you do not have to guess when you are going to die!

I did as much research as I could on the best ways to invest money. I read many books and tried to keep an open mind, even though I was in the real estate industry. I looked at the stock market, at bonds, at starting a franchise, at REITs, and at tax liens. All the research I did pointed towards rental properties as the best investment. The great thing about real estate is that if you invest for cash flow, you have money coming in every month for as long as you own the properties.

The cash flow on my rental properties comes in without eating away at the principle balance of my investment. If I earn $5,000 per month from rental properties, that $5,000 is going to keep coming in every month until I sell or refinance my properties. The cash flow will most likely increase as rents go up and as I pay off my mortgages over time. With rentals, I do not have to calculate when I am going to die or worry about outliving my savings. Instead of guessing how long I am going to live, I can calculate how much monthly income I need and buy enough investment properties to meet that need. Once I hit whatever monthly number I need or want, I will be financially free. I can retire, start a new business, or if I really want the finer things in life or to leave a legacy, I can keep going.

Rental properties do not have to be a ton of work either. You will earn income while doing minimal work every year for the rest of your life. You can hire a property manager and let someone else worry about repairs and vacancies. I spend almost no time on my rentals (except when I first buy them) because someone else manages them.

Many investors end up quitting their day jobs and concentrating on investing in rental properties at a very young age. They buy a couple of properties and realize what a great investment they are. I know many real estate investors who quit their day jobs before they were 40 and now live solely on their rental income. How much money would you have to put into the stock market to accomplish that? I invested about $300,000 in my rentals to generate $8,000 per month, and I am 37. To create that much cash flow every month via the stock market, I would have had to invest millions.

## Rental properties can be the best route to passive income

I won't sugar-coat things: purchasing and locating your first investment property takes money and discipline. Once you learn how to invest in properties that will generate passive income, the process becomes much easier. The more properties you buy and the sooner you get started, the easier it gets. It is possible to buy three properties per year for ten years if you are smart with your money, use techniques to buy with little money down, and use your cash flow to buy more properties. Many people may find this difficult to accomplish, but it is possible with hard work, a budget, and a willingness to act fast. Even if you can afford only one property each year for ten years, you can bring in significant passive income.

These numbers may seem ridiculous, but it is entirely possible to make that much money with rentals. Not everyone will do it because it is not easy. Finding the right properties, saving money to invest, and finding the right lenders takes work. In addition, staying on track takes discipline.

My current rentals all generate 15% or more in cash-on-cash returns. Those returns do not include appreciation, equity paydown, or tax savings. I consider those factors bonuses on top of my cash flow. While you may not be able to get quite as high a return as I do, rentals can still be a fantastic investment for almost anyone if you invest the right way.

## I am not a frugal guy

My blog, InvestFourMore.com, could be considered a financial blog since I talk a lot about investing and retirement. However, my blog is not like most financial sites you come across. Most retirement blogs are based on living frugally and making a little money last a long time. Personally, I want to buy as many rentals as possible so I can retire as early as possible with as much passive income as possible. I do not want to penny pinch and worry about what I can afford. I want to be happy and able to afford whatever I want for my family and myself.

If you want to be successful in anything, it takes sacrifice. I saved money for a long time when I was younger. I never had a car payment until I was 28, and I still have never bought a new car. Does that mean I do not enjoy life? No! I own a 6,600-square-foot house and a Lamborghini Diablo. I am a strong believer in investing in what you love. Not only do I invest in rental properties and flips, but I also invest in things that make me happy. I am not talking about buying an SUV every year to keep up with your neighbors. I am talking about figuring out what really makes you happy and investing in those things. Some people may be happy with living abroad for years on a tight budget. Others may be happy with a condo on the beach, and some people may want more.

When I stopped letting society tell me what I should invest in, how much money I should be happy with, and which things should make me happy, I became a much happier person. I started setting incredible goals, pushing myself further, and achieving more. Things I thought I would never get in my entire life came to me before I was 35. I am definitely not done.

This book is not about goal setting and self-improvement, although I think those are vitally important to success. My point is you do not have to live frugally and give up the things you love to retire early and be financially free.

# Why rental properties are a better path to retirement than the stock market

In a recent survey, 59% of people said they are afraid they will outlive their retirement. People should worry about outliving their retirement if they use traditional methods, such as the stock market, to prepare for retirement. However, there are many ways to prep for retirement, including ways that safeguard you from running out of money. Rental properties are already providing me with great income that will last my entire life. I will never have to worry about outliving my savings.

Rental properties can take a great deal of cash to buy initially, but in the end, you can make much more retirement income with rental properties than with the stock market.

## Why do Americans worry so much about outliving their retirement?

With traditional retirement methods, you save as much money as possible over as many years as possible. The longer you save, the faster your money will grow thanks to compounding interest. Compounding interest is fantastic for growing your money, but compounded interest is not the reason traditional retirement methods are scary. The scary part is that after you retire and stop saving, you start spending your savings.

If you use a retirement calculator from any retirement website, you must enter how long you think you'll live and your target retirement age. The calculator assumes you will use the income your savings produces plus the principal balance until you run out of money. If you plan to live to 80 but end up living to be 85, you might have to go back to work or cut back on spending in your later years.

## What return will you get from the stock market?

Retirement calculators require an average yearly return to determine how much someone needs to retire, which is usually a suggested yearly return of 7 to 10%. Historical average stock market returns are over 7%, but many retirement calculators still suggest a higher return. Remember, a historical average of 7% does not guarantee a future gain of 7%. We saw negative returns in the 2000s and huge returns more recently. The longer you invest, the more likely you will see historical averages. The shorter the time you invest, the more likely you will see big gains or losses. If you want to retire early, you'll hopefully realize big gains...not big losses.

The uncertainty in the stock market makes it a very scary way to invest. A difference of a few percentage points in returns can mean running out of money five or ten years sooner than you had planned.

People have varying amounts of time to dedicate to investing. I am a real estate agent, which is a huge advantage. The average investor may not realize returns of 15% when they buy rental properties, but they can realize returns of 10% or higher if they take the time to learn to invest. Returns on rentals are based on supply and demand of rental properties in local housing markets. In my experience, rental rates in most areas are much more stable than the stock market. Even during the last housing crisis, when we saw housing prices plummet, rents did not drop nearly as much.

Another thing to consider is those returns are based solely on the cash flow from rental properties, not any appreciation, tax advantages, or equity paydown. Returns end up being much higher when you consider the tax savings and equity pay down. Appreciation is a nice bonus as well, but you will not actually see that money unless you refinance or sell the property.

## Why stock market returns are not as high as they appear

7% is a good return to many people, but I want a better return. I like the 15 to 20% cash-on-cash returns I realize from my rentals. The 7% historical stock return is not really the true return because it does not consider inflation. If you consider inflation, the return drops to 4.4%. You will also have brokerage fees when you invest in the stock market, and many 401ks have fees in addition to the brokerage fees! Check out Tony Robbin's book: MONEY Master the Game to get the full picture of the fees they charge you.

Rental properties also naturally hedge against inflation. When inflation rises, housing prices and rental rates naturally rise. My rents will keep increasing over time as inflation increases, and I will not have to deduct the historical inflation rate from my returns. In fact, inflation actually increases my returns. I get loans that allow me to put 20% down. If I buy a $100,000 rental property, I put $20,000 down. If the house value rises $35,000 over ten years, (this would be the increase with 3% inflation) my increase in equity would be higher than the inflation rate. My increase in equity would actually be 8% each year because I did not buy the house with 100% down.

## Why you can retire earlier using rental properties than you can with the stock market

If you want to retire at 65 and assume you will live to 85, you will need enough savings to cover 20 years. If you want to retire at 45, you will have to have enough savings to last 40 years. Not only will you have to save much more money to last the extra 20 years, but you will have much less time to invest and save, which means your money will not grow as fast. Compounding interest has a bigger effect on your money the longer you invest it.

If you invest $100,000 and earn a 7% return on your investment, it will grow to just under $200,000 in ten years. If you invest it for 20 years, it will grow to $386,000. If you invest it for 30 years, it will grow to $761,000. The huge advantage to compound interest occurs in the later investing years. If you can invest that $100,000 for 40 years, it will grow to almost $1.5 million.

When you retire young, you do not have time to see your money grow exponentially, and you will have to invest a huge amount of money for it to last 40 years. For me to produce $6,000 per month from the stock market for the next 50 years, I would need $2.5 million saved already! The funny thing is most retirement calculators do not even let you enter a retirement age below 50. Producing that same $6,000 monthly income from rental properties took me less than $300,000.

## Does the stock market offer better returns than real estate?

There have been many discussions about whether the stock market or real estate produces better returns. Many proponents of the stock market simply point to its historical returns compared to those of real estate. It is true that the stock market has out-gained the housing market over the years. The problem with this argument is that you are comparing housing prices to stock market prices. If you are buying a house as an owner-occupant with cash, the historical gain of housing prices may be a good indicator of your return. However, real estate investors do not consider an owner-occupant purchase with cash a true real estate investment. Real estate investing is not about housing prices. It is about cash flow, leverage, and tax advantages, which housing prices do not account for.

The historic rise in housing prices since 1900 is only 3.1% per year. Stock market returns average about 7 to 10% per year before inflation. Looking at those figures (which is what many stock market proponents do) makes it seem like the stock market blows real estate out of the water. However, real estate investing is completely different from buying a house and hoping for appreciating value.

## What are the advantages of real estate investing?

- Real estate investors should be investing for cash flow, not appreciation. Only counting the housing price increase is like saying stock market investors cannot count any dividends they made on their stocks.

- Real estate investors tend to use leverage or loans to buy rental properties. The overall housing market index does not take into account any leverage. It assumes an investor buys a house solely with cash.
- Even if an investor buys a house solely with cash, they will still make money from rental income. The only situation I can think of that would meet these scenarios is an investor who buys land, never rents it out, and holds on to it assuming it will go up in value. However, most investors still make some income from land, whether it is a Conservation Reserve Program (CRP), mineral rights, or farming.
- Real estate investments can be depreciated; stock market investments cannot. The tax savings from depreciation can equal thousands of dollars per year, blowing that 3.1% out of the water.
- You can buy real estate below market value, which you cannot do with the stock market.

The only way to get just the 3.1% return from the housing market is by buying as an owner occupant. However, you would have to pay cash for the property because as soon as you use leverage, you will be putting much less money down and increasing the return on the cash you have invested. There are problems with assuming that an owner-occupant paying cash will only make 3.1% on the money they invest as well.

- People must have a place to live. If they do not buy a house, they will have to pay rent. You cannot take the money you would have used to buy a house and stick it in the stock market. You would have to use it to rent a house, which would give you a guaranteed 0% return.
- In my market, renting is more expensive than buying a house. Even when you consider the taxes, insurance, and maintenance that homeowners must pay, buying a house is usually more cost effective.
- When you buy a house using a loan, you can deduct the interest from your income taxes. You are also paying money towards your mortgage, and you have a house of your own. Life is not all about the exact return you get on your investment. Consider the fun factor. Consider what the

pride of owning your own house is worth.

After comparing real estate investing to buying a personal residence, there is almost no situation where you would only earn the 3.1% return the housing market has seen since 1900. There are more factors to consider when buying or selling a house. When you sell a house, you must pay selling costs, which may include paying a real estate agent. You must pay title insurance and closing costs. However, if you live in a house for two or more years as an owner-occupant, you may not have to pay any taxes at all on the profit you make. This goes to show there is much more to real estate returns than the historical housing market average gain, especially if you invest in rentals.

## Why does investing in rental properties beat the housing market's historic return?

I did not buy my rental properties for appreciation; I bought them for the cash flow they produce. With a $25,000 to $35,000 investment, each of my rental properties have produced close to $500 per month in cash flow, which produced about 15 to 20% cash-on-cash return. That cash flow is completely independent of the increase in the value of the house. The values of my rentals could go up 40% or they could go down 40% (some of my rentals are worth double what I bought them for after 4 years), and that could have no effect at all on my cash flow. There is a chance that a huge downturn in the housing market could produce lower rents. However, in my market, the last housing crisis did not cause rents to drop significantly.

Getting 15% returns from the cash flow on my rental properties isn't easy. One of the reasons I get such great returns is I can buy real estate below market value. I can buy a house for $120,000 that has a fair-market value of $150,000. That does not make sense to many, but some sellers want to sell quickly, a house may need repairs, or other circumstances create opportunity to buy below market value. You cannot buy stocks below market value. Yes, you can buy stocks that are "undervalued," but that is different from buying below market value. Market value is what someone would pay for something today in an open market. Undervalued means someone thinks the market has not valued something correctly based on the fundamental financials. When buying undervalued assets, you are hoping the market changes its mind or the asset performs better, causing the value to increase in the future.

Being able to buy rental properties below market value allows me to get better cash flow and gain instant equity. When I make 15% on the cash flow from my rental properties, I do not even consider the returns from buying below market value. I bought my 11th rental property for just over $109,000 and made about $12,000 in repairs. I could have sold the house for at least $150,000 after fixing it up. If you take $150,000 minus the repairs and purchase price, I would make $29,000. For those experienced in real estate, you know I do not get to keep that entire $29,000. I would have to pay a real estate commission, title insurance, recording fees, and closing company fees to sell. On a $150,000 sale, those costs would equal about $7,000 (I am a Realtor, so I would not have to pay a listing agent).

I came away with an instant $22,000 in equity when I bought and repaired this house. I spent about $32,000 on the down payment and repairs, which means I would make about 65% if I ever decide to sell. People may say I have not realized that return if I do not sell, and that is true. However, the same thing can be said for the stock market...except the stock market is not producing 20% in cash flow while I hold the asset.

## What has the return been on my rental properties?

If you consider the cash flow I earn and the instant equity I gain when I buy a house, I make a great return on my rentals. We have not even considered the increase in yearly value that comes with average housing prices as well as many other factors.

I put 20% down when I buy a rental property, and I pay down my mortgage every month. On my 11th rental property, I paid about $1,500 toward the principal the first year. That amount increases over time as the principal goes down because more of my monthly payment goes towards principal and less towards interest.

When you consider the tax advantages of rental properties (which I will discuss shortly), I make even more money. I can depreciate my 11$^{th}$ rental property over 27.5 years, which equates to about $1,050 in tax savings every year.

With those two factors, I make $2,550 a year, which equates to 8% in returns on my $32,000 investment. If you total the returns I make from cash flow, buying below market value, the tax advantages, and equity pay down, I am up to 93%. I have not even considered the appreciation or annual housing price increases yet. To be honest, my returns will not be that high every year because I will only make the 65% for buying below market value when I first buy the house. That still creates a 28% overall return every year, even after buying below market value is taken out of the equation.

**Real estate returns** are not limited to the annual housing price gain. If someone tries to convince you that the stock market is a better investment than real estate because of the annual housing gains compared to annual stock market gains, you can point out why that is a false comparison. Annual housing market gains are a very small part of the advantages of real estate.

## What are the tax advantages of rental properties?

This book is meant to offer a broad overview of the tax advantages of rental properties, not specific advice. I am not an accountant or an attorney. If you are looking for tax advice, please talk to a tax professional. Many online tax calculators and estimators can assist you as well. This book gets much of its information from the IRS tax code on rental properties.

Not only does a great rental property provide plenty of cash flow, but rental properties also have incredible tax advantages. The IRS allows most rental property expenses to be deducted or depreciated, and you can also depreciate the structure of the property. It is very common for a rental property to produce cash in hand but, thanks to depreciation, show a loss on your taxes.

## Is mortgage interest on rental properties tax deductible?

The interest you pay on a rental property can be a deduction on your tax return. You cannot deduct the entire payment because part of your payment is equity paydown, which is not deductible. Paid-down equity is not considered a business expense since the money is used to reduce debt and is not spent on repairs or maintenance.

## How does the IRS treat rental property depreciation?

The IRS treats rental property as a depreciable asset. They assume the rental property will degrade until it falls down and is worthless. This is very good for the rental property owner since most properties will not become a pile of rubble if they are maintained.

The IRS says a house will last 27.5 years, which means an investor can deduct the cost basis of the rental property in equal increments over 27.5 years. To calculate the amount that can be depreciated each year, divide the cost basis by 27.5.

The cost basis only includes the structure of a rental property, not the land. If you buy a rental property on a lot for $100,000, the entire $100,000 is not the cost basis. You must deduct the value of the land from the purchase price to get your cost basis. You can also add many of the closing costs to the cost basis, such as abstract, title, recording, and other fees. The entire list is on the IRS website.

If, after all expenses, I make $3,000 on a rental property, I can use that $3,000 any way I want. However, it most likely will not show up as $3,000 in taxable income due to depreciation. If the cost basis of my rental property was $100,000, the depreciation would be $3,636 per year for 27.5 years. The $3,636 would counteract all the income I made and show a loss of $636! Even though I have $3,000 more in my pocket due to the money my rental property generated, I pay no taxes on that money and may even be able to counter other income with that loss.

## What is the disadvantage of depreciating a rental property?

If you depreciate a rental property over 20 years then sell the house, you will receive a large tax bill from the IRS. The depreciation can be recaptured, which means you must pay back all those taxes you saved if you sell the property for more than the current cost basis. The cost basis is calculated by taking the original cost basis and deducting any depreciation.

Even though you must pay back those tax savings, paying those taxes 20 years down is still better than paying them now. With inflation, money is worth less in the future, and you can invest that money for 20 years until you must give it back to Uncle Sam. Think of it as a no-interest loan from our government! There are also many ways to avoid depreciation recapture.

The easiest way to avoid paying back the tax savings is to never sell the rental property. After 27.5 years, you will not be able to use the depreciation tax break anymore, but you also will not have to pay back any of the previous tax savings if you hold the property forever.

Another way to avoid the depreciation recapture is to use a 1031 exchange. If you sell your rental property, the IRS allows you to exchange that property for a similar property without having to recapture any depreciation. I write much more about 1031 exchanges later.

If you happen to pass away while you own rental properties, the properties will pass to your heirs. When your heirs inherit the properties, the cost basis becomes the current value of the properties, not the original owner's cost basis. That means there will be no depreciation recapture. Planning to hold your rental properties until you die is not a bad strategy tax wise. *There are some limits and restrictions based on the estate tax.*


## What other rental property expenses can be deducted?

Since rental properties are considered a business, travel expenses, account- ing fees, management fees, and many more expenses are also deductible.

If you make repairs on your rental properties, those are also deductible, but improvements are not. Repairing a leaky faucet is deductible, but adding a second story is considered an improvement and is not deductible.

Even though improvements are not deductible, that doesn't mean you cannot count them on your taxes. Improvements can be depreciated like the rental property itself. Improvements are depreciated over differing timeframes ranging from 3 to 20 years. You do not have to wait 27.5 years to see the full tax benefit of most improvements.

The IRS has different rules for people in the real estate business and those that are not. If you spend more than half your time on rental properties, you are considered to be in the rental property business. There is no limit to the deduction or losses you can take on your rental properties if you are in the business.

If you are not in the rental property business, you can take a maximum loss of $25,000 depending on how much money you make. The more money you make, the less of a loss you can count towards your other income. The deductions and depreciation will still counteract the money you make on the rental properties, but it might not help reduce your regular income taxes.

## How much money can you make on rental properties?

When I was younger, I kept telling myself I did not need the finer things in life. I was happy with whatever I had and could afford. I told myself I did not need expensive things because I did not believe I could ever afford the things I really wanted. A few years ago, as I became more successful, I completely changed my thought process. I now believe I can achieve and acquire whatever I want, and I was doing myself a disservice by masking my true desires. Rental properties have been a key component to my ability to chase my dreams. Because of the steady cash flow rentals provide, I am much more comfortable spending money on myself, and I don't worry about money.

One of my passions is automobiles. I love classic and exotic cars. I purchased a 1986 Porsche 928 a few years ago, and I absolutely love that car. In 1986, the 928 was the most expensive car Porsche made, but I purchased it for just $6,000. I think the 928 is one of the all-time bargains for classic/exotic cars. Unfortunately, not all classic/exotic cars are bargains.

My all-time favorite car is a Lamborghini Miura, which was built in the late sixties and early seventies. The Miura was the predecessor to the famous Lamborghini Countach, which is also one of my all-time favorite cars. A Countach runs at least $100,000 in today's market, and a Miura is somewhere in the $500,000 range, if not more. Not only are these cars extremely expensive, but maintaining them can cost thousands of dollars per year. Finding someone who knows how to maintain or work on a Lamborghini isn't easy.

I first wrote this part of the book back in late 2013. If you want to know how crazy the car market is, a Miura will now cost about $1.5 million and a Countach about $400,000! At the end of 2013, I set a goal to buy a Lamborghini Diablo in 2014. I changed my goal from buying a Countach because prices increased so much that the Diablo was a better value, and really, a better car. In May 2014, I bought a Monterey Blue 1999 Lamborghini Diablo. It is a gorgeous car, and you can read all about it on my blog. Many think buying a car like that is about the stupidest thing you could do. However, it was a passion of mine for many years. The car has been a great marketing tool and has increased in value by about 75% since I bought it!

## How long-term rentals give me more stability to go after what I want

I knew if I ever wanted to be able to afford a Diablo, Countach, or Miura, I would have to make a lot more money or earn very high returns on the money I was investing. I have been able to do both, and a lot of that resulted from my decision to start investing in long-term rental properties. I have purchased 16 rental properties, and I am making over 15% cash-on-cash returns on all of them. I know rental properties by themselves probably won't generate enough money for a Lamborghini, but they provide a financial security that is tough to beat. I know that money will be coming in month after month, which does not happen with traditional jobs or businesses.

My super-aggressive goal is to own 100 rental properties by 2023. I created this goal back in 2013, and I am a couple of years into it. With my 16 rentals to date, I am a little behind on my projections, but I am confident I will get there. You can see my plan on my blog at:

Even though I am a little behind on my goal, I know the goal has gotten me further along than if I did not set a goal. It has pushed me to buy more and to work harder than if I didn't have any goals and was just floating along.

## What is the cost of a rental property?

I go over the exact costs of buying a rental in a later chapter, but let's assume it costs $30,000 to purchase and repair one rental for now (you can buy your first rental for much less money using strategies I will talk about later). You also do not have to invest $90,000 per year to buy three rentals within that time because you can begin refinancing rental properties after you own them for a year (in some case 6 months) and take the cash out to invest in more rentals. I usually buy my properties for about $100,000 and put 20% down. I make repairs that range from $5,000 to $15,000. On some houses, I can get the seller to pay for some of my closing costs. As an agent, I also save a commission on many of my purchases. For the most part, I can get about $500 in monthly cash flow from my rental properties with financing in place.

Depending on your local market, rents in your area, and your property taxes, you may be able to make more or less than I do. As I mentioned before, making this much money from rentals isn't easy. You may have to make sacrifices to realize these numbers, such as investing in another market, getting your real estate license, or even living in potential rental properties.

## How much money can you make within ten years?

If you could buy three rental properties per year for ten years, you would have about $15,000 coming in every month at the end of those ten years based on very simple math. If you bought the properties with 20% down and made repairs on all of them, you would have about $900,000 invested into those properties to make that $15,000. This sounds like a good investment, but there are more things to consider.

The exciting thing is that to make the math simpler, these numbers are not adjusted for inflation, rent increases, or appreciation.

- **Appreciation:** I do not count on appreciation, but it is a nice bonus. The median value in my area has gone from $120,000 in 2012 to $260,000 in 2016. If that trend continues, it can be a game changer.
- **Inflation:** Over time, real estate values have always risen. Lately, rents have also risen. The great thing about rental properties is that when rents increase, your mortgage payment stays the same. Rentals are a great hedge against inflation.

While you might not be able to buy three properties—or even one—each year, they are still a great investment. If you could buy just one rental property that generates $500 each year, you would have, at a minimum, $5,000 per month coming in after ten years. That assumes rents never increase for that entire ten-year period.

When you get a great deal on rentals, it also gives you more options to buy properties in the future. I have refinanced 7 of my rentals over the last four years. They still cash flow well, even after the refinance, and I have been able to take out over $250,000 in cash. This has allowed me to buy more houses more quickly without having to save all the down payment funds. Even though I have spent a lot of cash to buy and renovate my houses, I have gotten much of that back through refinancing properties.

## Conclusion

Rental properties are an awesome investment. When you buy below market value, buy with cash flow, and take advantage of the excellent tax rules, they can make you a lot of money. People may say real estate is a bad investment because the housing market only increases 3% per year, but they have no idea what they are talking about. The right rental property can make you more than 15% cash-in-pocket every year. When you factor in other advantages like equity paydown, tax savings, appreciation, and forced appreciation, your returns could be much higher.

# 3

# What Are the Risks of Investing in Real Estate?

Getting started with investing in rental properties is difficult. It is not a get-rich-quick scheme; being a successful investor takes a lot of effort and determination. However, I think the difficulty rental investments pose is great. If it were easy, everyone would do it, and the returns would be much lower.

I would estimate that only 2% of those who set out to invest in real estate ever buy a rental property or a flip. I do not want to scare you off, but becoming a great investor takes time and effort. Once you have figured out your niche and have some experience with purchasing rental properties, it gets much easier. But if you do not take the time to learn the fundamentals, you can make some huge mistakes and lose money.

The biggest mistakes people make are overestimating returns and incorrectly managing property. However, other mistakes can also cause rental properties to be a bad investment.

Many investors are afraid of failure because they hear so many nightmares about bad tenants and investors who lost money. That fear of failure prevents them from ever investing in real estate and realizing the wonderful benefits rental properties can bring.

When investing large sums of money into rental properties, a little fear is

OK. Use that fear to your benefit. Make sure you have researched the market, returns, and the kind of property you want. Once you have educated yourself about what a good deal is, you must be able to pull the trigger once you find that good deal.

## Are you a failure if you do not succeed right away?

I hate the word "fail!" I do not ever like to use it because it means you gave up. Many people face setbacks. They lose money; things do not go as planned; or they change course. That does not mean they failed. I have many goals, and I do not reach all of them. In fact, I set my goals so high that I'll likely miss some of them. Big goals help me achieve more and keep working hard to accomplish them. Do I consider myself a failure because I did not reach those goals? No. I look at how much further I got because I had goals, and I think about how I can improve things to reach those goals in the future. Sometimes, I realize a goal was unrealistic or was not worth my time and effort, so I change it.

My point is that you can only fail at investing in real estate if you either never try or give up. Most people do not do things perfectly the first time, and becoming proficient at something takes experience and practice. Many real estate investors get stuck in the education phase and never buy a property. You cannot succeed if you never play the game. Other investors end up accidentally owning a rental property or losing money on their first flip and give up. They proclaim real estate is a horrible investment and say they will never do it again. If you gave up on everything you were not successful at right away, you would not be able to walk, talk, read, drive, or do countless other things.

On my podcast (InvestFourMore Real Estate Podcast on iTunes or my blog), I interview many successful real estate investors. Many of those investors lost money or had a really rough time with their first deal. However, they did not give up—they used their experience to learn and do better the next time.

## Why are there so many stories about people losing money on rental properties?

I think most who have ever expressed—to friends or family—interest in buying rentals have encountered negativity. Someone always seems to know a cousin, uncle, or long-lost friend that lost their entire life savings in real estate. When I started in the business, I even had other real estate agents tell me how bad an investment real estate was.

The reason most people tell you real estate investing is a bad idea is they do not understand it. Do not assume real estate agents or your lender know about real estate investing. Most agents never invest in real estate and do not understand what a good investment it is. Before you base major financial decisions on someone else's advice, make sure that advice is good. Those who tell you how bad real estate is have probably never invested themselves and are retelling stories that may or may not be accurate.

There are many types of real estate investments. Someone hears a bad story about a flip, a rental, or a partnership, and they associate that story with every type of real estate investment, even though they are completely unrelated.

If you hear a story directly from someone who lost a large amount of money investing, get the entire story. Most people who lose money in real estate did not know what they were doing, or they took on huge risks to try to get rich quick. If you educate yourself and follow certain guidelines, it is hard to lose money.

Current investors may tell you how horrible real estate investing is, but if it is so bad, why are they still doing it? Many people who own rentals will tell you that rentals are a pain and not worth the trouble. So why do they still own them? Usually, they are making money and don't want to sell because they love the income, or they do not want more competition and discourage others from buying.

I am not saying that everyone who loses money in real estate does not know what they are doing or are trying to discourage the competition. It is entirely possible to lose money in real estate...even if you know what you are doing. I have lost money on fix-and-flips, and I have flipped more than 100 houses. If you are going to take someone else's advice, at least make sure you get the whole story and that it applies to your situation.

## How can you lose money investing in real estate?

Truth is, you can lose money many ways. Educate yourself and work hard and you'll likely make money rather than lose it. I have listed the most common reasons investors lose money below:

- **Investors do not know the numbers.** Real estate is all about the numbers. You must know what your cash flow will be, how much money you need to invest, and what your returns will be. You need to know how much you can afford and how much to keep in reserves. Most investors who lose money do not look at the numbers close enough. They do not consider all the costs when figuring returns on rentals, and they do not figure all the costs on flips. They also underestimate the time it takes to flip a house or to make repairs. My biggest pet peeve is when people ask me, "Is this is a good deal?" but haven't calculated any of the numbers. I had a blueprint student (a coaching program I offer) who was unhappy with my answers when he asked me if a rental property was a good deal. I asked him what the house would be worth after repairs, what the repairs would cost, and what the rent would be. He did not know any of those numbers and was mad that I could not tell him if the house was a good deal! No one can do the work for you. You must be able to run the numbers to be a successful real estate investor.

- **Investors try to save money by doing work themselves.** Many investors try to save money by managing properties or repairing houses themselves. They assume they will save money by renting houses, making repairs, or managing the entire process. The biggest problem is most first-time investors do not know how to manage a property because they have full-time jobs and are not contractors. Picking good tenants takes time. You also must stay on them to pay rent and visit

26

the property to make sure they are taking care of it. Most horror stories come from investors who rented to the same tenant for several years yet never drove by the house. If you think you can rehab a house by yourself on the weekends and within a couple of weeks, think again. You can save money by doing things yourself, but make sure you have the time and are qualified to do the work.

· **Investors assuming prices will increase.** Most investors who lost money in the last housing crisis were over-leveraged and assumed prices would continue to increase. I think we are also seeing that same scenario take form in today's market. Finding good deals and houses that will cash flow is difficult. Finding flips that will generate income is also tough. When you start fudging the numbers to buy houses, you are asking for trouble. When I buy rentals, I make sure they generate plenty of cash flow no matter what the market is doing. When I buy flips, I assume I will sell for what they are worth today, not what they might be worth in six months.

· **Investors start investing by accident.** Many people get their first rental property by turning a house they lived in into a rental. They never intended to rent out the house, and they did not look at rental numbers before they bought, but circumstances caused them to move and rent out the house. Surprise! The house was not a good rental because it was not intended to be a rental. You need to make sure any house that you rent out will make money. You cannot rely on appreciation.

There are many more ways to lose money in real estate investing. However, I only consider it a failure if you gave up and failed to learn anything from your experience.

## Why do people avoid investing in real estate?

Many people will lose money investing in real estate because of the reasons listed above. Many more will never invest in real estate at all, even though they know it is a great way to build wealth and have every intention of investing. Why do people never get the ball rolling?

- **No money.** Investing in real estate, even with no-money-down loans, takes money. If you don't have money, you'll have trouble getting started (it is possible to get started with nothing, but do not expect it to be easy), but that doesn't mean you cannot invest—you just need to get money! Either learn to save more money or make more money. I can pretty much guarantee there is someone out there in a worse financial situation than you are who was able to save money and buy a house. You'll have to make sacrifices and work hard, but it is better than having no money the rest of your life.
- **Analysis paralysis.** Many investors educate themselves about everything, yet they never buy a property. Education is important, but after a certain point, you will have enough knowledge and information to invest.
- **Too much work.** Most people are not willing to do the work it takes to invest successfully in real estate. Learning your market, finding deals, getting a team of professionals to help you, and saving money takes time. Most people simply give up when they realize it will not be easy.
- **They are talked out of it.** We have already discussed this, but many people listen to the naysayers and do not invest because they think it is a bad investment. Do not let someone else tell you the best way to invest your money. Figure it out for yourself.

Most aspiring investors never buy a property. They talk themselves out of it because it is too hard or they cannot get the money together. There are ways to invest with little money. Many investors will teach you online or in books how to buy with less cash. If you are not willing to work hard at life, you will not get very far. If you want to invest in real estate, do not let someone else decide that you should not or allow a lack of money to be an excuse. Get out there and do it. While there are ways to lose money investing in rentals, if you do your homework and know how to run the numbers, the chances of losing money decrease greatly.

# How risky are investment properties?

Many people automatically think there must be huge risk involved with real estate because you can make so much money with it. There is risk in real estate, just like any other investment. If you have a long-term plan built to withstand market fluctuations, there is little risk when investing in long-term rental properties.

One key to a low-risk rental strategy—or any successful real estate strategy—is to buy a property below market value. Buying below market value enables you to create instant equity, increase your net worth, and protect yourself against a downturn in the market.

Let us look at my fourth rental property as an example. I purchased it for $109,000 in 2012. I put about $35,000 cash into it for repairs, down payment, and other costs. My loan was about $88,000. My breakeven was $123,000 to get my full investment back. That house was worth at least $145K fixed up and probably closer to $150K or more when I bought it. Since I bought below market value, prices would have to drop 20% before the property would be worth less than what I had into it. Prices would have to drop even further (more than 40%) for the value to drop below my loan balance. Even if prices nosedived in the next year, I would still be okay.

## Cash flow reduces the risk with rentals

I consider cash flow the most important factor in my long-term rental strategy. I plan to live off the cash flow from my rental properties. When I buy a property and fix it up, I expect at least $500 per month in cash flow.

My rents range from $1,100 to $1,600 per month, and I make $500 on almost all of them. For me to see negative cash flow, my rents would have to drop more than 40%! House prices could possibly fall 20 or even 40%, but rents did not drop 40% when the housing market crashed. In fact, many places saw only minimal drops in rental rates because rental rates are not based on house prices: they're based on the supply and demand of rental properties in any given area. If we ever see rental rates drop 50%, either the economy has completely crashed or some life-altering event has changed a country or region forever. No matter what you are investing in, you are going to have major problems.

My strategy focuses on single-family rental properties that are less than 50 years old. The older a property is, the better the chance it will need a major repair. I have enough cash flow coming in to account for major repairs, but houses that are more than 100 years old can have issues that could wipe out all equity. It is rare, but a foundation or structural problem can make a property uninhabitable and cost tens of thousands of dollars to repair. By purchasing newer properties, I lessen the chances of running into repairs that could wipe out my profit for a year...or even two.

## You must have reserves in the bank

Another reason investors get into trouble is they have just enough money to buy a rental property. They save only for the down payment and the needed repairs. When they cannot rent out the house right away or a major repair comes up, they do not have the money for the extra expenses. Most banks require six months in reserve for mortgage payments on all properties. I think this is the minimum savings you should have before you invest. If you have plenty of cash flow and reserves, you can weather the storm if prices drop or the rental market declines. With plenty of cash flow and reserves in the bank, you will not have to sell your rentals if values drop. We had a drop in prices during the housing crisis, and many investors with rentals went bankrupt. However, many others made it through the crisis just fine and are doing very well now that the market has recovered. The difference was the investors who made it through the downturn had equity, cash flow, and reserves.

# Should you invest in rental properties?

Everyone reading this book lives in or on some type of real estate. I would think most of you are interested in real estate because you spend most of your time in some type of real estate. I personally love houses and architecture, and I love fixing up properties (my contractor does the actual work). I think it is important for people to be excited and interested in their investments. If you do not care about a stock or a mutual fund, you probably are not going to do much research or spend much time researching the financial data on that investment. Investing in rental properties requires a good deal of due diligence to ensure a good investment. If you do not care about houses and are just in it for the money, you may not do as well as others who love the business.

You can still succeed in real estate even if you do not care about real estate, but you will need to discipline yourself. This is not a get-rich-quick scheme. Real estate can make you rich much faster than the stock market can, but it may take a little more effort.

## Do you have the right attitude?

Many people fear change. It is perfectly normal to be nervous or apprehensive when investing in rental properties. Houses are expensive, and buying one is a big deal! If you let fear get the best of you and start thinking there is no way you can succeed, you probably will not be successful. Our minds have a funny way of helping us succeed or fail depending on how we feel. If we are positive about our chances and believe we can accomplish something, we are more likely to succeed.

Letting others convince us that our goals and dreams are not possible or are flawed is easy. We tend to listen to them, even though we have more knowledge and experience on the subject. We let our minds convince us that the naysayers must know something we do not, and if we embark on this new adventure, it will lead to ruin. Do not listen to them! Be confident in your ambitions and in your future. They would probably love to be starting something new and exciting but are too scared to do it themselves.

I am not against gaining knowledge and education from the experts. I can sit and listen to experts talk about real estate all day long. If someone thinks real estate is a bad investment because he or she knew someone who once lost money on a flip, I will politely ignore everything he or she has to say. Have confidence in your decision, and do not doubt that if done right, investing in real estate is a fantastic path toward wealth.

## Are you willing to learn and change?

I have been in real estate my whole life. My dad has been an agent since 1978, and I have been helping him since I was three years old. Yet I still learn new things regarding real estate all the time. I thought I was an expert on investing and knew just about everything there was to know before I started my blog. I was wrong—there was so much I did not know in so many facets of real estate. I think every real estate investor can continue to learn better techniques and ways to invest if they are willing. You do not have to know everything, but you do need to know the basics. You do not have to learn everything at once, but you must be willing to learn new ideas and accept that what you thought about real estate may not be reality. Sometimes the best teacher is experience and getting in the game even when you do not know everything.

## Are you disciplined enough?

Becoming a great real estate investor takes money, time, and patience. If you are not willing to do what it takes to get funding, find properties, and choose a good team, you may not succeed. You will need discipline and perseverance to work through the hard times. I love the book *The Art of War* by Steven Pressfield because it defines resistance as that thing that keeps you from greatness. Every time you are close to finishing a project or reaching a milestone, there is always something that pops up to stop you. It could be an unexpected phone call, work task, or taking a break that turns into a day off. The book talks about overcoming resistance and pushing through it. If you can recognize resistance and either ignore it or push through it to complete your tasks, you will accomplish so much more. Most people stop when they meet resistance and will not give that extra effort. If you think you are close to something great or making a breakthrough, do not give up when you meet resistance. Resistance is a sign that you are close to your goals and close to a breakthrough.

If you do not have a lot of money to invest right away (which most people do not), you may have to make changes to your lifestyle. You may have to start a budget, cut down on expenditures, or find ways to make more money. I personally like finding ways to make money because I hate budgeting and cutting back! Making your first purchase may take a long time, but do not get discouraged. If you tend to give up easy, you may not be able to last long enough to make it in real estate. Once you make your first purchase, it all becomes easier and everything starts to fall into place. It took me years to invest in real estate after the idea got into my head. It does not have to take years, but it can take time, and that is okay.

The key to any successful real estate investing strategy is to purchase properties below market value. Purchasing houses for market value that are actively for sale on the MLS is relatively easy. The difficult part is finding the great deal, acting fast, and getting it under contract. Finding motivated sellers that do not have their houses listed on the MLS is a great way to find deals but takes a lot of work and patience. Do not get discouraged if you cannot find the right deals immediately. One of the reasons it takes so long to start investing is you must first learn what a good deal is and then be patient while looking for it.

If you give up easily and find yourself quickly moving from opportunity to opportunity when they do not pan out, real estate may not be right for you.

## Do you have enough time?

You must have spare time to be a real estate investor. You must do research, look at houses, manage repairs, and rent out your houses or find a property manager. If you are constantly tied up with work or family, think about whether you have the time to add something to your plate. If you do not think you have time for something new, you may be too busy or need to change your life. Investing in real estate may be a great first step toward increasing the amount of spare time in your life. I am constantly working on gaining more free time and delegating tasks to others. Time is our most valuable commodity because we cannot buy more of it. If you have no time, try creating a time budget for yourself. I take all the hours in the week and allocate time for sleep, work, leisure, family etc. Looking at where you spend your time now is a great way to decide if your priorities are in the right place.

A great way to instantly increase your time is by focusing. I am horrible at trying to do too many things at once. Ultimately, multitasking takes me longer because I make more mistakes and forget what I am doing. It is hard for me, but I force myself to focus on one thing until I am done or until I have spent a certain amount of time on it. I do not check email, browse the Internet, or do anything else until I am finished with that task.

Hiring help is a great way to increase time and usually increases your results as well. Whenever I hire a new assistant, I delegate tasks I do not like doing. When I am not working on those tasks, I am happier and get more done. I also have more time to focus on the things I like doing or the tasks that make me more money. A great piece of advice I recently heard is to never work below your income. If you are worth $100 per hour, do not do tasks you can delegate for $20 per hour. Focus on things that make you that $100 per hour or more and let someone else do the less-important work.

## Are you a people person?

Being a people person is not a requirement, but it sure helps when investing in real estate. The more people you know in real estate, the better your chances of succeeding. Even other investors will help you out if you are willing to go to local investor meetings. Real Estate Investor Associations (REIAs) are a fantastic place to learn about investing in your market and a great way to network. I do not go to as many REIA meetings as I should, but when I do go, I meet wholesalers, like-minded investors, real estate agents, and lenders. Those people may not be able to help me now, but who knows how they may be able to help me in the future.

If you are going to be a real estate investor, you will have to deal with agents, title companies, inspectors, appraisers, contractors, and other investors. The better you can get along with everyone, the more you will succeed. If you really do not like dealing with people, you can always collaborate with or hire someone who does like to network.

I am a natural introvert myself. When I was younger, I was that kid who hid behind his parents and would not talk to anyone. Even in high school and college, talking to people was hard for me. Eventually, I realized that there was nothing to be afraid of, and I forced myself to come out of my shell. I have even spoken in front of hundreds of people at real estate conferences. It is scary, and I get really nervous, but doing it and knowing I conquered a fear feels amazing. If you want to be successful, sometimes you must get out of your comfort zone.

## Do not give up!

This section is not meant to discourage you but to educate you. Getting started in real estate investing isn't easy, but it all gets much easier once you get your feet wet and start investing. Real estate is so rewarding, and I believe the benefits far exceed the work it takes to get started. Successful investors do not need to work or manage houses, and they have the freedom to do anything they want. Many investors continue to invest and manage their properties even when they do not need the money because they love it! I hope you choose to invest in real estate and are as successful as or even more successful than I have been.

Remember—if it was easy, everyone would do it, and there would be much less opportunity for those willing to put in the work.

# 4

# How Do You Know What Makes a Good Rental Property Investment?

Rental properties can be great investments if you do it right. The big question is how do you know what a good rental property investment is. This is not an easy question to answer because every market and investor is different; everyone has different financial situations; and everyone has different goals. What may work for me may not work for you.

I use many fundamentals to judge rentals. These can help you decide if an investment is a good one. The main things I look at are:

- Did I buy it below market value and by how much?
- How much does it cash flow each month?
- What are my cash-on-cash returns?
- What do the prospects look like for the market in which I am buying?

When coming up with these numbers and projections, I must make sure I am calculating everything correctly. People calculate cash flow incorrectly all the time. Cash flow is somewhat of a guessing game because you cannot predict all the expenses. However, methods exist that allow investors to have a pretty good idea of what the actual returns will be.

# How do you determine the cash flow on rental properties?

Determining the cash flow on rental properties seems simple, but many people do not include all the expenses. Each rental property will need maintenance and will be vacant at some time. You must account for these costs. An investor must factor vacancies and maintenance into expected returns, even if a house is in good condition and the vacancy rate in the area is low.

I have a great cash flow calculator on my website: https://investfourmore. com/calculators/rental-property-cash-flow/. There is a place to enter vacancies and maintenance. When you own rental properties, you may not have a lot of vacancies or maintenance every year. In other years, you may have many vacancies and a lot of maintenance that you will make up for during the good years.

If you plan for years that may have a lot of vacancy and maintenance costs, they will not hurt as much, and you will still make money.

## How do you account for vacancies?

Vacancies are times when your property isn't rented out or generating rent. Vacancies occur when a tenant moves out or stops paying or you cannot rent the property out as soon as you had hoped. You will not be collecting rent during vacant months, but you will have expenses like utilities, mortgage payments, taxes, and insurance.

Two of the costliest rental-property scenarios are tenant evictions and non-paying tenants. Evicting a tenant can take months and thousands of dollars.

One of my tenants had heart surgery and could not work. He fell behind on rent, and I did not have the heart to evict him. We worked out a deal where he moved out, but he owed me over $3,500 in back rent. If you have a tenant who will not pay rent and will not leave, you could pay much more for an eviction. Each state's eviction rules and laws are different, and the costs and time it will take varies.

## Why do you have to factor in maintenance?

I repair all my rental properties before I rent them out. When I first rent out my properties, they most likely will not need very much maintenance because they are in great shape. However, I also buy houses that are 30, 40, or even 50 years old. Although I repair houses before renting them out, I do not rebuild them, and things eventually break. Tenants break things, and their security deposit may not cover all the damage.

My cash flow calculator determines maintenance costs based on the age of the house and how much rehab has been done. The more work that a house has had done, the less maintenance it will need. The newer a house is, the less maintenance it will need because the major systems are of better quality and will last longer. I prefer to buy rental properties that are 50 years old or newer because they have a much smaller chance of needing major work.

The most important factor when keeping up with maintenance is the quality of the tenants and oversight by the property owner or manager. The better the tenants take care of a house and the more a property owner monitors the property, the less maintenance there will be. The most-damaged rental houses I have seen had been rented to the same tenants for years, and the property owners never checked on the house.

Even if a house does not need any maintenance for years, a big expense could pop up and wipe out all the good years. A roof could cost $5,000 to $10,000. A tenant could trash the paint and carpet, which could easily cost $5,000 or more. The big repairs are why we account for maintenance in our returns, even if a house may not need any other repairs for years.

## How much money should you plan to spend for vacancies?

The tricky part about accounting for vacancies is deciding how much money you need to allocate for future vacancies or evictions. A good rule of thumb is to count on 10% of the rent. 10% would be just over one-month's rent and would account for one vacant month, any utilities, and other costs you incur while the house is vacant. On my rental properties, I have been very lucky and proactive, and I usually rent them out right after a tenant moves out. In Colorado, we have had very low vacancy rates, and I have seen about a 5% historical vacancy cost on my rentals.

Here is the vacancy table I use:

| Single Family | 5% |
| --- | --- |
| College Rental | 10% |
| Multifamily | 10% |

These rates can vary greatly based on the location of your rental property. If you are in an area that has very high vacancy rates, the expense on a single-family house might be 10%. On a multifamily, it may be 15%. Different neighborhoods and differently priced rentals may also have varying vacancy costs.

## How much should you plan to spend on maintenance?

Planning for maintenance costs is very difficult because you never know what will break or how well a tenant will treat a house. In my cash-flow calculator, the maintenance costs on my tiered scale range from 5 to 30% of the collected rents. The 5% figure is for an almost-new house with all the systems in great condition. The 30% is for a house that is 100 years old and has outdated systems and no recent remodels. Maintenance costs will vary greatly depending on the type of house you buy, its age, its condition, and how well it has been taken care of.

Here is the table I use for my cash-flow calculator:

|  | Good | Average | Needs Work |
|---|---|---|---|
| 0-10 Years | 5% | 10% | 15% |
| 10-50 Years | 10% | 15% | 20% |
| 50 Years+ | 15% | 20% | 25% |

## How do you determine total cash flow?

Let's use one of my rental properties as an example. This rental is paid off and has no mortgage. However, I do have a line of credit (LOC) against it (I often use LOCs for my fix-and-flips).

| Rent | $1,400 |
|---|---|
| Taxes | $60 |
| Insurance | $50 |
| Maintenance (rent x 10%) | $140 |
| Vacancies (rent x 5%) | $70 |
| HOA Fee | $13 |
| Property Management | $112 |
| **Total Cash Flow** | **$967 per month** |

If I had a mortgage on this property, which I did when I first bought it, my cash flow would be $967 minus whatever the principal and interest payments would be. It is also important to remember that most lenders will escrow the taxes and insurance. Escrowing means rolling costs into your mortgage payment, so make sure you are not counting them twice if the lender is including those costs in your payment.

When I bought this house in 2010, I paid $96,900 for it, and my payment at the time was about $350, including principal and interest. That would make my cash flow about $600 per month once I account for the mortgage payment.

# What is the 50% rule when used for rental property expenses?

The 50% rule states the expenses (not including mortgages expense) on a rental will be 50% of the rent.

 Many investors use this rule to judge profitability. However, using a blanket rule like this is not the best way to analyze a rental property. Here is an example of what the 50% rule would say the expenses are on one of my properties.

| Rent | $1,600 |
|---|---|
| Expenses | $800 |
| Mortgage | $740 (with tax and ins) |

According to the 50% rule, I make about $60 per month on this property. However, my cash flow calculator shows I am making over $500 per month on this property. What is the difference? The cash flow calculator includes all the expenses—it does not use a blanket rule. Here are the expenses on this property using my calculator:

| Property Management | $128 |
|---|---|
| Taxes | $83 |
| Insurance | $50 |
| Maintenance | $160 |
| Vacancies | $80 |
| **Total Cash Flow** | **$501 per month** |

The difference between my estimates and the 50% rule is $300 per month or $3,600 per year. Are my expenses really this low, or am I just making stuff up? I analyzed my rentals last year, and my expenses were almost exactly what I had estimated them to be. I have owned rental properties since 2010, and my estimated expenses have been very close to my actual expenses. This was not just a one-year anomaly.

## Why would the 50% rule show the expenses are so much higher?

Numerous factors lead me not to like the 50% rule, and I think it can overestimate expenses. The biggest reason I do not like the rule is it assumes all rentals will have basically the same expenses in every state and on every type of property.

- **Property Taxes:** Property taxes in every state can vary by a huge amount. In Colorado, my taxes are less than $1,000 per year on most of my properties. In other states, those same properties would have taxes five times that amount. **Difference in expenses on taxes: $80 versus $400 per month.**
- **HOA dues**: If you own a condo or townhome, chances are you have HOA dues. Many single-family houses have them as well. I have one rental with an HOA, and the rest have no HOA fees. Some HOAs can charge hundreds of dollars per month. **The difference in HOA expenses: $0 versus $200 per month**.
- **Vacancies:** Different types of properties have different vacancy rates and so do different towns. In Colorado, we have had extremely low vacancy rates. In some cases, and during some years, vacancy rates have been under 1%. In other parts of the country, the vacancy rate is over 10%. Single-family houses typically have lower vacancies than multifamily. College rentals will have much higher vacancies than other types of rentals. Some properties may have vacancy expenses of 5% and others may have 15% or higher. **The difference in vacancy expenses: $80 per month versus $240 per month.**
- **Maintenance:** Properties will need work, even if they are brand new. The amount of work will vary based on the condition and type of property.

Multifamily residences usually have more wear and tear than single-family, and college rentals can have much more wear and tear. The older a property is, the more maintenance it will require. The worse shape a property is in, the more maintenance it will require. The maintenance expense can vary from 5% to 30%. **The difference in maintenance expense: $80 versus $480 per month**.

Other expenses will make a huge difference as well (like insurance). If the property is in a flood or hurricane zone, insurance will be much higher. As you can see, the expenses on similarly priced rentals that may cater to different tenants in different areas of the country can vary from $400 (once you add insurance and property manager) to $1,160 per month! If we used the same $1,600 in rent that I am receiving on my example property, my expenses could be anywhere from 25% to over 70% of the rent. These are extreme examples, but they show how different properties will have much different costs.

Another problem with the 50% rule is it uses the rent to determine the expenses. When I bought my fourth rental property in 2012, it rented for $1,300 per month. Rents have gone up to $1,600 per month over the last three years, and it may rent for more than that if I were to get a new tenant. Look how much the expenses changed due to the rent increase:

· With monthly rent of $1,300, the 50% rule says my monthly expenses are $650.
· With monthly rent of $1,600, the 50% rule says my monthly expenses are $800.

Did my expenses really go up by $150 due to higher rent? It could be argued that since the rent is higher, my vacancy expenses would be higher because when a month's rent is missed, I lose more money. I agree with that, but here is how much my vacancy costs would increase using different vacancy rates.

- **5% vacancy:** monthly expenses would increase from $65 to $80
- **10% vacancy:** Monthly expenses would increase from $130 to $160
- **15% vacancy:** Monthly expenses would increase from $185 to $240

Even with 15% of the rents accounting for vacancies, the monthly increase would only be $75, not $150. With a 5% vacancy allowance, the extra monthly cost is only $15. Maybe the other expenses would be higher with the higher rent. My property taxes have gone up slightly (less than $10 per month); my insurance has not increased; my maintenance has not increased; my property management has increased. The monthly property management increase is about $22. On certain properties, the monthly expenses could possibly go up by $150 when the rent changes (if many other things also change). Expenses possibly wouldn't change much at all, which is the problem with the 50% rule. It is a blanket rule that does not account for the different expenses on different properties.

The 50% rule might be dead-on for some properties, but for other properties, it could be wrong by hundreds of dollars. Therefore, you cannot rely on a blanket rule to calculate expenses. You need to write everything out or use a cash flow calculator. Knowing the exact expenses will make you a better investor and help you figure out what is and is not a good rental property.

## Are the 2% or 1% rules good ways to judge rental properties?

The 2% rule is a general guideline many investors use to determine if a rental property is a good deal. The basics of the 2% rule say the monthly rent should be 2% or more of the cost of the property. I don't believe the 2$ rule is a good judge of rental-property value. The rule is too vague and does not account for many variables, just like the 50% rule. Good rental-property deals are all about the numbers in a particular market, and the 2% rule assumes that all costs are the same with every property in every market.

## What exactly are the 2% and 1% rules?

The 2% rule is very simple. If a house costs $100,000 with no repairs needed, the monthly rent should be $2,000. If the house costs $100,000, and you must do $20,000 in repairs, the repairs would make the cost basis $120,000, and you would have to rent out the house for $2,400 per month. The 1% rule is exactly the same, but the rent would be 1% of the purchase price or cost basis.

If you think the 2% rule requires incredible rent-to-purchase-price ratios, you are right. If you think it is also virtually impossible to find properties that meet the 2% rule, you are also right. I know 2% rental properties exist, but they are usually priced very low (often under $50,000). You can make money with low-priced rentals, but you can make a lot of money on more expensive houses that do not meet the 2% rule. The 1% rule is much more achievable, and most of my properties come close to meeting it. You still cannot use a blanket rule to buy rentals.

I do not like the 2% rule because it only states what rent should be based on the cost basis. So many other variables need to be considered. The expenses from rental properties are what most people underestimate, and the 2% rule was created to make sure investors don't underestimate expenses. If you use the 2% rule when buying properties, you will make money if you can find properties that meet the guidelines. More likely, you will never find a decent rental property that meets those guidelines unless you live in an area with very low prices. The problem is the rule is so extreme that it makes it impossible for most people to buy a rental property.

Taxes are different in every state. Each rental property is different, and even some homes that meet the 2% rule will have a tough time generating money depending on the circumstances. My rentals don't come close to meeting the 2% rule but still generate a lot of money. My rentals are much closer to the 1% rule, but I would not use any rules when trying to decide if a rental property is a good deal.

Properties that meet the 1% rule may be a better investment than properties that meet the 2% rule. Sure, 2%-rule properties will generate more money on paper, but they are usually lower-priced rentals. Lower-priced rentals come with more turnover, more maintenance, more vacancies, and can be harder to finance.

This shows why it is so important to run the numbers yourself and not to rely on a rule. I never used any rules when I bought my rentals. I calculated what my cash-on-cash returns would be based on all the expenses and expected rents. If you take shortcuts, you may miss out on some awesome deals or invest in some horrible ones.

## Why you should not count on appreciation

I base my strategy on cash flow, not on appreciation. Do I want my properties to appreciate? Yes! It allows me to refinance more easily and possibly pull cash out to buy more properties if I need to. However, I do not need my rental properties to appreciate to make money and get good returns.

One of the biggest mistakes investors make is buying rental properties that generate little or no cash flow and hoping the houses will appreciate. In my mind, this is not investing: this is speculating that the market will increase in value. I never buy a property with my only profit potential being appreciation.

Positive cash flow allows me to bring in income as soon as I rent out the house. If house values go down, it does not hurt me because I am making money from cash flow, and I do not need to sell the house. In fact, I do not want to sell because the property is generating income every month.

The biggest problem with buying a rental property with negative cash flow is investors usually underestimate their expenses. The fact they are buying a property with negative cash flow means they are usually stretching their buying criteria to make the deal.

Many novice investors do not account for the unknown because they really want to make a deal work. Justifying numbers that don't make sense is very easy when you are a new investor looking for your first deal. When I started investing in rental properties, I underestimated expenses all the time. I used minimum repair and vacancy expense numbers hoping that things would work out. When you underestimate expenses, you let emotions make the deal, which is a big mistake. If you really want to make a deal work and you fudge the numbers to get everything to line up correctly, you may end up with negative cash flow every month.

## Even if you plan for negative cash flow, most investors cannot maintain it

Most investors quickly tire of writing checks on properties with negative cash flow. As I just discussed, most investors underestimate their expenses, and with negative cash flow, that can mean they are paying out hundreds of dollars each month on one property. While those investors are waiting for the house to appreciate, they are losing thousands each year due to negative cash flow. The investor realizes very quickly that hoping the housing market will increase while they continue to lose money doesn't make sense. The investor's only choice is to continue to dump cash into the property or to sell at a loss. Even if the investor can sell the house for as much as they bought it for (or slightly more), selling costs will eat up all the profit.

Selling costs usually total 6 to 10% of the value of a house. Investors got into trouble during the housing crisis because they were investing based purely on anticipated appreciation without regard for cash flow or long-term scenarios. When you buy for appreciation, it takes huge market gains to make the money back you spend on selling costs and expenses.

The simple way to avoid shelling out cash every month on a rental is to invest in a house that cash flows. If values go down, rents may go down as well, but unless your margins are tight, you will still cash flow, and you will not have to sell. The easiest way to lose money in real estate is to have to sell your property quickly in a buyers' market. The only buyer may be an investor like me who is looking for a great deal!

## Predicting the real estate market does not work for me

House prices historically appreciate, but that does not mean you can predict when and by how much prices will go up. In the last decade, house prices in the United States have gone through a huge upturn, downturn, and then another huge upturn. I like to make money by buying a house below market value. However, many investors live in an area with extremely high real estate prices, and they invest hoping for appreciation. I understand why investors buy for appreciation because it is very hard to find cash-flowing rental properties or houses with enough room to flip in highly competitive markets. Investors justify their decision to invest for appreciation because they feel they are in a highly desirable economic location. I do not like to invest for appreciation because there are so many factors beyond our control that affect housing prices. I love it when my houses appreciate, but I do not need them to appreciate to make money.

## Why do some housing markets appreciate more than others?

Real estate markets constantly increase and decrease in value, with some markets fluctuating much more than others. California has seen huge increases in real estate prices...and huge decreases. Check out this graph of the historical home prices in Southern California from aboutinflation.com.

Los Angeles CA Real Estate Inflation Adjusted Index Trend Historical graph 1953 - 2013

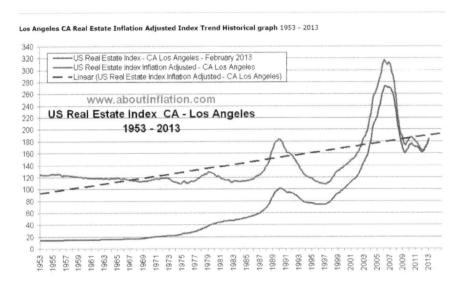

This shows some fluctuation over the last 60 years in Southern California. This graph does not show the large increase in house values recently, but prices have shot up again. Many investors feel California has many things going for it: great weather, a good economy, and an increasing population that will continue to push prices up. However, California had those same things going for it when the market crashed. Markets with the highest population growth and the best economies usually see the highest appreciation. However, areas with the highest appreciation also see the largest declines in values when the market turns.

If you look at the graph below, you see a much more stable real estate market in Dallas. Companies like Toyota are relocating there, which is leading to more new house inventory. Prices in Dallas did not appreciate as much as California, but they also did not decrease as much. Even with steadily rising prices for decades, Dallas saw a sharp decrease in prices during the housing crisis. If you buy and hold properties long enough in stable or declining markets, your house will most likely appreciate given enough time. When you are investing for appreciation without any cash flow coming in, how long can you hold properties until they pay off?

## What are the risks of buying for appreciation?

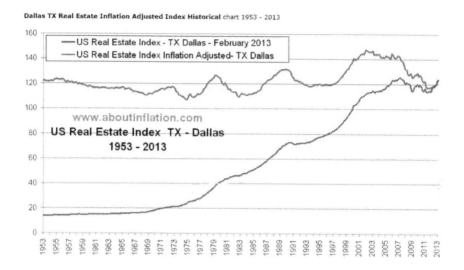

Dallas TX Real Estate Inflation Adjusted Index Historical chart 1953 - 2013

The Dallas and California markets show the differences between highly volatile markets and stable markets. Most people who buy rental properties or flips for appreciation are doing it because they cannot buy for cash flow or a profit in their current market. They are seeing huge value increases, and rents do not come close to making up for the prices they must pay for properties. They hope the appreciation will continue so they will be able to sell for a profit in six months or a year. The problem is that prices do not always continue to rise, even in very stable markets with a great economy and high buyer demand.

If you are counting on appreciation for house flips, you are running a very risky business. Many investors used this strategy before the housing crisis and went bankrupt when the market turned. If you buy a fix-and-flip with enough profit to make money using current market prices, you should be okay, even in a market downturn. I flipped houses before and after the last housing crisis, and my county had the highest foreclosure rate in the country for a while. If you buy rental properties hoping for appreciation and the market turns, you are stuck with a property that makes no money that you cannot sell. Many investors also did this with rental properties before the housing crisis and went bankrupt when the market turned.

There is an easy way to avoid being someone who loses all their rental properties to foreclosure: buy for cash flow, have reserves, and don't expect appreciation as your only way to make money.

## Is it possible to predict which housing markets will appreciate and when?

Many investors look at every economic indicator and think they can predict which markets will appreciate. Are there plenty of jobs, local colleges, emerging technologies, etc.? They feel good economic indicators and a strong housing market will promote even higher housing prices. I do not believe this to be the case because there are so many variables to consider with the housing market. Many investors betting on appreciation went bankrupt in the last housing crisis because all the economic indicators looked strong. What factors will affect housing prices?

**Interest rates**: If interest rates rise, it could dramatically affect how much house people can afford and could negatively affect housing prices.

**National economy:** The national economy was a huge part of the last housing crisis: unemployment skyrocketed and people could not afford their houses anymore.

**World economy:** It does not seem like China's economy could hurt the U.S. housing market, but it can. The Chinese economy can affect the U.S. stock market, and a decline in the U.S. stock market could cause concern for the economy, which affects the housing market.

**Building supplies:** If building-supply costs continue to rise, new construction prices will continue to rise. If there is a shortage of already constructed houses on the market, people turn to new construction. The cost of new houses can greatly affect the cost of already constructed ones. An oversupply of new houses can cause local housing markets to decline greatly.

**Lending guidelines:** The housing crisis was caused in part by loose lending guidelines. People could finance over 100% of the value of their houses, and when values stopped going up, people went underwater. Lending guidelines changed after the housing crisis, making it harder to get a loan for a while.

**Foreclosures:** The more foreclosures there are, the lower prices are because supply increases. I doubt we will see the huge price decreases we saw during the housing crisis, but a large increase in foreclosures could easily cause prices to stop appreciating and decrease. With looser lending guidelines, there is a greater chance of more foreclosures in our future.

Given all the local, national, and international factors that affect housing prices, I think it is difficult for an individual investor to predict what housing prices will do. Prices could continue to rise, or they could fall sharply if one of these variables changes.

## Are you the only one betting on appreciation?

Some investors believe their local economy is so strong that they can withstand the national variables that cause prices to decrease. In highly competitive markets, many investors are looking to invest, and they all may be justifying mediocre investments with the same reasons: the schools are great; everyone loves it here; the weather is awesome; so the housing market must keep going up. How do you know if prices are already too high for what the local economy can support? Those investors are pushing prices up even higher than what the local economy and buyer demand can support. There may even be large hedge funds betting on that same appreciation pushing prices higher. Just because a market has a great economy and high buyer demand, it doesn't always mean prices will go up. Affordability and many other factors are also big factors.

## Can you predict housing prices in stagnant areas?

Predicting which housing markets will appreciate (and when) is very difficult, but it is easier to determine which housing markets will not appreciate. If an area has no or negative growth, it will be almost impossible for housing prices to increase in value. House prices increase because there are too few houses for the number of people looking to buy. If there are too many houses for the current population, housing prices will decrease and continue to decrease until the houses are removed or more buyers come to town. Many areas in the Midwest have very stable populations, and they see almost no appreciation because there is always an ample supply of houses for sale. Because so many people moved away, Detroit removed houses to decrease the housing supply.

Housing prices constantly go up and down. It is very hard for anyone to predict exactly when and by how much they will appreciate. Prices may keep going up for one year, two years, or more, but they may also start decreasing in a few months. The United States economy is doing pretty well now, but that could change very quickly based on the climate, oil prices, the world economy, and thousands of other factors. The great thing is you can still make a lot of money in real estate relatively safely by buying below market value and buying for cash flow.

## How much cash flow do you need?

Another question investors must ask themselves is how much cash flow they'll need from their rental properties? How much cash flow do you need to be secure? How much cash flow do you need to justify spending money on a rental property? How much cash flow do you need to reach your financial goals?

Positive cash flow is a great thing, but how much is enough? Obviously, the more cash flow the better, but awesome cash-flowing properties do not exactly grow on trees. The return a person requires to justify spending a specific amount of cash on a rental property is a personal decision. I like to see $500 in monthly cash flow from my properties, which I purchased for $80,000 to $140,000. If you are buying less- or more-expensive properties, your cash-flow requirements may be different. Another way to look at the returns is the cash-on-cash return.

I like to see over 15% cash-on-cash returns, but I love to see closer to 20%.

Some people would be happy with 15, 10, or even 5% returns on their cash. Remember, you will usually have higher returns on rental properties than just the cash-on-cash percentage once you factor in mortgage paydown, tax advantages, possible appreciation, and buying below market value.

## What are cash-on-cash returns and how do you calculate them?

People rarely hear the term cash-on-cash return outside of the real estate world. Stocks and most investments are judged by ROI (return on investment), not cash-on-cash. Determining the ROI on rental properties is very difficult because, until you sell a rental property, you will not know the actual return on your investment. The cash-on-cash return is a much easier number to calculate because it looks at the cash return from rental properties compared to the cash invested.

The way I calculate cash-on-cash return may not be the exact way an accountant would calculate it, but this technique is the best way for me to judge the returns I am getting.

## Why is it hard to calculate the ROI on rental properties?

ROI stands for return on investment, which is usually a good way to judge investments. With ROI, you sum all the money you made from your investment and divide it into the cash invested. If you make $50,000 on an investment that cost you $500,000, you have made an ROI of 10%.

ROI includes your total investment versus your total returns. Rental properties have many awesome benefits. There are tax benefits thanks to depreciation, leverage, cash flow, appreciation, and the ability to refinance take out cash.

My rentals have increased my net worth by well over $1.5 million. However, if I sold my rentals, I would have to pay selling costs and high taxes. I would not get all that cash back, and I would have to divide what is left of that money along with my cash flow and tax benefits over the years I have owned my properties to see what my yearly ROI is Right now, my estimation of the selling prices and costs are an educated guess, and I have not realized any of that gain.

## How is cash-on-cash return calculated?

The cash-on-cash return is calculated by determining the cash flow or rental income and dividing it by the initial cash invested into that property. If you spend $25,000 on down payment, closing costs, and repairs and earn $5,000 in cash flow, your cash-on-cash return is 20%. To make it easy, I created a cash-on-cash calculator on my website: https://investfourmore.com/calculators/rental-property-cash-flow/.

Determining cash-on-cash returns seems simple, but some situations make it difficult. The biggest problem is deciding when to start calculating the cash-on-cash return. If you buy a rental property that needs repairs, it may not be ready to rent out for weeks or even months. You will pay the down payment and closing costs when you buy the house, but you will not pay the contractor until work is completed. You also will not collect rent until the house has been repaired and rented out. I like to start calculating the cash-on-cash return once I have paid all expenses and the house has been rented out.

The cash-on-cash return does not tell us everything like the ROI will. It does not factor in any appreciation or tax benefits. The cash-on-cash return also does not factor in the equity pay down on loans, which can be a significant amount of money. I like to calculate my cash-on-cash return on my rental properties, and I consider the other benefits a bonus. If a new rental property provides at least 15% cash-on-cash return, I know I will make a lot of money on that property.

## How do you determine how much cash flow and what kind of returns you need?

When you are trying to figure out how much return you need, here are a few things to consider:

- What is your end goal? Do you want to retire in ten years? Do you want to pay for your children's college? Do you want to build an empire? Do you want to be able to make more than you would in the stock market? Your end goal will help you determine how much in cash you need each month.
- Once you know how much money you want every month from your rentals, you must figure out how soon you need to get there. Is it five years, ten years or longer?
- How much money will you have to invest in rentals? The less money you have and the higher your goals, the more cash flow you will need.
- After you consider all these factors, you can start to build your own plan for how many properties you want and how much each property will need to generate.

## Conclusion

There are many ways to invest in rental properties, and many people have lost money investing in real estate. Most of the people who lose money did not invest wisely. They were betting on the market to improve, which is speculation...not investing. Even when you look at the investors who lost houses during the housing crisis, it was not as bad as many people think.

The total number of loans that foreclosed or started the foreclosure process through 2011 was about 7% for real estate investors who took out loans from 2004 to 2007. These loans were taken out when prices were the highest, loans were easy to get, and loan-to-value ratios were the highest. The loans should have produced the worst results for investors. About 1 out of 14 of the worst loans ever originated failed. Some investors had many houses, which meant 1 out of 14 loans went into foreclosure, not 1 out of 14 investors.

Even in the worst housing crisis we have ever seen, few investors lost houses. The horror stories you hear about are blown way out of proportion. If you invest the right way with cash flow, buy below market value, and cushion yourself with plenty of reserves in the bank, rental properties are not that risky.

# 5

# How Do You Know What Type of Investment Property to Buy?

Now that you have an idea of how to calculate the cash flow on rental properties and what a good rental property investment is, how do you know what type of property to buy? There are condos, single-family houses, college rentals, and multifamily properties. Many investors and gurus say one is better than the other, but which is better depends on you. What is your market like? What are your goals? And what can you get a great deal on? The next few sections will go through the different types of properties you can invest in along with the pros and cons of each.

## Are single-family or multifamily properties a better choice?

Many investors assume multifamily properties are the better investment because they are built to produce income for property owners. I invest in single-family residences because they give me great returns and are easy to find and manage. However, many successful investors also invest in multifamily properties. I believe the better investment depends on what you are looking for and what you can buy in your market.

## Can I buy single-family houses below market value?

The main reason I get great returns on single-family rentals is that I only buy properties that are below market value. Good deals are hard to find, but they are out there if you know how to find them. I try to buy properties at 70 to 80% of market value. Usually, the properties are cheap because they need work or have very motivated sellers. Not only do I make money as soon as I close because I bought the property below market value, but I usually also add value through repairs or improvements.

I have purchased rental properties through REOs, short sales, fair-market sales, and estate sales. Some of the keys to buying properties below market value are making offers quickly, having cash, strong financing, and having a good reputation for closing on properties. There must also be an ample supply of houses for sale. In my market, there are many more single-family than multifamily properties. The law of averages states I should be able to find more deals for single-family residences simply because there are more of them.

In some areas, multifamily properties produce great returns, but in my area, I can actually make better cash-on-cash returns by purchasing and renting out single-family properties. The rent-to-value ratio is higher on single family residences than it is on multifamily.

## Why can I make more money with single-family properties?

In Colorado, there is no way I could make over 15% cash-on-cash returns with multifamily residences. If I were to buy single-family properties at market value, I could not make 15% either, but there are so many more single-family properties available that it gives me a better chance of getting a great deal.

The CAP rate on multifamily residences in Colorado is around 5%. The CAP rate on single-family properties, which I buy below market value, is around 8% (sometimes higher). I do not know for sure why the CAP rate is so high on multifamily properties in Colorado. I would guess it is because we have a booming economy and great market appreciation, and large institutional investors are buying multifamily properties with cash. Those large investors are not as concerned with getting awesome returns as small investors are. Large investors are looking for modest returns and a safe place to park their money.

In other areas of the country, CAP rates for multifamily properties are 10% or higher. Therefore, knowing your market and formulating your own investing strategies is important. Doing exactly as I do doesn't make sense for everybody. You need to know your market and what the return will be for different types of assets.

## What are the advantages of single-family properties?

Single-family rentals are easier to manage than larger complexes. With a single-family rental, I do not have to pay any utilities. Tenants pay them all. In multifamily properties, the property owner is usually responsible for the water and, sometimes, electric and gas. Many tenants feel a single-family rental is their own house, not just an apartment or place to live. They usually take good care of the property and even fix and repair items themselves. They also tend to stay longer and renew their leases year after year. My parents have rented a single-family house to the same family for 14 years!

Single-family properties are usually less expensive than large complexes with multiple units. Large complexes bring in more rent, but because of that, they are much more expensive (at least in my area). The down payment, repairs, and maintenance expenses are usually lower with a single-family property than with multifamily properties. Because single-family properties are cheaper, investors may find them easier to buy than a multifamily property.

Single-family properties historically appreciate more than multifamily properties. Multifamily properties are valued on the rents and condition, while most single-family properties are valued on supply and demand. If rents go up in an area, multifamily housing prices will rise as well, but only if rents are raised to meet market rental rates.

Single-family properties are easier to sell. If an investor wants to cash out an investment or needs to sell for another reason, single-family properties have a larger buyer pool. They arc typically sold to owner-occupied buyers but may also be sold to investors. There is always a market for owner-occupied buyers, and there are many more of them than investors. When you own a multifamily complex, the only buyer is another investor. Single-family properties are much easier to sell because the buyer pool is so much larger.

## What are the advantages of multifamily properties?

Multifamily properties offer many advantages. As I mentioned, some areas see higher returns on multifamily properties than on single-family properties. Multifamily properties are valued on the income they produce, which can create opportunities. If a multifamily property is under-rented or you can make improvements that greatly increase the income, you can greatly increase the value of the property.

Many investors buy large multifamily buildings that are run-down or contain tenants who are paying rent that is too low for the market. They slowly repair the property and raise rents, which greatly increases the value. The nice thing about this strategy is you do not have to hope market rents or values increase: you can force the value to increase by increasing the income the property brings in.

If you buy multifamily properties, you will have more units under one roof, which some investors consider an advantage. You will usually bring in more rent per square foot with multifamily properties, which means the maintenance may be lower over time. You must couple this with the fact that rents are usually lower for multifamily properties, and in my experience, the tenants do not take as good of care as an apartment as they would a single-family house. Buying many single-family properties is also safer than buying one apartment. If you invest everything in one building, and that building is condemned or damaged, you won't earn any rent. I have seen apartment complexes be condemned because of meth, and there was no insurance payout or way for the owner to collect rent for months.

You can buy multifamily properties with conventional or FHA mortgages if there are less than 4 units. You can only have one FHA mortgage in most cases. Getting more than four conventional mortgages is tough, and it's impossible to get more than ten conventional mortgages. Because you are buying more units with one loan, you may be able to buy more multifamily units with FHA and conventional loans. Many other loan options are available for single family and multifamily housing, and I'll discuss them later.

If you are a beginning investor looking to buy with little money down, house hacking a multifamily property can be a great way to get started. House hacking involves living in one unit and renting out the other units to take advantage of owner-occupant loans. I talk much more about this in a later chapter.

## Are college rentals a good investment?

College rentals can generate a lot of money but are very different from rental properties that are geared towards families. I have 16 rentals as of the writing of this book, and all but one of them (a duplex) are single-family rentals. The duplex could be considered a college rental since it has one college student in the basement and a family in the upper unit. I have been around college-rental properties my entire life since my parents and my sister both have college rentals. In fact, my sister used to manage over 100 college-rental units when she was a property manager. I used to help her manage those properties when I was in high school.

Many areas see higher rents for college rentals, but college rentals can take a lot more management and maintenance than single-family properties.

## What is a college-rental property?

A college-rental property is any property that is rented to college students. Most college rentals are located close to a college and are marketed specifically to college students. College rentals can be multifamily apartment buildings, single-family houses, houses that have been converted to multifamily properties, or a retail space with an apartment above or below it.

If you are investing in college rentals, make sure your college rental is zoned correctly. Many cities only allow a certain number of unrelated people to live in a single-family residence, which means that it may be illegal to rent a four-bedroom house to four college students if the house is zoned as single-family. If a house is zoned for multifamily, renting a six-bedroom house to six unrelated people may be perfectly fine. Always check the zoning before investing in college-rental properties as it will greatly affect the value. Do not assume a house is zoned for college students because it is close to a college. I have seen properties across the street from large universities that were zoned as single-family. If the city finds out you are using the house illegally, you may be forced to evict your tenants.

## Why do investors want to buy college rentals?

If a property is near a college, an investor will usually earn more rent from college students than from a family. Most college students will pay a premium to be close to school and to live with their friends. You could rent out a single-family property that is far from the college, but you cannot count on that house always being occupied, and you probably will not get a premium on the rent. Since college rentals demand more rent than a single-family property, many investors feel they can make more money renting to college students. In my experience, the higher rent will not always make up for the increased expenses that come with a college rental.

I was a college student, and I can say from personal experience college students do not always take care of their residences. They may not intentionally destroy a house (although some will), but they are young and inexperienced and don't know how to take care of a house. When college students rent a house, they may be on their own for the first time. They might not know how to take care of a house, even if they have the best intentions. My sister has had multiple students turn off the heat in the middle of winter for Christmas break. The pipes froze and burst, causing thousands of dollars in damage. This happened multiple times, not because the students tried to freeze the pipes, but because they were trying to save on heating costs and did not know any better.

College students may not have learned how to clean well. Therefore, the house will see more wear and tear than a single-family rental. Many families take pride in their houses, while college students only need a place to live and party. A family might take care of minor repairs without even telling the property owner. A college student may call the property owner for everything that could and does go wrong.

Unlike single-family residences, most college-rental owners pay some utilities and yard care. Many college rentals are houses that have been divided into multiple units and do not have separate water meters. The students will expect the property owner to pay water, and possibly other utilities, if they are not on separate meters.

## College-rental properties have more turnover than single-family rentals

The same tenant has lived in one of my single-family rentals for three years. On the other hand, college students are always moving and rarely stay in one residence for more than a year. When you rent to college students, you must expect high turnover, and you must have new tenants ready well before the current tenant moves out.

College students rent during very specific times. Most college rentals are leased in the spring after school is over or in the fall right before school begins. If a property is vacant during these periods, it may not be rented at all, or the property owner may have to drastically reduce the rent. The best college renters are usually searching for a place to live months before they must move to make sure they get a good place. Therefore, houses must be shown while they are being rented. The better your renters are, the better a house will show, and the more rent you will get.

Most college rentals are sold to other investors, unlike single-family rentals, which can be sold to either investors or owner-occupants. Because investors buy college rentals, they want to buy a property that is already rented out and is generating cash flow. A house that is not rented out will be worth much less than one that is.

College rentals may bring in more income than single-family rentals, but they have many more expenses and are more time consuming. I prefer single-family rentals due to lower expenses and less hassle. Just like multifamily properties, college rentals can also be harder to sell because investors are the main buyer pool.

## Are condos a good investment?

Finding a great rental property can be tough. In many markets, prices are increasing, and making money on a single-family house or multifamily building is difficult. One option is to buy the cheapest house you can find and make it a rental. You can also buy a townhouse or condo and turn it into a rental property since they are typically less expensive than single-family detached homes.

Condos and townhouses can be great investments, but you must look at the numbers closely. Condos have many costs that you will not have with single-family properties (like HOA fees). The appreciation may not be as high on condos, and some very scary issues can cause a great condo or townhouse investment to become a nightmare.

### What are condos and townhouses?

A condo is a unit within a large complex of apartments or other condos. There may be units next to, above, or below you. You rarely have any yard other than a shared space with other units.

A townhouse might have a small yard and may have units next to it but not above or below. Townhomes are typically worth more than condos because they have fewer connected neighbors and some land. Both condos and townhomes are worth less than similar single-family properties.

## How do HOAs work?

Almost every townhouse and condo has an HOA (homeowners' association). The HOA takes care of the shared land, and most take care of the exterior maintenance and landscaping. Many HOAs also pay for the water and may provide common amenities such as a pool, clubhouse, or tennis courts. Some single-family properties may also have a neighborhood HOA. The HOA fees are usually much higher on a condo or townhouse because the HOA takes care of many more items. Here is a list of many things that an HOA handles on single-family detached properties, patio homes, condos, and townhomes.

| | Condo or Townhome | Patio Home | Single Family |
|---|---|---|---|
| Common Area | Yes | Yes | Yes |
| Land-scaping | Yes | Yes | No |
| Water Service | Yes | Possibly | No |
| Exterior Maintenance | Yes | Possibly | No |
| Exterior Insurance | Yes | Possibly | No |
| Clubhouse and Pool | Yes | Possibly | Possibly |
| Trash and Snow Removal | Yes | Possibly | Possibly |

A patio home is usually a single-family detached house with an HOA that maintains the lawn. HOAs for condos and townhomes are more involved, which makes them much more expensive.

In Northern Colorado, HOA fees for most single-family detached houses are around $400 or less per year. Monthly HOA fees on condos or townhomes are usually at least $100 and in some cases $400. HOA fees can be even higher in larger cities with complexes that have security and many more amenities. Only one of my rental properties has an HOA, and it costs $300 per year.

## Is an HOA on a rental property bad?

I have no problem with having an HOA on my rentals. The HOA takes care of the common amenities in the neighborhood, and I have never had a problem with them. The only other responsibility of this HOA is to make sure all the houses in the neighborhood comply with HOA rules and regulations. Many HOAs do not allow work trucks to be parked outside or excessive junk to be stored in the yard. For many people, this is a good thing, and for others, it is not. As a property owner, I appreciate having another set of eyes on the property, and I like to know if the tenants have junk everywhere or are not mowing the lawn.

I do not think having a small HOA with few responsibilities is a bad thing. A larger HOA will provide many benefits, and even though a larger HOA will be more expensive, it will lower many property owners' costs. The HOA will pay for exterior insurance and maintenance, which will reduce expenses. It will handle yard maintenance and snow removal, which can also lower expenses. In my case, I invest in single-family properties and have the tenants take care of the lawn and pay all utilities, so an HOA does not save me much money.

The drawback to large HOAs is they can charge special assessments if they need extra money for major repairs or if they have financial problems. I know of property owners whose HOA fees increased greatly in a one-year span because the HOA had to repaint the exterior of the entire complex. Monthly fees increased from just over $100 to $200 for every condo in the complex. Another HOA imposed a $30,000 special assessment on every single condo in a complex to pay for improvements. This particular property owner was planning to flip the condo, and he lost all his profit because of this assessment.

An HOA cannot impose a special assessment or raise fees without agreement from the HOA members, but in many cases, members do not show up to HOA meetings to oppose the changes. If a condo or townhouse has a fixed HOA fee, the HOA can still increase monthly fees or require special assessments.

## Do condos and townhomes appreciate as much as detached houses?

Another factor to consider when buying a condo or townhouse is property value. Condos and townhomes are less expensive than detached houses because they cost less to build and demand for them is not as great. Single-family properties come with more land and have lower HOA fees. An HOA fee reduces the amount a borrower can qualify for when getting a loan. Usually, condos and townhomes with the highest HOA fees are worth less than similar condos or townhouses with lower fees because fewer buyers can afford them. A $100 monthly fee could reduce the amount a buyer can qualify for by as much as $20,000.

Even though I invest for cash flow when I buy rental properties, I still consider possible appreciation or depreciation. Some people prefer a condo to a detached house, but most people want a detached property. In my area, condos are the first to start losing value in a down market and the last to increase in value in an appreciating market. While condos and townhouses can appreciate (and often do) single-family detached houses tend to appreciate more.

## How can FHA rules affect condo prices?

FHA will loan on condos and townhouses, but they have very strict rules. If investors own more than 50% of the units in a particular complex, FHA will not loan to anyone in that complex. FHA is a very popular loan, and it can greatly decrease values in a complex if the units cannot be sold using FHA.

As you can see, you must consider many factors when investing in a condo or a townhouse. The number one factors should be cash flow and buying below market value. You must remember to factor in the HOA fees and the possibility they may increase in the future. If you buy a condo in an older complex that will need work soon, you may see a huge increase in HOA fees or a special assessment. If many investors decide to buy units in a complex, the value of every unit might drop due to FHA rules, and you will not be able to expect as much appreciation.

You can make money with condos, but given similar returns between a condo or townhouse and a single-family detached property, I will take the detached house every time.

## Is buying cheap rental properties wise?

I prefer single-family rental properties that are slightly below the median sales price in my area. Other investors make money buying multifamily rentals or inexpensive rentals. There is no best way to invest for everyone, but there may be a best way to invest for you based on your market, goals, money available, and many other factors.

When I purchased most of my rentals, the median price was about $200,000. I have purchased rental properties that cost anywhere from $80,000 to $140,000. I buy my properties below market value and make repairs, so they are actually worth $150,000 to $200,000 when I rent them out. I would not consider these cheap rentals because they are not the bottom of my market. In my market, the lowest priced houses cost $50,000 to $70,000.

Even though I purchased some of my properties for less than $90,000, buying properties that fit my criteria for under $110,000 today is almost impossible. When I bought my first rental properties, I could have purchased many them for under $50,000 (some as low as $30,000). The definition of cheap rental properties varies in every market, but if I had to define it, I would say properties under $50,000 are generally considered cheap rentals.

## Why are returns different for differently priced rentals?

Rental properties that cost $50,000 or less will have vastly different returns than properties that cost $200,000. Typically, the lower-priced rental will have more maintenance and more turnover as well as lower appreciation over time. There are exceptions to this rule, which I see in my market. If I had bought rentals costing $30,000 in my market a few years ago, I would have made a killing today. Those properties are now worth many times more what they were just three or four years ago.

However, my market had not seen prices as low as they were four years ago since well before 2000. I would not expect every market with $30,000 houses to see the appreciation we did. Many areas that have $30,000 houses for sale have seen low or stagnant prices for years. When you buy cheap rental properties, you are usually not betting on appreciation—you're investing for cash flow. Often, the rent-to-value ratio on lower-priced rental properties is better than on more expensive ones. That high rent-to-price ratio is what makes low-priced rental properties attractive to buyers, even with more maintenance and turnover.

## Why is the rent-to-value ratio higher on less-expensive rentals?

Rental rates are determined by the supply and demand for rental properties in a given market. Rental rates are not determined by housing prices or building costs. Large apartment buildings usually have the lowest rental rates. If there is a shortage of apartment buildings in a given market, rental rates will usually rise. Eventually, when rental rates get high enough, new apartment buildings pop up very quickly to meet the demand because

BUILD A RENTAL PROPERTY EMPIRE

investors see the need for more units. However, no matter how many apartments are for rent, there will always be people who want to rent single-family houses.

When there is a shortage of single-family properties for rent, builders usually do not build more houses to meet that demand, especially at the low-end of the market. Builders simply cannot build cheaply enough in most markets to make newly constructed rental properties a viable business. Builders target owner-occupant buyers when they build new houses. When there is a shortage of single-family rental properties in an area, rents will increase, but unlike apartment buildings, new construction does not ease the supply shortage.

Most low-priced rental property markets are found in the Midwest, and you may see properties sell for $30,000 that can be rented out for $600 to $700 per month. That is a great margin when you consider my properties rent for $1,200 to $1,500 per month.

The rent-to-value ratio may be higher on low-priced rentals, but that does not mean cash flow is higher. The expenses on a lower-priced rental are most likely going to be a higher percentage of the value of the property. Here is an example of how an investor might calculate the costs on a higher-versus lower-priced rental property. These numbers were generated from my cash-flow calculator on Investfourmore.com. I am using these numbers based on a higher-priced rental property I could buy in my area and a lower-priced rental that could be bought in another state.

**Higher-priced rental bought for $130,000**
  Rent: $1,500
  Maintenance: $225
  Vacancies: $150
  Taxes: $60
  Insurance: $60
  Property Management: $120
  Total expenses: $615
  **Cash flow: $885**

72

**Lower priced rental bought for $35,000**

Rent: $700

Maintenance: $140

Vacancies: $70

Taxes: $40

Insurance: $50

Property Management: $56

Total expenses: $356

**Cash flow: $344**

Looking at these numbers. The low-priced rental blows away the high-priced rental when bought for cash. If I were to get a loan on the high-priced rental property, the mortgage payment would be approximately $500 per month. That would drop my monthly cash flow to below $400, and if I had to make repairs to this house before I bought it, my cash investment would be similar to the $35,000 the low-priced rental property costs. The returns are not that different between the two but are slightly higher with the high-priced property. We do need to look at the numbers closer to see why low-priced rentals have different expense ratios than high-priced ones.

- **Age**: In my cash-flow calculator, I devote a higher percentage to maintenance costs on older houses. The older house will likely need more maintenance. However, with lower-quality tenants, you may need to factor in an even higher maintenance allocation. Cheaper properties tend to be older.
- **Lower expenses due to lower rent**: The rent is much lower on the cheaper property, which makes the expenses much lower for vacancies and maintenance. The entire maintenance allowance for the year on the cheap property is $1,680, and it's $2,700 on the more expensive property. If the properties were the same size, accounting for maintenance costs that high on a more-expensive house wouldn't make sense, but the cheaper rental is most likely smaller, so I think those figures are a decent representation.

- **Maintenance**: I used the same maintenance percentage for both rentals, but this may be misleading. The more expensive property is rented for more money, and lost rent would be higher than the cheaper property. However, in my experience, more-expensive rentals have more stable tenants. An eviction costs the same no matter what type of rental you have, and the likelihood of an eviction is higher with the less-expensive rental. The yearly vacancy cost for the expensive rental comes to $1,800. The same cost on the lower-priced rental is $840. I think the costs should be similar for both properties.
- **Insurance**: insurance costs are based on risk and replacement costs. The insurance cost will be lower on a smaller house...but not by much. If insurance on a $130,00 house is $600, it will not be $200 on a $30,000 house. It may be $400 or $500 per year, which is a higher percentage of the cost compared to the value of the property.
- **Property Management:** property management fees should be similar on each property.

When looking at the percentage cost of the expenses on the two properties, the cheaper property's expenses are over 50% of the rent, and the expensive property's expenses are just over 40%. The expenses may not be high enough for the cheap property because vacancy and maintenance costs may be more than what an investor assumes they will be.

While the cheap rental property may look like a slam-dunk on the surface, it has more expenses and may take more management. That does not mean the properties cannot generate money or that it will not be a good investment.

## What are the disadvantages of buying low-priced rentals?

With ratios this good, there must be a reason not everyone invests in low-priced rentals. In fact, there are many reasons many investors do not like low-priced rentals.

- **Higher turnover:** when you rent out the lowest priced houses in a market, you tend to get less-than-ideal tenants. There is a greater chance of evictions, damage, and other problems.
- **More maintenance:** often, the lowest-priced rentals in a market are older houses. The older a house, the more maintenance it will need, and lower-quality tenants can do more damage to a house.
- **Less appreciation:** I do not like to invest for appreciation only, but increases in house values doesn't hurt. In most cases, the lower the house's value, the less appreciation it will see.
- **Buy below market value:** I buy all my houses below market value, which gives me instant equity. However, 20% on a $30,000 house is only $6,000, while 20% on a $100,000 house is $20,000. You earn less equity when buying cheaper houses below market value.
- **Getting a loan:** due to more risk and less profit, most banks do not want to loan on cheap properties. Getting an investor to loan on a $30,000 house is very difficult.

## What are the advantages of buying low-priced rentals?

Cheaper properties aren't all bad. Lower-priced rentals offer other advantages in addition to the higher rent-to-value ratio.

   **Smaller houses:** Lower-priced rentals are typically older, which means more maintenance. They are typically smaller which means maintenance costs less. Painting a 700-square-foot house will cost a third less than painting a 2,000-square-foot house. There are fewer windows, a smaller furnace, a smaller roof, and less floor space. Smaller houses may need maintenance more often, but that does not mean the total maintenance costs will be more than on a larger rental.

- **Can buy with cash:** you can spend the same amount of money buying inexpensive rentals with cash as you would with a loan on a higher-priced house. When investors already own multiple rentals, are foreign, are investing with an IRA, or show low income on their taxes, getting loans is difficult. Paying with cash is an easy way to buy rentals when you cannot get a loan.

· **Less chance of loss:** with less-expensive houses, there is usually less appreciation, but there is also a smaller depreciation loss. Inexpensive houses can go down in value, but if values drop 30% on a $30,000 house versus a $100,000 one, your losses will be much less.

## Is it better to buy low-priced or higher-priced rentals?

There is no right answer for everyone. You must figure out for yourself which type of property is right for you. I like higher-priced rentals because they are not as old, have less maintenance, less turnover, and sometimes, better appreciation. I also have no problem getting loans on my rentals, even with ten mortgages (more on that later).

If you are in a position where getting a loan is harder, lower-priced rentals might be a better option. I prefer to buy local rentals at below market value, but if those are not available, I would try buying an out-of-state property. If you are having a hard time finding good rentals in your market, a cheaper turn-key property could be a good option (we will talk about turn-key properties later).

If you are looking at less-expensive properties in your market, you must consider many factors. Calculate how much you will make with less-expensive versus more-expensive properties. Consider historical values, which property is a better deal, and how much management each property will require. If you still cannot decide, buy one of each and see which one you like better!

## Can vacation rentals be a good investment?

My wife and I recently went to Turks and Caicos, which are incredibly beautiful islands in the Caribbean. While there, we were tempted to buy a vacation rental. It seems like every time we go on vacation, we think about buying a vacation house, but this time we gave it more thought. Turks and Caicos was our favorite vacation destination, and prices were relatively affordable.

We thought about buying a vacation house because we love it there and plan to go back repeatedly. At first, vacation rentals appear to be a wise decision if you visit the same destination often enough. The plan would be to buy a house or condo on the beach, stay there a few times per year, and rent it out when we are not staying there. However, when we looked at the investing side of a vacation rental, we were reminded why it is not always a wise financial decision.

## How much money can you make from vacation rentals?

Staying on the island is very expensive. Our one-bedroom condo cost $400 to $500 per night. It had direct ocean views, a balcony, two baths, and a full kitchen. You can buy similar condos in the same building for under $400,000. On the surface, that looks like a great return on your money: buy a place for $400,000 and rent it out for $12,000 per month. That blows the 2% rule out of the water, and the rent-to-value ratio is much higher than what I earn on my rental properties!

One reason I was intrigued by real estate in Turks and Caicos was the rent-to-value ratios. We stayed on Florida's gulf cost a couple of times in the last few years. On our last trip, we paid $2,400 for one week in a three-bedroom, oceanfront house. That house recently went up for sale for $1.6 million. The rent was lower on the Florida beach house, but the value was over three times higher than the Turks and Caicos condo. This shows how much rents and values can vary in different markets.

The problem with vacation rentals is the cost to manage and maintain them. I pay a property manager 8% of my rents. The cost for a property manager on vacation rentals is 20% to 50% of the rents! The management fees on the units we looked at were 40%.

Short-term rentals are also vacant much more frequently than longer-term rentals. There are high and low seasons, and you cannot expect to see peak income year round. The total income on one unit in 2014 was $72,000 and another was $62,000. These units were identical, adjacent units, but the income differences show the volatility with vacation rentals. It also shows that you cannot count on $400 per night every night. Weekly rates will be lower; the unit will be vacant many night; and off-season rates will be much lower.

The actual monthly income is not $12,000. It's closer to $6,000 once you factor in the vacancies and off-season rates.

## Why are management fees so high on vacation rentals?

I used to manage my rental properties myself, but once I got to seven rentals, I started to run out of time. I couldn't manage my properties, flip houses, run a real estate team, and write my blog! With a property manager, my properties have become almost completely passive except for the purchase.

Managing a vacation rental is an entirely different situation. Vacation rentals take much more marketing, much more active management, have more inquiries from renters, need more cleaning, and are more like a hotel. Managers need to be able to check people in at all times and even be a concierge in some cases. More responsibilities and work means you must pay much higher fees.

Property management fees on the Turks and Caicos condos are $20,000 to $30,000 per year alone! We have not even talked about the other expenses that come with a vacation house.

## What expenses would a vacation house have that a regular rental would not?

When you invest in condos, you must also consider HOA or maintenance fees. On beachfront condos, HOA fees can be very high. There is a pool, maid service, parking lot, and towels. Properties near the beach have extra expenses. The beach must be maintained, and buildings weather faster due to salt and wind. The occasional hurricane can really cause problems. Monthly HOA fees on beachfront condos can easily run $1,000 or more.

Vacation rentals must be furnished, have dishes, silverware, linens, televisions, and everything someone would need while staying there. Over time, these items must be replaced and upgraded to keep the rental unit desirable. If you are charging $400 each night, it must be very nice.

Vacation rental owners must pay for all utilities as well. The electric, gas, cable, water, and internet add expenses and will most likely cost more in exotic places such as the Caribbean. Fresh water comes from rain and desalinization, not wells or rivers. Internet, cable, and electric all cost more.

If you want an oceanfront property, I guarantee it will be in a flood zone. You will need flood insurance, which is much more expensive than regular insurance.

Here are the total monthly costs of a beachfront vacation rental compared to a regular single-family rental (assuming they rent for the same amount or you have multiple single-family rentals that rent for the same as one vacation rental):

|  | Vacation Rental | Single Family |
|---|---|---|
| Rent Received | $5,833 | $5,833 |
| HOA Fees | $1,000 | $0 |
| Property Mgt | $2,333 | $467 |
| Utilities | $60 | $0 |
| Credit Card Fees | $60 | $0 |
| Travel Agent Fees | $300 | $0 |
| Maintenance | $600 | $600 |
| Taxes | $0 | $416 |
| Insurance | $500 | $400 |
| **Total Costs** | **$4,993** | **$1,883** |

These are not all the costs, but they're meant to show the huge differences between a long-term rental and a short-term vacation one. I did not include vacancies because the rents I used for the vacation rental are actual returns.

Keep in mind that with a single-family rental property, you will have much fewer vacancies than with a vacation rental.

Here are a few more vacation-rental costs that I have not discussed:

- Most people book vacation rentals with a credit card, and you must pay processing fees to accept credit cards.
- You pay travel agents a commission to book a vacation rental for you.
- Insurance costs could vary greatly. I assume five single-family rentals were needed to create that income, but insurance may be more or less depending on the number of properties. Flood insurance is much higher on each property.
- Taxes are very skewed in this vacation-rental scenario. In TCI, there are no property taxes, but there is a 15% tax on all property purchases. You would have to add $60,000 in taxes to a $400,000 purchase. Over five years, that would average out to $1,000 a month.
- The utilities on the condos we looked at were not very high because the HOA took care of the water, electricity, and cable. They also handled the exterior maintenance but not the interior maintenance. Obviously, vacation-rental expenses eat up almost all the income. If you consider the huge initial tax bill, all the income is used on the vacation rental, and this is if you pay cash!

## What about all the money you save when you go on vacation?

The reason most people consider a vacation rental is they think buying a vacation house will save them money. Even though you actually lose money on this particular vacation condo, buying it may make sense if you stay there often enough. You will save thousands on every vacation, right? The problem is, every time you stay at your vacation rental, you take it off the rental market. You could be renting to someone else, and you lose rental income.

Is owning a vacation house really an advantage if you stay there a week or two each year? Will you also feel obligated to vacation in the same spot each year? What if you must use your vacation time on a wedding, graduation, family reunion, funeral, or another occasion? Most people do not use their vacation properties as much as they think they will. This is one of the reasons timeshares are such a horrible investment.

The numbers I have used so far assume you are paying cash for a vacation rental, and you are still losing money! If you get a loan, you will lose even more money. Do you want to tie up $400,000 or more in a vacation rental that you use a couple times each year? $400,000 would give me over $7,000 in monthly rental income because I can use that money with financing to buy a lot of properties. That $7,000 would more than pay for a couple of vacations per year in some nice places! Not to mention getting financing in another country, or even another state, isn't easy.

## When would buying a vacation rental make sense?

There are some instances when buying a vacation rental would make sense, but they can still be very risky.

If you wanted to invest strictly for appreciation, a vacation rental might make sense. Prices can go down on vacation properties the same as other houses.

If you were going to live in a vacation house for months out of the year, it might make sense.

If you were going to manage the property yourself, you could make money. However, you must spend a lot of time on marketing and management.

Even in these scenarios, there are other risks, such as beach erosion, natural disasters, political changes in other countries, insurance changes, and giant half-finished resorts next to your condo!

On the surface, a vacation house may seem like a great investment. They are not making any more oceans, and there is only so much beachfront property. If you must tie up huge sums of cash to buy the property, but you lose money every month, is it worth it? For me it is not worth the risk, the money it would take, and the loss of flexibility with my vacation choices. I love Turks and Caicos, but that does not mean I want to spend every vacation there for the rest of my life.

There are many different types of vacation properties and many different locations. Some investors may make a lot of money with their vacation houses, but you must look at the numbers closely. You also should remember that laws and regulations can change. In Florida, many areas require at least a one-month stay, which makes it tough to rent out a vacation rental. In Anaheim, where we stay at a vacation rental for Disneyland, they passed an ordinance making it illegal to have vacation rentals!

## Is investing in commercial real estate wise?

Commercial and residential real estate investments are very different, and learning the ins and outs of each takes time. Commercial real estate may be a great investment for some, but I prefer residential real estate, and I think new investors are better off with residential rental properties. However, if an investor is well versed in commercial real estate and is willing to work hard, there is a lot of money to be made.

One reason I like residential rental properties is I am a real estate agent who specializes in residential properties. Because I deal with residential properties all day long, I am more familiar with residential rentals than commercial ones. I know how to buy residential properties below market value, and I know my rental market very well. I also invest in residential properties because, in my area, residential rental properties tend to give better returns than commercial ones.

## Are residential rental properties easier to understand than commercial ones?

Buying a residential rental property is straightforward once you learn your sales and rental markets. You need to know the cost of the house, how much it will cost to repair, how much it will be worth, and for how much it will rent. Even though residential rental properties are not complicated, learning how to invest in them and make money still takes time.

Commercial properties, on the other hand, are much more complicated than residential ones. With commercial rental properties, you need to know the same things as you do with residential ones, but figuring out those numbers is much more difficult. Factors that affect rent and value are the type of tenant that best suits your building, the length of the lease, how solid your tenant is, and the future desirability of your building. All of this is important with residential but much more so with commercial. The reason these factors are more important with commercial is that they have a huge impact on the property's value, whereas owner-occupied-buyer demand drives single-family residential property values.

Residential property value is calculated by determining how much similar properties are selling for. Many more residential properties sell than commercial ones, and finding sold residential properties that are similar to a house you own or are looking to buy is easier. Residential property values are derived using the sales-comparison approach, meaning similar sold properties are used as a comparison.

Commercial properties are rarely valued using the comparison approach because there are far fewer commercial properties, and finding similar recently sold properties is more difficult. Most commercial properties are valued using the income approach, which is much more complicated than the sales-comparison approach.

The income approach uses the income a property generates. Most commercial properties and some multifamily residential properties are valued this way.

The income approach takes the profit a property generates each year and multiplies it by a cap rate to arrive at the property's value. The cap rate is not a set figure but varies in different parts of the country and for different property types. When buying commercial property, knowing market-cap rates is very important.

## What is cap rate and how do you determine it?

If you have researched investment properties, you have probably heard the terms cap rate and net operating income (NOI). The cap rate on an investment property is a measure of what the returns will be, assuming you pay cash. I do not use cap rates on my investment properties because they don't factor for financing costs. I prefer to use the cash-on-cash return, but the cap rate can still give you a basic idea of a property's returns.

NOI is the net operating income on a rental property and does not factor in debt service. NOI can be another indicator of rental property returns but can also be easily manipulated.

Cap rate equals NOI divided by the price of a property.

For example, if you buy a house for $100,000, and it generates annual net income of $10,000, the cap rate is 10% ($10,000/$100,000=10%). Cap rate can be figured very easily, but the tricky part is knowing how accurate the income numbers are on a particular property.

NOI is how much the rental property will generate after expenses.

Debt service is not included, but property management, taxes and other expenses should be included. The NOI can easily be manipulated because different investors use different expense numbers. Some investors include allowances for vacancies and maintenance, while others do not. If a property is self-managed, the property owner may not include any expenses for property management. Make sure you do not blindly trust NOI figures.

Here are expenses that should be included:

- Property taxes
- Property insurance
- Property management fees

- Utilities paid by property owner
- Ongoing maintenance paid by property owner
- Vacancies
- Expected maintenance expenses
- HOA fees
- Any onsite management

## How can the cap rate vary greatly on the same property?

If the NOI does not include all expenses on a property, the cap rate will be artificially inflated.

If a property generates yearly gross income of $10,000, that is great, but you have not accounted for expenses yet. Accounting for only property taxes and insurance (which I have seen), the NOI might be $8,000 and the cap rate 8%. However, when you add property management, expected maintenance, and vacancies, the income may only be $5,000, which would only be a 5% cap rate.

Cash flow or cash-on-cash returns are more important because cash flow tells you exactly how much money you are going to make, including expenses and debt service. Our cash-flow calculator even helps you determine what the monthly maintenance and vacancy costs may be. Cash-on-cash return will tell you what percentage you are making on the money you have invested, which is much more important than cap rate.

## What can the cap rate tell you about different markets?

The cap rate gives a very basic idea of the return rate. If you are looking to invest in remote properties, the cap rate can give you an idea of the returns in that area. Average cap rates in the country can range from 5 to 15%. There are many other factors to consider when determining where to buy, but cap rate can give you an idea of the returns in different areas.

Cap rates can also give you an idea of the different returns on single-family versus multifamily properties in an area. In Colorado, the cap rate for a multifamily property tends to be around 5%. For a single-family residence, cap rates are around 8%. I buy my properties below market value and see cap rates at 10% or higher on my single-family rentals. In other markets, those percentages may be reversed on single-family and multifamily properties.

## Why does the cap rate on commercial properties change?

If you have a 20,000-square-foot warehouse leased for 10 years to a tenant with almost no risk of default, that cap rate will be different from an office building that is half-vacant with mediocre tenants in the other half.

The cap rate will be lower for the property with the stable tenant because you have a better chance of that tenant paying rent through the end their lease term, and the lease is longer. The office building will have a higher cap rate because there is much more risk involved, and renting out vacant units will be difficult. Cap rates vary based on the tenant type, lease length, the tenant's credit rating, the property's condition, and market conditions.

As you can see, commercial-property valuation is complex. You must know the market cap rates for a building, a tenant, and your market. These cap rates are not always easy to determine if you are not very experienced in the commercial real estate market. If you overpay for a commercial building, selling it, or refinancing it, could be very difficult. Properties that look like an awesome deal may be priced low due to a bad tenant or an uncertain future.

The other problem with valuing properties using the income approach is that you are using information from the current owners for expenses and income. If the owner fudges numbers or forgets a few expenses, the property may look much more valuable than it really is.

## Residential properties are usually more stable in a down market

Everybody needs a place to live, but not everyone needs a store or wants to own a commercial investment property. Another reason residential properties are safer than commercial properties is there will be always be a larger buyer pool for residential properties. Even when the market is bad, people will still buy or rent houses because they need a place to live.

In the commercial market, people may close their shops, work at home, or get another job if the market turns bad. Commercial real estate investors may have trouble getting a commercial loan and will not buy in a down market. This means that selling a commercial property in a down market may be incredibly difficult, especially if it is vacant. In a down market, you may have to rent out or sell a residential property for less money, but you may not be able to sell or rent out a commercial property at all.

Longer leases can be a good thing for investors, but there is a reason commercial leases are longer. Commercial properties typically take longer to rent out and are harder to rent out than residential properties. Property owners want a longer lease in place on commercial properties because of the difficulty in leasing them. The cap rate varies so much with commercial properties because when a commercial property goes vacant, it can stay vacant for months or even years. An investor must consider how long the current lease is and how stable the current tenant is. A ten-year lease is great, but even ten-year tenants can go bankrupt, and you are left with a vacant building. Since commercial buildings are usually very specific to the tenant, leasing space out or retrofitting a building for a new tenant can take a lot of work and time.

A commercial lease is very complicated. A commercial tenant has many lease options: a gross lease, triple net, double net, modified gross, etc. Cap rates will change again based on the type of lease and the costs the tenant is paying.

Financing residential properties can be difficult, but many lenders will loan on them. Typically, you can get a 15- or 30-year loan on residential rental properties. With commercial properties, the loan amortization is going to be less than 30 years, and most commercial loans will have a balloon payment. A balloon payment means the entire balance of the loan will come due after a certain amount of time (perhaps 5 or 10 years). The investor must pay off the loan when the balloon payment comes due, which is not always easy. Many commercial investors count on being able to refinance their loans when a balloon payment comes due, but that is not always possible. If the lending market becomes tighter, an investor's financials change, or the commercial market changes, refinancing may not be possible.

## What opportunities are there in commercial real estate?

Even though commercial real estate can be a very tricky business, there is opportunity to make a lot of money. There are no black-and-white valuations of commercial properties because there are so many factors to consider with cap rates. That means the people who really know what they are doing can spot good deals or a way to increase cap rates. If you have a property that is worth $200,000 based on a 10% cap rate, it is generating $20,000 per year in income. If you can create a more stable lease or rent to more attractive tenants, the cap rate may drop, making the property more valuable. If the property was generating $20,000 per year and had an 8% cap rate, it would be worth $250,000.

An investor could also find a better use for a commercial building, which may increase the income or lower the cap rate. A warehouse may not have a good cap rate in a certain market because there are vacant warehouses everywhere. That warehouse could be turned into self-storage units, which are in short supply, increasing the income and lowering the cap rate. Increasing the value of a commercial property could be as simple as taking a vacant building and finding a good tenant on a long-term lease.

For most investors, residential properties are much simpler and easier to understand than commercial properties. Understanding the commercial world and how it functions in the market in which you want to buy takes a lot of time and work. I currently stay away from commercial properties, but I will not rule out investing in them in the future. The most attractive part of commercial investing to me would be increasing the value of properties and quickly turning them (like my residential fix and flips). There are so many unknowns with long-term commercial properties because lending can change, financing terms are different, and vacancies can last a long time.

# How do you know which neighborhood to buy rentals in?

When you buy rental properties, the property's location is extremely important. Landlords who have properties in different neighborhoods can charge different rents, have houses with different levels of maintenance, and see different turnover rates. Investors can be very successful in every type of neighborhood, but an investor must know what to expect before buying a rental property. If an investor bases their expected returns on a neighborhood with stable tenants and high rents but ends up with high turnover and lower rents, the returns will suffer and the investor could lose money!

If an investor knows they will have to deal with high turnover and maintenance, they may get great returns in those neighborhoods. The trick is knowing what type of neighborhood your rental property is in. If you have lived in a town your entire life, you may know the neighborhoods well. Many people are not able to invest in the town they are most familiar with due to relocation or rental property returns. How can investors figure out which neighborhoods they want to invest in when they are unfamiliar with the town?

## Why can't you trust a real estate agent to recommend good neighborhoods?

A real estate agent may seem like the first choice for determining a good neighborhood. However, I am a real estate agent, and it is illegal for me to tell anyone that a neighborhood is good or bad since that is considered steering.

It is illegal for me to recommend neighborhoods because my opinion of a good neighborhood may be different from someone else's. If people used my judgement to determine a good neighborhood, they would all buy houses in the same neighborhoods. If everyone bought houses in the same neighborhoods, values in some neighborhoods would be pushed up and values in others would be lowered.

Not everyone wants to live in the same area. We all have different reasons for living where we do and why we think some neighborhoods are better than others.

Not only do real estate agents shy away from offering general opinions on neighborhoods, but many do not talk about crime rates, school ratings, or demographics such as ethnicity. It is also illegal for agents to talk about many of these characteristics. You may be frustrated that your real estate agent will not give you the neighborhood information you want. It is not because they are a bad agent...it is because they cannot legally do it.

Since a good neighborhood is relative to what buyers are looking for, it is up to each buyer to figure out what a good neighborhood is to them. A buyer needs to figure out what they want in a neighborhood first. Neighborhood characteristics that a buyer should consider are:

- Crime rates.
- School ratings.
- House prices.
- Age of houses.
- Size of houses.
- Size of the town.
- Proximity to large population areas.
- Local economy.
- HOAs.
- Types of houses (multifamily or single-family).
- Tax rates.

Many more characteristics will affect values and rent rates in a neighborhood. If you want to buy rental properties, the returns you get are going to be determined in large part on how well you research and judge neighborhoods. Remember, you are not judging a neighborhood on whether you would live there but on whether it would be a good investment.

## How can investors decide what neighborhood is best for rental properties?

Since every market is different, there is no set formula for a great rental property—it boils down to the numbers. You may get higher rent-to-value ratios on low-priced houses, but you might have more turnover and maintenance on those houses. You might have less maintenance and turnover on high-priced rentals, but the cash flow may not be as high. I personally like to find a happy medium with good cash flow and low maintenance and turnover.

Once an investor knows what type of neighborhood they want to invest in, here are some tips for verifying the neighborhood will meet expectations.

- Call the local police department. Often, the local police will tell you what the crime rates are and even tell you which neighborhoods have high crime.
- Drive through neighborhoods on the weekends and in the evening. This will give you an idea of the upkeep of houses and traffic.
- Check websites that give neighborhood information statistics (such as City Data).
- Ask friends or people you know who live in the town in which you want to invest. If you do not know anyone in that town, try to meet some people! Non-real-estate agents can give you their opinion and much more information on neighborhoods.
- Talk to people in the neighborhoods in which you want to invest. When you are driving around looking at houses and you see someone doing yard work or walking their dog, ask them what they think of the neighborhood.

Determining the best neighborhoods to invest in isn't easy. Each investor's idea of the perfect neighborhood will be different based on their expectations on returns, willingness to make repairs, familiarity with a location, and much more. If you do not know a town or neighborhood well, make sure you do your due diligence before you buy.

## Conclusion

The type of investment property you buy depends greatly on your personal goals and the market you want to invest in. I have had awesome luck with single-family rentals, but they do not work as investments in every market. Others see amazing results with multifamily properties, and some have tremendous results with commercial properties. Single-family properties are usually the easiest to start out with and the easiest to understand. They are also the easiest to sell if you ever get into trouble.

# 6

# How Do You Buy Real Estate Below Market Value?

One of the keys to my investment strategy is buying houses below market value. This is not easy, and you cannot just call up a real estate agent and ask them to find you awesome deals from the MLS. Buying houses below market value takes patience, hard work, the ability to act fast, and nerves. If you learn how to buy correctly, you'll have a lot of fun and will make a lot of money.

I have bought every house I have owned, except for the first one, below market value. I bought my first house in 2002. I was 22. I bought it for $188,000 and put at least $10,000 in materials and a lot of sweat equity into it over seven years. In 2009, I managed to sell it for $190,000. Talk about a huge disappointment! I learned that I could not depend on the market to increase to make money in real estate. I had to buy below market value and force equity into the property.

For my next house, I bought a foreclosure from the Public Trustee. We bought this house for $220,000 by borrowing money from my sister and father-in-law (I had to pay cash at the sale). I was able to refinance the property and pay them back in full. My wife and I lived in that house for three years, and thanks to an awesome deal and some market appreciation, we sold the house for $350,000. That was a tax-free profit since I lived in the house for at least two years. I used that money for the down payment on our current house.

## How do you determine market value on real estate?

Market value is one of the most important factors in determining what a good investment property is. When you are fixing and flipping houses, it is obvious that market value is the most important factor to determine a profit. Actually, ARV (After Repaired Value) is the most important factor because you want to know what the house will sell for when it is fixed up. When you are buying long-term rental properties, the market value may not be as important as it is on a fix and flip. However, you still need to know the market value of a long-term rental for many reasons:

- You may have to sell it one day. There are many reasons why you may have to sell, even though you may not plan to when you buy the house. You could have a financial setback, a medical problem, a relationship issue, or some other emergency. You may decide you do not like investing in rentals or you may need the money for an incredible opportunity. I want to buy 100 rental properties, but if a better opportunity comes along and I need to sell some of my rentals, I will have no problem selling them for much more than I bought them.
- A great way to obtain money to buy more rental properties is to refinance your current properties. Almost every lender will want less than a 75% loan-to-value ratio on an investment property refinance. The best way to gain equity is to buy houses below market value. The more equity you have in a property, the more money you will be able to take out when refinancing. I have refinanced 7 rental properties over the last four years and taken out over $200,000 in cash. They still have great cash flow, even after the refinance, because I got great deals on them.
- In order to get loans on multiple rental properties, you have to know a great bank and be able to convince that bank it is a good idea to invest in you. A bank will look at many factors when lending to investors. Most

importantly, they want to know that the investor is in a good financial position. If you own eight properties with little or no equity, that is not a good position. Owning eight properties with 50% equity is a great financial position to be in, and a bank will be more willing to give you a loan.

The easiest way to determine market value is to hire a professional. I am a real estate agent, and I provide comparative market evaluations for sellers all the time. I also provide values for investors and buyers. The trick for the new investor is convincing an agent that you are a serious investor and they are not wasting their time. The easiest way to overcome this problem is to buy a house, but that is not realistic for a beginning investor who is trying to figure out values.

My advice is to be perfectly honest with agents. Tell them you are new and you are trying to determine market values. It helps if you have done some work first and can ask them if the value you came up with seems accurate. Then buy them lunch or give them something in return. Simple gestures like buying lunch can make a huge difference in convincing someone to help you.

Do not ask the agent for ridiculous things or make huge requests. Do not ask for 100 values or sales comps from the last two years for an entire town. I recently had an investor ask me for all the cash sold comps in the last year for metro Denver. Then he wanted me to put them all on an Excel sheet and email them to him. I had never talked to this investor prior to this request, and I was just a little put off that he expected me to put in hours and hours of work for him. He gave me no reason to do this work and did not even tell me why he wanted this information. To top it all off, I am not even in the Denver market!

## How to come up with a house value when you are not an agent

I mentioned that it would be good to have your own value in mind when talking to an agent, but how do you come up with a value yourself? Valuing a house is not easy unless you use a website like Zillow. However, Zillow is not always accurate. Some of the values were as much as 40% off when I compared my own property's values to Zillow values! I would not trust Zillow to provide house values, although you can get some great information from Zillow.

I use sales comparables to determine property value. I compare multiple sales in the last six months that are as similar as possible to the house I am valuing. As an agent, I can easily pull up any sold comps I want from the MLS. If you are not an agent, finding sold comparables isn't as easy. You can find sold comps online at Zillow and a few other websites, but you do not get all the information you need with those.

Zillow uses all the sold comps it can find: foreclosures, short sales, and sometimes trustee sales. The reason this is important is you do not always know if those were market sales or just sales. A trustee sale price could simply be the amount the bank was owed and not a market value. You also do not know what the condition of the sale was, any concessions, or the financing terms. You do not know how long a house was for sale, how many price changes there were, or if it was a short sale or REO. These are vital details that are necessary to make an accurate valuation.

A non-agent investor may be able to determine a range of values from online comps, but you still need to talk to an agent to make sure your values are accurate. If you have a great agent, they will probably offer you sold comps in an area and make your life much easier!

Active listings may also be used to value properties. This method isn't easy because an active listing does not mean it will sell for the asking price or if it will sell at all. Active comps do give you an idea of what is for sale in a neighborhood and what the competition is. I use active comps along with sold comps to value properties. You can use active comps for a broad value but not a solid value. The best way to use active comps for values is to track them over time. Keep track of the asking price, when they go under contract, and for how much they sell. When you know the history of a sale on a website like Zillow, that comp becomes much more valuable.

## Adjusting for values on an investment property

When you find sold and active comps that are similar to your subject, your work is not done. You must then decide if you need to make adjustments for the differences between the comparables and the property you are valuing.

If you are valuing a house with a one-car garage and the sales comps have a two-car garage, you must make an adjustment. If the bedroom, bathroom, room count, square footage, views, location, or anything else is different, you need to make adjustments. Determining the adjustment amount is the tricky part. More-expensive houses have different adjustment amounts than less-expensive ones. Different areas of the country put more value on certain amenities than other parts of the country. I am not going to tell you how much to adjust because I am not in your market.

Again, a real estate agent can help you determine how different amenities add value. When you look at enough houses and comparables, you should start to get an idea of how much value features and size add. Getting to know your market and accurately determining values and adjustments will take time.

Here are a few adjustments I would make on my $150,000-price-range rentals.

- 1- versus 2-car garage: $4,000 to $7,000 adjustment
- 3 versus 2 bedrooms: $2,000 to $4,000 adjustment
- 1,500 square feet versus 1,200: $6,000 to $12,000 adjustment

A $2,000 adjustment for a bedroom does not seem like very much, but you must realize the house also has more square footage that would add value as well. You should look at the entire picture when making adjustments to ensure they make sense.

## How to buy bank-owned properties (REOs) below market value

REO (Real Estate Owned) is a term for properties banks have taken back through foreclosure. REO properties are usually listed in the MLS (Multiple Listing Service) by an REO listing agent. I am an REO listing agent myself, and I can tell you that each bank handles their REOs very differently. Some banks repair houses before they list them, and others do not fix anything. Some banks are willing to negotiate quite a bit on their prices, and others will hardly budge.

REOs are getting harder and harder to find due to the improving housing market. There are still some great deals, but the deals are usually on houses that need many repairs.

If you find a great deal on an REO, do not be surprised if you find yourself in a highest-and-best situation. Many banks ask for highest and best when they receive more than one offer on a property. There is a ton of competition for REO properties right now, and multiple offers are common. Highest and best gives every buyer who made an offer a chance to raise his or her offer and hope it is good enough to get the property. In many highest-and-best situations, the winning offer is higher than the actual asking price. I will discuss highest and best in more detail later in this chapter as many sellers now use it.

Many banks prefer a cash offer from an investor and, sometimes they actually prefer an owner-occupant buyer. Sellers like Fannie Mae, Freddie Mac, and Wells Fargo only allow offers from owner-occupant buyers at the beginning of the listing period. This can be frustrating for investors looking for a good deal, but there is no way around their owner-occupant restrictions. Pretending to be an owner-occupant when you will not be occupying the property is against the law.

You need a real estate agent to buy almost any REO property. Buyers see vacant REO properties and think that, if they can just talk to the bank, the bank will sell it to them well below market value. The truth is that banks have strict guidelines for how they sell houses, and they almost never sell them without putting them in the MLS system. Trying to contact the bank to get them to sell it to you is almost always a huge waste of time unless it's a very small local bank.

Getting a great deal on REOs has become tougher as the banks have strict requirements on who can bid and when they will review offers. A lot of my techniques do not work well on bank-owned properties because speed is not always important. However, banks will negotiate much more on properties that have been on the market an extended timeframe. If a property has been for sale for 60 days or more, banks will sometimes look at low offers.

## How can you get a great deal on a HUD home?

HUD (Department of Housing and Urban Development) homes can be an incredible opportunity for investors. However, some investors are apprehensive about bidding on HUD homes because purchasing a HUD home is much different from purchasing a traditional listing or even an REO. HUD also gives priority to owner-occupant buyers over investors. Once you know the HUD system, submitting bids and buying HUD homes becomes very easy. I happen to be a HUD listing broker, and I know the HUD system very well.

HUD homes are properties that have been repossessed by the bank after going through foreclosure. HUD homes were previously purchased with government-insured FHA loans. Many houses that have FHA loans and go through foreclosure go back to HUD. When HUD becomes the owner, they sell the property through local listing brokers such as myself and list them on www.hudhomestore.com. Hudhomestore.com lists all HUD homes for sale that are not currently under contract. Once a HUD home has an accepted bid, it is taken off Hudhomestore.com, and the status in MLS is changed to under contract. HUD homes are sold in an online auction format, and all bids must be submitted online by a licensed real estate agent who is registered with HUD.

## When can investors bid on HUD homes?

HUD has very strict owner-occupancy restrictions on the houses they sell. HUD has two main classifications for their properties: FHA insurable and uninsurable. On FHA insured HUD homes, only owner-occupants, nonprofits and government agencies can bid the first 15 days that the house is on the market (typically called the owner-occupant only period). For uninsured houses, the owner-occupancy only bid period is the first five days. Investors can bid on HUD homes on the sixteenth day for insured properties and on the sixth day on uninsured HUD homes.

When a HUD home goes under contract, HUD stops the daily count for a house being on the market. If a HUD home goes under contract on the eleventh day and that contract falls apart, the house would come back on the market 11 days into the bid period. Therefore, some HUD homes have been for sale for 30 days but are still in the owner-occupant period. An investor can see whether a HUD home is insured or uninsured on the Hudhomestore website.

- If a house is listed as only available to owner-occupants, an investor can see when they can bid by looking at the period deadline. The period deadline will tell you the last day of the current bid period.

HUD typically changes the price on HUD homes every 35 to 50 days the house is actively on the market. HUD does not have a new owner-occupant bid period when they change the price on a house. Investors can bid the first day after a price change.

## What are the penalties if investors bid as owner-occupants on HUD homes?

A HUD home is federal property, which means that any crime committed involving a HUD property is usually considered a felony. HUD makes it clear that any investor who bids as an owner-occupant is **subject to two years in federal prison and up to $250,000 in fines**. HUD does prosecute investors who have been caught buying in the owner-occupant period. HUD also may take the real estate agent's ability to sell HUD homes away. HUD and other investors watch these properties and report investors who are breaking the rules.

It is also a felony for investors to make repairs to a HUD home before they buy it or to move anything onto the property before closing.

## Why are HUD homes a great way for investors to buy houses below market value?

HUD orders an appraisal on each of their houses before they are listed. That appraisal usually becomes the list price and determines how much HUD will take for the house. For whatever reason, many HUD appraisals come in very low compared to market value. If a HUD home makes it through the owner-occupant bid period, they can be a great opportunity for investors. Uninsured HUD homes (houses that need more than $5,000 in repairs) do not qualify for FHA loans. The more repairs that a HUD home needs, the better its chance of making it to the investor bid period. Investors are much more likely to buy uninsured houses. I have sold many HUD homes to investors who were able to flip the house or get a great deal on a rental property because the house needed a lot of work.

HUD uses different formulas in different areas of the country to determine how much less than list price they will accept. In Colorado, HUD usually does not take less than 90% of the list price unless a house becomes an aged asset. HUD considers a house to be an aged asset if it has actively been on the market for more than 60 days. In my market, once a HUD home becomes aged, HUD may accept 80% of list price. If a HUD home is on the market for an extended period, they may take even less. However, the discounts are figured on a case-by-case basis, and there is no across the board rule. In other parts of the country, I have seen investors buy HUD homes for 80% of the list price in the first month. On some aged assets, investors are getting HUD homes at 50% or less of list price.

If HUD receives a bid that is close to the price they will take, they may counter a buyer. Submitting a low offer never hurts; the worst HUD will do is decline your bid. HUD does not blackball investors who submit many offers. in fact, HUD encourages all bids no matter how low they are. The only exception is when an investor is submitting the same bid every single day. There is no need to resubmit a bid over and over, which may annoy HUD. HUD keeps track of the bids and usually notifies buyers of a price change or if they will now consider a bid that was too low in the past. I would still submit new bids if the price changes.

Speed is the key to an investor getting a HUD home. Many investors are waiting for HUD homes to make it to the investor bid period, and most good deals will receive bids the first day investors are eligible.

Investors can also use a trick on uninsured houses to gain an advantage over other investors. HUD opens bids the next business day after the five-day owner-occupant bid period is over. HUD does not open bids first thing in the morning; they usually open them mid-morning or later depending on how busy they are. At the beginning of the sixth day, an uninsured HUD home will be available for investors to bid on, even though HUD may be accepting an owner-occupant bid later in the day. Investors should always try to get their bid into the system on that sixth day because HUD homes tend to fall out of contract more than other properties.

If an owner occupant cancels their contract, HUD moves on to any acceptably priced backup offers in their system before they put the house back on the market. If the contract is cancelled, an investor who bid on the sixth day could have their bid accepted before any other investors get a chance to bid.

Investors should always have their real estate agent mark "yes to backup position" when bidding on a HUD home. There is no penalty to buyers who choose to mark this but later decide they do not want the house. There is also a chance that HUD will accept an investor's low bid if HUD changes the price on the house and that low bid is now within an acceptable range.

## How does HUD handle inspection periods with investors?

A very important point to remember is HUD does not return earnest money to investors if they cancel their contract. HUD clearly states that they consider investors "savvy," and if an investor cancels due to inspection items, the earnest money is forfeited to HUD. If an investor is using financing and their loan cannot be completed, they may get half of their earnest money back. I always tell investors to expect to lose their earnest money if they cancel a HUD contract. HUD also does not pay for title insurance or any closing fees that other sellers typically pay.

HUD homes can be a great deal for investors who know how the system works. Getting used to the system and learning HUD's dates and procedures can take some time. Many investors shy away from HUD because it is different and can be confusing. This creates more opportunity for the investors who are willing to learn the HUD system. My best advice is to find an agent who knows the HUD system very well.

## How to buy short sales below market value

Short sales are another great way for investors to find deals. Short sales are owned by private parties who are selling the house for less than they owe the bank. To sell the house, the bank must agree to take less money than what they are owed.

Historically, short sales could take up to six months or even a year to close because lenders were so slow to make a decision. In the last couple of years, banks have gotten much quicker at making decisions, and some short sales are approved in two weeks or less (some banks still take months). With many short sales, the first party to make an offer will get the house. You must act very quickly when a great short sale comes on the market. Remember, even if the seller accepts your offer, there is no guarantee the bank will approve the offer. It is wise to wait to perform an inspection or start the loan process until you have written approval from the seller's bank that your short sale offer is accepted.

You must be careful when buying off-market properties as short sales. Banks are very strict about which offers they accept. If a buyer and seller are using a short sale to sell a house but not disclosing all the terms to the bank, it could be considered fraud. A couple of years ago, short-sale fraud was the most investigated crime by the FBI. Most banks require that short sales be listed on the MLS by an agent. Also, the buyer and seller cannot be related, and the properties must sell for close to market value. A good real estate agent can help buyers navigate the short-sale process.

## How to buy fair-market sales below market value

Fair-market-sale houses are owned by a private seller who has enough equity in to sell without having to involve the bank in the decision making (short sale). Finding great deals on fair-market sales is more difficult because sellers are usually not in a huge rush to sell their house below market value. There are some cases where you can find a great deal on a fair-market sale.

I have purchased estate properties that were great deals. Often, estates just want to get rid of the house because they have issues or creditors that need to be paid quickly. I have also purchased a house that the seller had recently bought as a foreclosure. The house needed a lot of work, and the sellers did not have the money needed to complete the repairs. The market appreciated enough that they could sell the house.

Investor-owned houses present another situation where an investor can buy below market value. An investor-owned house is usually rented out, and although it may be perfect for a first-time homebuyer, the first-time homebuyer cannot wait three months for the tenants to move out. The only choice for the investor is to sell the house to another investor for a discount.

Some investors also try to flip houses but run out of money and must sell before the house is completed.

Houses in rapidly appreciating markets also create opportunity. Some real estate agents may not keep up with current prices. I have bought many houses that were underpriced by the agent, and I was the first to make an offer.

I buy many of my flips and rentals as fair-market sales. We will talk about strategies for buying these properties in the section about making offers.

## How to get great deals from the MLS

Some investors will tell you finding rentals or flips on the MLS is impossible. I buy almost all my flips and rentals from the MLS. Even if you are not an agent, you can still get deals from the MLS, but you must have a great agent (more on that later). Short sales, REOs, fair-market listings, and estate sales can all be bought from the MLS. We have talked about what those properties are, but this section will go into detail on exactly how I buy those houses.

There are many deals on the MLS if you know how to find them, and in my opinion, buying from the MLS is easier than from other places. I used to buy many of my fix and flips from trustee sales, but there is so much competition that prices are higher at the trustee sale than on the MLS! I would rather buy from the MLS, where I can complete an inspection, see the house, and get a loan.

I am still buying REOs and short sales, but more of my purchases have been traditional or estate sales. Prices are rising in many areas of the country, and that creates investor opportunity. With rising prices, more fair market sellers are able to sell their houses.

A fair-market sale is one where the house is not in an REO or short-sale situation. Many homeowners bought foreclosures and houses in disrepair in the last few years, while prices were lower. Not all homeowners had the money or time to repair the house once they moved in. Some of those homeowners need to sell a house that is in poor condition. A house that needs repairs creates opportunities. The more work that is needed, the bigger discount it takes to get a house sold. One of my rental properties was a fair-market sale. It needed a lot of work and was a great deal. I bought it for $88,000, and two and a half years later, it was worth $170,000. You can find detailed numbers and videos on all my rentals on investfourmore.com.

## How can rising house prices create opportunity on the MLS?

With rising prices, real estate agents or sellers sometimes underprice houses. I recently bought a couple underpriced houses, and my offer was either accepted right away, or I won in a multiple-offer situation. Houses may be underpriced because the real estate agent did not know the true value of the house due to an appreciating market or because the owner wanted to sell quickly.

A couple of my rental properties were underpriced fair-market sales. I purchased one for $130,000 and with only $3,000 of work, it was worth $180,000. I purchased the other for $99,000, and with a minimal amount of work, it was worth $150,000. If a real estate agent is not paying attention to market price increases; if a house needs some work; or if the sellers simply want to sell their house quickly, it could mean opportunity for investors.

Some sellers get into trouble and cannot make their payments for various reasons. If the market is stagnant or declining, these houses must be sold as short sales or they become foreclosures. When the market is strong, sellers are able to sell their houses, but if they must do it quickly, they may be very motivated.

Being a real estate agent gives me a huge advantage when submitting offers quickly. I check the MLS many times per day. As soon as I see a great deal, I look at the house as soon as possible. If I like the house, I have my assistant write up an offer and send it to me with DocuSign, which allows me to sign the contract electronically on my phone. I then submit my offer to the seller almost immediately. By being an agent, having an assistant, and using DocuSign, I can send an offer less than an hour after a house is listed. Acting quickly is one of the most important things you can do when buying from the MLS.

Many REO sellers will not accept an offer right away, but many short sales and fair-market sales will. Most banks, when selling their REOs, have a five-day or longer period before they will review offers. HUD and some banks have owner-occupied periods when a house is first listed where only owner-occupants can make offers. This is why short sales and fair markets sales can sometimes be better deals than REOs.

No matter what you do, submitting an offer takes longer if you're not an agent. One way to speed things up is to ask your agent to set up property alerts. In my MLS, I can set alerts to send an email as soon as specific properties that meet my given criteria are listed. I set these alerts so I will not miss a great deal on the MLS. I bought buy my last fix-and-flip thanks to a property alert that told me a house was back on the market. Investors can use sites such as Zillow and Realtor.com, but their listings are not always updated quickly. Zillow also has many listings on their site that show as being for sale but are actually under contract. The best way to be able to submit offers quickly is to have a great real estate agent...or to be one.

## Offer the most you can in multiple-offer situations

If you find a great deal, do not be cheap! Do not try to lowball an already great deal. Offer the most you can while still making your desired profit. You also do not want to stretch your limits when you make an offer. Buying a house that won't make you money doesn't make sense.

I may try to offer a little less than I want to pay if I think I can get my offer in before any others. If the house is an amazing deal, I offer full price or sometimes even higher than full price in hopes that the seller will sign my offer before any other offers come in.

When some sellers (most REOs) get more than one offer, they will ask for highest and best. They want every buyer who sent in an offer to make their very best offer, and the seller will choose the best offer. In a multiple-offer situation, I do not pay attention to the list price. I offer the most I can that will still make me my desired profit. Sometimes, I offer less than the listing price, and sometimes I offer more. Do not be scared off by a multiple-offer situation!

Buyers always tell me they do not want to get in a bidding war. Why not? A bidding war means that a house is priced great and many people want it. Why would other people being interested in a house make you not want to buy it? Too many people let their emotions get in the way, and they feel the seller should have just accepted their offer and ignored the other offers. Do not let your emotions stop you from getting a good deal! Withdrawing your offer in a highest-and-best situation makes no sense.

## Make your offer more appealing by using cash or few contingencies

I am an experienced investor, and I am in a great place to be able to offer cash on a property if necessary. I also have a great portfolio lender that does not require an appraisal on loans under $100,000. Most sellers want quick and easy closings, so a cash offer is usually the most enticing to them. If you must use financing, use as few contingencies as you can. I can remove the appraisal contingency on most of my financed offers, and I will even remove my inspection contingency in some cases.

On my last three deals, I removed my inspection contingency, and I know that helped get my offer accepted. This is risky for someone who does not know what to look for in a house, but if you are getting a good enough deal and know what to look for, it may be a good strategy. A cash offer with no inspection contingency will often get accepted over a higher offer with financing and inspection contingencies. However, some sellers, such as HUD, only care about the net price to them and do not care if you use cash or a loan.

## Use real estate agent mistakes to your advantage on the MLS

I have bought many houses from the MLS that were listed incorrectly. I bought a house from HUBZU where the listing didn't include a basement. In fact, the house had a full, finished basement with two bedrooms and a bath. I recently bought a rental listed as a three-bedroom, two-bath house that was actually a five-bedroom, two-bath house. You must know your market, pay attention to the listing photos, and confirm the information in the listing. Do not be afraid to look at many houses to find the few that are listed incorrectly. The more market knowledge you have and the more experience you gain, the easier spotting the mistakes will be.

## You need to be flexible when buying from the MLS

If tenants live in a property, the buyer cannot occupy some houses until months after the sale. In these situations, competition is reduced because most owner-occupants will not want to buy a house that they cannot move into right away. Tenants can often be difficult when you are trying to show the house, or they may not keep the house looking nice, which decreases the amount the seller can get. The worse the tenant is, the better deal a buyer can get!

## How do you know when one seller is more motivated to negotiate than another?

When you flip houses or buy rentals, you must get an awesome deal to make any money. 97% of the houses on the MLS will not work for flipping because there is not enough profit after all the costs are considered. Some houses listed on the MLS can be awesome deals, but the list price does not indicate how much the seller is willing to take. I do not advocate submitting low offers on every house hoping one seller will accept 50% of list price. However, some sellers will take significantly less than asking price if you know what to look for.

- **Aged listings**: Some houses sit on the market for months without selling. Often, the sellers priced the house too high, it was hard to set up a showing, the house needed major repairs, or other factors caused the house not to sell. Not every aged listing can be bought for much less than asking price, but some can. HUD homes that are on the market more than 60 days can sometimes be bought at a significant discount. Some sellers will not lower their price when their house does not sell but may take less than asking price. Submitting low offers on houses that have been on the market a long time doesn't hurt, but look for other signs as well.

· **MLS comments**: Some comments in the MLS descriptions shout: *make a low offer!* If you see the words "as-is," "seller motivated," "quick close preferred," "cash deal," "no financing," "will not go FHA," "out-of-state owner," "needs work," "needs TLC," or anything else that indicates the house needs work and the seller wants it gone quickly, they may be more willing to negotiate.

· **Fast price changes**: If a house does not sell right away, the seller will usually lower the price. I see house prices lowered around the 30- to 60-day mark in most cases. However, occasionally I see a house pop up on the market, and in only seven or ten days, the price changes. This indicates to me that the seller wants it gone quickly! The bigger the price change, the quicker they want it gone.

· **Back on the market**: Houses go under contract and then come back on the market all the time. However, in some cases, a contract falling apart can indicate a house with major problems, or it can also motivate the seller. When I see a house come back on the market at a decent price, I will ask the agent why it came back on the market. Sometimes, the agent will indicate it was buyer financing or a problem with the inspection. In some cases, the agent will indicate the seller wants to get rid of the house because they were expecting it to sell and the contract fell apart. A house coming back on the market and the price changing at the same time indicates a very motivated seller! If a house repeatedly goes under contract and then comes back on the market, the seller may be motivated by a cash offer with no inspection to get the deal done.

## How low should you offer on a house?

As I mentioned earlier, if the house is already an awesome deal, do not be afraid to offer list price or higher if the numbers work. Many of my deals were houses that I bought well below list price because I saw some of the situations mentioned above and knew that the sellers were motivated.

I rarely, if ever, submit an extremely low offer. I have never submitted an offer that was 50% or less than list price. When I submit a low offer, it is usually about 70 to 80% of list price. Offers lower than 70% of list price usually offend the seller, and even a 70% offer might offend them. I do not submit low offers on every house on the MLS, but I select listings that I think will be more likely to negotiate.

When I make my first offer, I do not offer the most I can pay. I leave some room for negotiation because the seller is most likely not going to accept my low offer. I recently bought a house listed for $109,900. This was a good price, although not for a flip because of the work needed. Seven days after the house was listed, the seller lowered the price to $104,900. I noticed in the comments that the house needed TLC, was dirty because previous tenants had just moved out, and would not qualify for financing. This was music to my ears! I knew the seller was motivated because they would not spend $150 to clean the house. I offered $80,000 with no inspection and a cash closing in 20 days. The seller countered at $85,000, which I happily accepted. The seller will often want to negotiate at least a little so they feel like they got the most money they could out of the house.

## What if the seller will not come down low enough to make a deal?

Not every offer I make is accepted. In fact, I don't end up buying most houses I make offers on. If you want to be a great real estate investor, you cannot be afraid to have your offer rejected or to see someone else get a deal you were hoping to buy. The fastest way an investor can get into trouble is paying too much for a house. If the seller will not come down to a price that makes sense for you, do not force the issue and pay too much! Even if the seller does not accept your offer, you still may get the house later.

If I make a low offer, I can usually tell how motivated the seller is. If the seller rejects my offer or acts offended at my offer, I forget about the house and move on. Negotiating back and forth is not worth my time if the seller is not coming close to my price. If the seller comes down significantly from their list price, I know I have a chance of getting something together. Sometimes, we cannot get together on the price or they accept another offer. In those cases, I am always polite and ask their agent to let me know if anything happens or if the seller is interested in my offer later. Often, the first accepted offer falls apart because it was an owner-occupant who later realized how much work the house needed, or maybe a wholesaler got the house under contract but could not find a buyer. Do not give up if another offer is accepted, and do not burn bridges.

## Should you try to negotiate with the seller on inspection items?

When I make offers, I do not ask for an inspection period. I have enough experience to know what major issues to look for and what repairs a house needs. I would not suggest waiving the inspection if you are a new investor. Waiving the inspection period gets me many deals, especially when a house comes back on the market. Many of the houses I am interested in have motivated sellers who want to sell the house fast. If they must put the house back on the market because of inspection problems, it costs them time and money. Every time a house comes back on the market, buyers wonder what is wrong with it, and the house will not command as high of a price.

If I make an offer without an inspection or financing contingency, the seller knows they will get my earnest money if I do not buy the house. This gives me an advantage, and I have bought many houses at a lower price than other investors were offering because I waved my inspection.

They assume they will be able to use the inspection to ask for a lower price and get the house cheaper. I do not do this because I feel it is not operating in good faith. While this tactic may work a couple of times, it will also give the buyer a reputation of always asking for a lower price on inspection. Another reason I get so many deals is that agents know me and know I do not play games. If I write a contract for a certain price, I buy the house at the price I say I will. Building a good reputation will give you a better chance of having your offers accepted in the future. If you are only going to buy a few houses, negotiating hard may make sense. If you want to be a serious investor, negotiating hard can hurt you in the long run.

Buying from the MLS is not impossible; it is actually my favorite way to buy houses. You cannot use the excuse that buying from the MLS does not work in my market, which is one of the hottest in the country. There will always be deals on the MLS if you know how to spot them and can act quickly.

## How to get great below-market-value deals from auctions

Buying a house from a foreclosure auction is another way to get a great deal, but it comes with risk. Auctions tend to have less competition because they have stricter requirements for buyers, and many times, you cannot inspect the house or even see the inside of it before buying. I have bought many houses from auctions over the years and made money on many, but I have also lost money on a few.

The fewer people you must compete with, the better chance you have of getting a great deal. Auction companies often have strict criteria for buying their houses.

- **Cash purchases:** Many auctions require the buyer to pay cash for houses on which they bid. Foreclosure auctions may require the buyer to have cash the same day they bid or before they bid on a property.
- **No inspections:** Many auctions do not allow buyers to inspect a house before they bid. In some cases, a house may be occupied, and the buyer cannot inspect the interior until they buy. I am currently buying a house that is occupied, and I have never seen the interior. If the house is occupied, you cannot just kick the occupant out. You must evict them or possibly honor their lease if they have one.
- **Non-refundable earnest money:** When you buy a house, you must submit earnest money to the seller. In a normal sale, if the financing falls through or you find a problem in your inspection, you usually get your earnest money back. With an auction property, if you back out of the contract for any reason, you usually do not get your earnest money back.
- **Short notice:** Some state foreclosure sales give buyers very little time to know what houses will be bid on and how much the starting bids will be. Other online auctions give buyers much more notice before an auction. In Colorado, we are given the property sale list two days before the sale.
- **Clear title:** many foreclosure auctions do not guarantee clear title. There is no guarantee you are even bidding on the first loan.

All these factors make it tough for most buyers to purchase houses from auctions. The majority of homebuyers are owner-occupants who need to get a loan. Most investors also need a loan to buy property, and auctions that require cash eliminate those buyers as well. Many buyers fear auctions because of the possibility of losing earnest money, the lack of inspections, and other issues. That usually leaves experienced investors to battle over the properties. Experienced investors know how much they can pay, can handle the risk, and can still make money. Some online auctions are less risky than foreclosure auctions, which can provide opportunities for less experienced buyers.

## How does the foreclosure auction work in Colorado?

Different types of real estate auctions come with varying degrees of risk. The riskiest are the local foreclosure sales because they require the quickest payment with the least amount of due diligence available. Every state has different laws regarding foreclosure auctions, which makes it very tough for inexperienced buyers. Make sure you know your local laws before bidding!

A foreclosure auction gives the public a chance to buy houses that are being foreclosed on by the bank or other lien holders. Before the lien holder can take possession of the house through a foreclosure, they must offer it up for auction. The bank or lien holder will make a starting bid, which may be what is owed on the loan including late fees and interest. The bank can also start the bidding at less than what is owed.

If no one bids on the house at the foreclosure sale, the house will go back to the bank. However, investors (or even owner-occupied bidders) can buy houses at the foreclosure sale if they bid more than the banks bid (assuming the bank is not bidding as well, which is possible). I used to buy most of my fix-and-flips at the foreclosure sale in Colorado, and I even bought a personal residence at the foreclosure sale. We stopped buying at the foreclosure sale for the most part because competition has increased, pushing prices too high. In my area, I can get a better deal on the MLS than I can at the foreclosure sale.

Here's how the foreclosure sale works in Colorado:

- The pre-sale list, which lists the properties going to sale and the starting bid, is published every Monday afternoon.
- The foreclosure sale is on Wednesday morning at 10 a.m. You can call the public trustees office before the sale on Wednesday to see if the properties you are interested in are still going to auction.
- The auction is conducted at 10 a.m., and all bidders must register in person at the public trustee office before the auction. The auction is live and goes very quickly.
- The winning bidders have until noon on Wednesday to come back to

the office with a cashier's check for the full amount of the bid. If the winning bidder does not show up, the second highest bidder is notified and given a chance to buy the property at their highest bid.
- There is a short redemption period (8 days) for junior lienholders in Colorado. A junior lienholder can redeem the property by paying off the first bid amount in full plus interest.

In Colorado, there is no guarantee you are bidding on a first loan or that you will get a clear title. The day before the sale, (Tuesday) we would get an O & E (Ownership and Encumbrance report) from the title company, check out the house as much as we could, and decide if it is worth bidding on the house.

## What are the foreclosure laws in other states?

The process for buying at the foreclosure sale I outlined is only for Colorado. Other states have much different laws, and each state handles their auctions differently. Here are a few differences you may run into:

- Some states require proof of funds before the auction. This requires bringing cashier's checks for the amount you want to bid.
- Some states give much less notice on which houses will go to the sale and what the starting bids will be. I have heard that, in some areas, you only have a few hours to research properties before they are sold.
- Some states have an owner redemption period where the previous owner has a certain amount of time to pay off whoever won the bid and get the house back. Some states have redemption periods that last as long as six months!

Make sure you know exactly how the foreclosure auctions work in your state before you bid. I have seen many new investors check out the auctions for weeks to see how they worked. I have also seen new investors bid on a second loan, not realizing there was a first loan. That investor was still responsible for paying off the first loan!

## How did I lose money on houses I bought at the foreclosure sale?

I have made a lot of money from houses I bought at the foreclosure sale, but I have also lost money because of the nature of the auction.

On one deal, I had the winning bid on a house at the foreclosure auction. I had an O & E that showed I was bidding on a first position note, and I viewed the house before the sale. I looked through the windows, and the house appeared to be completely vacant. After winning the bid, I learned the previous owners had filed a lawsuit against the bank claiming the bank did not foreclose correctly. The lawsuit had not been recorded yet, and I had no way of knowing about it. In the end, the lawsuit was thrown out, but it took the judge a year to look at the case, and I had to hold the property that entire time. After interest and carrying costs, I ended up losing money.

In many instances, I had to buy a house without seeing the interior. There are no open houses or showings when you buy a house at the foreclosure sale. Some investors try to get into houses before the sale, but if caught, they can be charged with trespassing or even breaking and entering.

When buying a house you cannot view, you have to consider repair costs. I usually bought houses from the auction for flips, so I knew how much my repair budget could be to make money. I would always assume a house would need new flooring, paint, appliances, fixtures, and at least $5,000 in other repairs depending on the age of the house. Sometimes, I got lucky, and the houses needed less work, but sometimes they needed more.

I also tried to talk to the occupants before the sale to get as much information as I could. Trying to talk to someone about buying their house they are losing to foreclosure isn't fun. Most people are actually friendly, and they will at least tell you if they are renting or own. Often, they have no idea how the process works, and you can build rapport by telling them how it works and what the timelines are.

## Foreclosure auctions versus online REO auctions

There are many types of auctions, and some banks use another auction to sell the house once they have completed the foreclosure. HUBZU, Homesearch.com, Auction.com, WilliamsandWilliams.com, Hudsonand-Marshall.com, Xome.com, and many more sites have auctions for REO properties that the bank already owns. These auctions have much different terms than the foreclosure sales, and buying from them is much easier. Online auctions for REO properties sometimes:

- allow financing.
- allow inspections.
- allow appraisals.
- give title insurance.
- pay a real estate agent commission.

The online auctions have different terms for different properties, and you must be very careful about what you are bidding on.

Buying a house at the foreclosure auction can be scary and very risky. I stopped because the prices increased to a point where the risk was no longer worth the reward. Colorado's foreclosure inventory has dropped significantly, and I think investors who counted on the foreclosure sale for inventory had to increase the prices they pay because they do not know any other way to buy. I would not rule out buying from the foreclosure sale, but I would also make sure you have multiple ways to get great deals as the market changes.

# How can you get a great deal from real estate wholesalers?

Recently, I have been buying most of my properties from real estate wholesalers. I usually buy from the MLS, but I had a goal last year to find wholesalers so I could diversify my business. Finding good wholesalers in my area (or them finding me) took some time. It can be frustrating because there are a lot of people who call themselves wholesalers who never wholesale a house. You must be diligent in your search if you want to find wholesalers who actually have great deals.

## What is wholesaling a house?

Wholesaling involves a real estate investor finding a great deal, getting it under contract, and finding another real estate investor to buy the property. A wholesaler could use a double close or an assignment to transfer the property to the new investor. The wholesaler usually does not do any work to the properties, and they do not use their own money to buy the property.

A double close involves the house being sold to the wholesaler and the wholesaler selling the house the same day to another investor. The wholesaler does not need any money to buy the house because the title company uses the money from the end investor to pay the original seller. Not all title companies will do this, but there are some that cater to investors and will. I have bought most of my wholesale deals using this technique.

An assignment is when the seller signs a contract to sell their property to the wholesaler, and the wholesaler then assigns that contract to another investor. The wholesaler will most likely use their own contract and not a state real estate contract with the seller. Not all contracts can be assigned. If you are dealing with REO properties or short sales, it is unlikely you can assign those contracts. Wholesalers make their money by charging more to the end investor than what they agree to pay the seller.

## How does buying a house from a wholesaler work?

When a real estate investor buys a house from a wholesaler, it is much different from buying a house from the MLS. The investor does not have much flexibility on closing time or other terms. Often, investors must put down a non-refundable deposit, and they get no inspection. The houses are sold as-is, and no repairs will be made. These terms can make getting a loan on a wholesale deal tough, especially if the lender needs an appraisal. Buying a wholesale deal as a new investor is tough due to all these restrictions.

Wholesale properties are not advertised on the MLS because most wholesalers are not real estate agents. They also do not want to pay real estate commissions. The wholesaler will find as many investors who may want to buy their property as they can and let them know whenever they have a deal. The wholesaler will usually send an e-mail to all their investors listing the price, repairs needed, terms, and what they think the house is worth. I never trust these numbers and always verify everything myself. The wholesaler compiles a list of investors who want to see the property and meets the investors at the house (usually more than one investor at a time).

Every wholesaler does business a little differently, so how they decide which investor gets the house can vary. In some cases, the first investor who says they want the house for the asking price will get it. Some wholesalers will use online forms to submit a contract, and the highest offer gets the deal. If there are not enough investors who want the deal, the wholesaler may negotiate their fee or try to get the seller to come down in price.

When I look at a property with other investors, I make sure to tell the wholesaler if I want the property as soon as possible. You cannot be timid and wait for the wholesaler to talk to you or finish talking to other investors. If you want it, tell them right away.

## Why do most wholesalers never complete a deal?

The tricky part in dealing with wholesalers is they never do a deal. Many people call themselves wholesalers because it is the most common type of investing taught. A lot of programs promise big money without using any of your own when you wholesale. A wholesaler sells houses to investors who want a great deal. They pay cash, get no inspection, and must be very flexible on many of the terms. Investors who buy from wholesalers want a huge discount from what they could buy on the MLS, or it is not worth their trouble. The wholesaler must get an awesome deal that leaves room for them and the investor to make money. Finding those deals takes a lot of time and effort.

I would estimate that 90% of wholesalers never find a deal good enough to sell. Here are some problems I see with many wholesalers:

- They may find properties they think are deals, but they do not know market values well. They overestimate market value, underestimate the repairs, and don't really have a deal.
- They do not know how much profit an investor needs. Many flippers go by the 70% rule, and many wholesale prices do not allow that much room for profit.
- They assume the repairs are the only cost and forget about carrying costs, selling costs, etc.
- They do not know how to market or have the money to market like they need to.

They will not tell investors they have never done a deal, so when looking for a wholesaler, you must be very careful. You can waste a lot of time with wannabee wholesalers who will never send you a deal. If you find the right wholesaler, they can be an awesome deal source.

## How do you find a great wholesaler?

There are many ways to find wholesalers, but they are not all effective. Here are some of the ways I have found wholesalers and ways I have heard of others finding them:

- **Real estate investor meetups:** Most areas of the country have real estate investor meetups, and they can be a great place to network. I have met many wholesalers at meetups yet have never seen a deal come from any of them. I am not saying that you cannot find a good wholesaler at a meetup, but that is where many newbies go.
- **Search online:** Many wholesalers have websites for investors looking to buy deals. You can search online for wholesalers in your area, but again, whether or not they have deals can be hit or miss.
- **Ask around:** Some of the best ways to find wholesalers is to network with other investors, but they may not be keen on giving you their deal source. Besides investors, ask real estate agents, title companies, and other people in the business. Many wholesalers will e-mail real estate agents to find buyers.
- **Look for marketing:** If a wholesaler is marketing, you know they are at least trying to find deals. Instead of looking for wholesalers, look for their marketing. Look for bandit signs, billboards, Craigslist ads, Facebook posts, and call the number. Most wholesalers market by advertising they will buy houses fast for cash. Tell them you don't want to sell your house but want to be on their buyer's list. If you receive a letter from someone wanting to buy your house, do not throw it away. Call them and tell them you are a buyer.

I found the wholesalers I bought houses from by accident. One of them sent me an email because I am a real estate agent, and they wanted to know if I had clients who were interested in buying their deals. Two other wholesalers found me online through my blog. I spent a lot of time actively looking for wholesalers, and the only ones that worked out found me!

Finding a wholesaler is not easy, but they can be a great deal source. Investors always tell me there are no good wholesalers in their area. While most wholesalers may not be very good, almost every market (if it is decently sized) will have wholesalers doing deals. If you are looking to buy in the larger markets, I may even know some awesome wholesalers I can introduce you to.

## How to buy off-market properties below market value

Many investors buy off-market properties that are not listed on the MLS. Basically, you use the same techniques a wholesaler uses to find properties, but instead of selling to another investor, you keep the house. Being able to purchase these types of investment properties takes money and time. Investors send out direct mail or postcards or advertise with signs that let people know that they buy houses. I am sure you have heard of "We Buy Ugly Houses." They use billboards, newspaper ads, and their giant trucks to advertise to potential sellers.

Some homeowners want to sell their house but do not want to list it on the MLS. The house could need extensive repairs; the sellers may not want anyone to know they are selling; the sellers may need to sell extremely quickly; or there may be other factors preventing a seller from listing on the MLS. The difficulty in buying off-market properties is finding motivated sellers who do not have their houses listed for sale.

- **Drive for dollars**: Driving for dollars involves looking for vacant houses. When you find a vacant house, you try to contact the owners to see if they will sell it you.
- **Direct mailing:** Direct marketing involves sending postcards and letters to people who may be interested in selling their house.
- **Networking:** Many people advertise they have off-market properties directly from banks. Please be careful, as banks almost never sell individual properties without using the MLS. You can use your network of investors, agents, and other professionals to find off-market properties.

- **Bandit signs:** The easiest way to start marketing to sellers is to stick out a few bandit signs, which are signs that say you buy houses. Investors like to put these on busy street corners or in neighborhoods they want to buy in. Many cities have made bandit signs illegal, and if your signs disappear, the city could be removing them, or another investor who wants less competition could be removing them. I do not use bandit signs because of real estate agent disclosure issues.
- **Websites:** If you can create a website to attract sellers in your area, it can be a great lead source.
- **Craigslist/for sale by owner:** Some owners also try to sell their houses themselves. They may list them on Craigslist or put a for-sale-by-owner-sign in the yard.

## How can you start a direct-marketing campaign?

The most lucrative way to find great off-market deals is by creating your own direct-marketing campaigns. Creating a direct-mail campaign is not easy, and there is a reason most investors will never venture into this field or will not stay long enough to be successful. I have my own direct-mail campaigns, and I have purchased and listed houses from direct mail. Since I am a real estate agent, I have a couple of different ways to use direct mail, but I must disclose I am an agent and be very careful when buying houses. I always have a seller sign a disclosure that states I am buying the house below market value and that I may profit from the purchase. **If you are an agent trying to buy off-market properties, check state laws**.

Direct mailing is one of the best ways, if not the best way, to find motivated sellers. Direct mail involves sending letters or postcards to people who may be interested in selling their house. There are many different mailings to use and many different segments to send that list to.

The first step in creating a direct-mailing campaign is coming up with a recipient list. I use List Source.com to come up with absentee owners in my area. I also use a company that gives me a list of inherited properties. We send different postcards to each list and update the lists a few times each year.

Once you have your lists, you must send letters or postcards to the recipients. I have seen many varying opinions on whether postcards or letters are better, and it seems to come down to testing. Everyone is in a different market, and different lists consists of different owners. With some owners, a postcard works better, and with other owners, a letter may work better. Try out different letters and postcards and see which one gets you calls from the most motivated sellers. Usually you want to say something about buying houses for cash, with no commissions, no repairs needed, and quickly.

One letter will not get the job done. You must send five letters or postcards to the same person before they will respond. You want to make sure you respond to calls right away. We have a dedicated number set up just for postcard calls so we can call them back whether they leave a message or not.

Setting up a direct-mail campaign takes a lot of work and persistence. Therefore, most investors will not do it or see a campaign through.

I recently started using a company that handles all my direct marketing for me, including taking calls! If you are interested in learning more about them, send me an email: Mark@InvestFourMore.com

## What do you say to motivated sellers?

The scariest part of any direct-mail campaign is talking to the sellers. Many upset people will call you, complaining about receiving mail asking to buy their house. Usually, when you talk to them and pleasantly explain you are buying houses in the neighborhood, they calm down. You will have to deal with some property owners who have nothing better to do than to yell and complain. One lady threatened to call the police if I did not stop sending her letters, but she refused to tell me her name or address, so I couldn't take her off my list.

You'll find many property owners hoping to sell their house, but they want full retail value without paying a real estate commission. You will also talk to motivated sellers who want to sell right away and are willing to take a lower price. I talk to sellers as much as I can to see why they are selling, how much they want, and when they want to sell. Often, sellers are happy just to talk to anyone who will listen.

Since I am an agent, I like to give sellers a couple of options. I am very honest with them and tell them that most of the time, they will get more money if they list on the MLS. Even knowing they will get more money on the MLS, some sellers still won't want to list, or the houses are in such bad shape that it makes more sense for me to buy them. Otherwise, as an agent, I can list the house for them and make money that way. If you are not an agent, you may be able to sell your leads to an agent, but a real estate agent paying a referral fee to someone who is not licensed is illegal in most states.

When you talk to a seller, you want to highlight the advantages of selling to you:

- No repairs needed
- No commissions
- No closing costs
- Fast closing
- Cash closing
- No showings
- No appraisal

These advantages are for an investor who can pay cash for houses and close very quickly. Some wholesalers will use these terms as well, assuming they can assign a contract to a cash investor who will buy the property. If you must get a loan, don't lie to the seller and claim you can buy with cash. Almost all the successful investors I talk to have a couple of things in common: they know their market like no one else, and they are honest and follow through on deals if they say they will buy a house.

# How to find an investor-friendly real estate agent

The most important person on an investor's team is a great real estate agent. Real estate agents can play a huge role in getting a deal, losing a deal, valuing a property, and many other factors that can make or lose you money. Finding a real estate agent who will return calls and respond quickly enough for an investor is difficult.

I am an agent, and I think it is a huge advantage for investors to be real estate agents as well. If you do not want to become an agent yourself, it is imperative you find a great agent to help you

There is a lot of information for new real estate investors to process. A great real estate agent can make the process much less painful and make investing much more enjoyable. Finding a great agent is tricky, but there are many things you can look for when searching for an agent.

## What is the first thing you should do to find an agent?

As with almost any professional service, the best way to find someone good is through referrals. The first thing I do when I need help from a professional is ask my friends, family, and co-workers for a recommendation. It is usually best to ask as many people as possible until you start seeing the same name pop up repeatedly. Even if you get a great referral for an agent, you want to make sure the agent knows what they are doing. I have been referred to agents that turned out horribly (when I was looking to buy out-of-state).

People become real estate agents for a variety of reasons. Some want a little extra money, some want free time, some think it is a way to get rich quickly, and others want to make a career out of it. You want to find the career agent who cares about their job and business, not the agent looking to get rich quick.

Answering the phone or returning a call quickly is the first sign of a good agent. The phone call from a potential client is one of the best leads for an agent, yet many agents ignore calls or take days to return calls  If you call a potential agent, they should either answer their phone or call you back within a couple of hours. Getting a call back quickly is important because investors need speed to get the good deals. If it takes an agent a day or two to call you back, that could mean the difference between getting an offer accepted and another buyer getting the property.

Sometimes, the busiest agents cannot answer their phone or return calls right away. The busiest agents are usually the best agents, but you must ask yourself if you want an extremely busy agent working for you. Once again, they may be a great agent, but if they have too many clients to act quickly, they may not be the right agent for you.

## When looking for an investor-friendly agent, make sure they are competent

After you find an agent who answers their phone, you still have a lot of work to do. You must make sure they know what they are doing. Test their knowledge by asking simple questions about the types of homes you are looking to buy.

1. Have you sold many REO properties?
2. Have you sold HUD homes? Does your office have an NAID number?
3. How do you suggest buyers handle multiple-offer situations?
4. How do short sales work?
5. If I were to sell one of my houses, how would you market it?

You should already know the answers to most of these questions, but you want to know if your agent knows. How confident are they when answering these questions? If they are newer and do not know everything, that is okay. They should tell you that they do not know, but they will find out. Real estate is a serious business, and there are severe consequences for fraud or mistakes. You do not want your agent pretending to know how to do things and getting you in trouble.

## Is working with a new agent smart?

Some people do not like working with new agents because they are inexperienced. New agents can make up for that inexperience with ambition. Most new agents are motivated and are excited about starting a new career. When I started out as an agent, I was very ambitious when working with buyers, and I worked very hard for the few clients I had. As I obtained more clients and more business, I could not give each client as much attention. I will be honest and say I am a horrible agent for investors now. I do not have time to show houses, write offers, or check up on offers. I hand off leads to other agents on my team who do have time. That is another thing a new agent has going for them: they most likely have plenty of time to work for you.

Many investors are very demanding of their agent. They need to act quickly and may make many offers before getting one accepted. If you are an investor who wants to make hundreds of low-ball offers, make sure you motivate your agent. They are only paid when they sell a house, not to make offers. If they think it is a waste of time to submit low offer after low offer, they are not going to work hard for you. Buy them lunch or dinner and discuss strategies. Show them you care and give them a reason to keep working hard. Even though lunch will not make up for the hours of time they spend, it may be enough to keep them going until you get a deal done and they make some real money.

## Is your real estate agent knowledgeable about rental properties?

If you are planning to buy rental properties, it helps if your agent knows the rental market and investment property market. It helps tremendously if they can help you determine rents or at least back up your thinking on potential deals. It gives you that extra push to move forward on deals, and they may see potential problems that you do not. You still need to know your market and be able to make decisions on deals yourself. Do not rely solely on your agent to determine what a good deal is. If they are not familiar with rentals, that is okay. Many agents do not have a clue about real estate investing; acting fast for you is much more important.

Good ethics are a very important issue for investors or anyone using a real estate agent. Many buyers want an agent who stretches the rules to get them deals. If a buyer or seller knows an agent is being unethical or breaking laws, the buyer or seller is also liable and can be held just as responsible as the agent. Even if the buyer or seller does not know their agent is acting unethically, they can still be held responsible.

HUD homes are a great example of how buyers and agents can get in trouble. If an agent helps an investor bid as an owner-occupant, both the agent and investor can face criminal charges. HUD homes are government property, which means any laws broken involving them are felonies. Buyers can face up to two years in prison and a fine of $250,000 for breaking HUD rules. Agents can lose the ability for their entire office to sell any HUD homes.

## Does your real estate agent have backup when they are not available?

Another very important thing to consider with any agent is whether they have backup. Agents go on vacation, get sick, and have accidents...just like everyone else. You want to make sure they have someone who can take over their business if they are unavailable. Many agents work on teams. This is a great way to know you will be taken care of if your agent cannot do it himself or herself. As I have mentioned many times, speed can mean the difference between getting and losing a deal. The last thing you want is for your agent to be out of town and unavailable to show you a house or make an offer for several days.

Finding a great agent can take a lot of work. If you are an owner-occupant who only buys one house every five years, an agent may not be that important. If you are an investor looking to buy multiple houses a year, a great agent can mean the difference in thousands and thousands of dollars. If you choose an agent that you think is doing a poor job, do not be afraid to fire them. I have had to fire agents who were helping me because I misjudged their abilities, work ethic, or character.

I have a network of agents across the country through my REO and investing groups. If you need help finding an agent, email me at Mark@investfourmore.com, and I will do my best to refer you to someone.

## Should you use multiple agents to find investment properties?

Being a real estate agent, I have a definite bias toward whether an investor should work with one dedicated agent or with multiple agents. I also can give the agent's perspective on how we work and how an investor can make an agent work best for them.

There are many different scenarios for how agents are paid, but there are no standard commissions or structures used. The most common scenario I see in my area for most real estate transactions is two real estate agents, one for the buyer and one for the seller. Usually, the seller pays both agents' commissions. For this example, I will use the HUD commission structure, which is 3% for the buyer side and 3% for the seller side. That can seem like a lot of money for one deal, but agents have many expenses.

Real estate agents must carry a lot of insurance. I carry Errors and Omissions (E&O), general liability, and umbrella insurance policies. Agents must pay for license fees, MLS fees, office expenses, and office space.

Most agents do not keep their entire commission, because they pay a percentage to their broker. In turn, the broker pays for staff, advertising, and other expenses. Commission splits can range from 50/50 to 90/10 depending on what the office pays for and the number of transactions the agent closes. Agents also receive no benefits! They pay all their health insurance costs and have no matching 401ks or any of the other benefits of a corporate job.

After factoring in all these expenses, agents do not make as much as people think. An agent usually only gets paid when they sell a house. Agents may make $5,000 on one sale, but they may also have spent 20 hours with another client who never bought a house, so the agent earned nothing for their time.

The reason I am outlining the way agents are paid is to show you that agents want to make sure that the investors they work with are serious and that they are not working for free. This can determine whether an agent sends good deals to you or to someone else.

## Using multiple agents to buy investment properties

Many investors like to use multiple agents to find properties for them. They feel the more agents looking for properties for them, the better chance they have of getting a good deal. They will talk to many agents all over town telling them that they are a serious investor and are looking to make some purchases. This strategy can work in some cases, but it can also backfire.

Most agents can sense when an investor or buyer is working with multiple agents, and a good agent will flat out ask any buyer if they are working with another agent. Agents are taught in ethics class not to steal other agents' clients. It is drilled into our heads that "stepping on another agent's toes" by showing houses or writing contracts for a buyer that has already looked at houses with another agent is very bad.

Because of this training, most agents will naturally shy away from any buyer that says they have seen houses or are receiving listings from other agents or do not have one agent but are working with whoever has the best deal. This does not mean agents will not help investors working with multiple agents, but they probably will not put a lot of effort into it.

Agents are usually able to show a buyer any houses listed in MLS, but if they have no connection to a buyer or feel the buyer is not committed to them, they do not have much motivation. They will usually call the investor if their own listing might meet the investor's needs, but that is about it.

Some investors also feel they may be able to get a better deal on a property if they work with the listing agent instead of their own agent. They feel if there is no buyer's agent involved, the listing agent will take a smaller commission, and the seller can net the same amount with a lower sales price.

This strategy can work on some houses, but the agents still often charge the full commission. The buyer also may not have proper representation when taking this route, which is risky. Most states allow the listing agent to represent both sides or act as a transaction broker. However, if the agent has known the sellers for years and just met you, whose interests will the agent really have in mind?

## Using one agent to represent you when buying investment deals

Real estate agents are taught that the best way to do business is to let a buyer choose an agent, and then that agent will work exclusively with the buyer. There are a couple of huge positive motivators for an agent to use this technique.

- Agents know that if the buyer makes a purchase, the buyer will use them, and the agent will be paid.
- Agents know if the buyer decides to sell a house, the client will use them, and the agent will be paid.

An agent who knows that they have a loyal buyer will work hard to send them new listings, search aged listings, and find other possible deals. They know if they find the right house, they will be rewarded with a commission check. They have much more motivation because they do not worry that the investor will use another agent on houses that they send the buyer.

Using multiple agents can work, but the investor making these techniques work is usually doing the property searches himself. He is not relying on an agent to send him listings or leads. He finds a good deal and then approaches the listing agent to try to make a better deal.

## Should you become a real estate agent?

Real estate has provided me with great income and the opportunity to own a business. When I became an agent in 2001, I did not invest in rental properties—I sold houses. When I started to invest in rentals, I could immediately see how big of an advantage being an agent gave me. I saved thousands of dollars in commissions, found better deals, and made more money because of my real estate license.

One reason I am getting such high returns on my rentals is I save thousands of dollars on each transaction by being an agent. I also do 10 to 15 fix-and-flips per year and save thousands of dollars on each of those transactions as well. Being a real estate agent has saved me over $70,000 in commissions every year. That does not include the profit I made on deals that I would not have gotten if I were not an agent.

If you plan to buy more than one or two rental properties per year, you may want to think about getting a real estate license. If you do nothing else with your license except buy your own rental properties, it will save you thousands of dollars in commissions each year. On every rental property I buy, I save money because I earn a commission as the buyer's agent. The commission may be 2, 2.5, or 3% per deal, but in the end, that adds up to a lot of money. If you buy three houses per year at an average price of $100,000, being an agent can save you $7,500 to $9,000 per year.

If you fix and flip those houses and sell them, you will more than double your savings because you will save a commission when you sell the house. On a recent fix and flip I bought for $105,000, I earned a 3% commission as the buyer's agent. I repaired the property and sold it for $175,000. When I list the house, I will save another 3% commission. On this one deal, I will save $8,400 because I am a real estate agent.

If you become an agent, you may not save as much money as I have. I have a large real estate team and pay a flat fee to my broker, which allows me to keep 100% of my commissions. If you start as a new agent, you most likely will not keep all your commissions, but it is still a huge advantage.

## Advantages of being an investor with a real estate license

Being an agent saves me commissions, and it allows me to get more deals. Here are some other ways that having a license is a huge advantage:

- As a real estate agent, you get access to the MLS and can do your own searches for properties without relying on an agent to find you the right deal. Having access to the MLS gives investors a huge advantage because they do not have to wait for an agent to send them listings. I search for listings at least five times per day and routinely make offers the same day a house is listed. An agent can also easily pull sold comparable information from the MLS to calculate property values. Calculating accurate values is one of the most important things an investor can do to be successful.

· As an agent, you can fraternize with other agents and people in the real estate world. The more people you know in the business, the more people you can inform that you are looking for property. Sometimes, the best deals are those that are brought to you, not the deals you find yourself. Let everyone you know that you are looking for investment properties, and you never know what will come up. I have bought many properties that were never listed on the MLS because of my contacts in the business.

· The IRS has limits on how much money you can deduct on rental properties if real estate is not your primary job. If real estate is your primary job, you may be able to deduct many more expenses.

· If you are an agent that does many deals, most agents will know who you are. If you have a good reputation for getting deals done, sticking to your word, and being dependable, other agents will want to work with you on tough deals. Many properties I buy have major issues and are tough to sell. Other agents know me and know I will do my best to get the deal done.

· I already mentioned the commission savings on investment properties, but there is another advantage besides just the savings. If I save $8,000 in commissions on a fix and flip, I can buy that property for $8,000 more than an investor who does not have their real estate license. That savings allows me to pay more money and get more deals than other investors while still making the same profit.

## How can you make money as a real estate agent?

I am biased, but I think being a real estate agent is one of the best opportunities out there. There are many, many forms of income in the real estate business. If you are motivated and dedicated to making it in the business, then you can make serious money. I will not go into details in this book (I wrote another book on how to be a successful real estate agent), but here are some of the different areas that can generate income.

**Property management:** If you want to be a serious investor, you will want a property manager to handle your rental properties at some point. If you start your own property management business, you can manage your properties and other properties as well. Not only are you saving 10% of your rent by doing your own management, but you can also make extra cash by managing other investor's properties.

**Retail Sales:** This is the most common way to earn money as an agent. Retail sales involve listing houses for private sellers and selling houses to buyers. If you are dedicated and treat this as a real job, you can make a lot of money. Many agents make over $100,000 per year, and the very best make much more than that.

**Commercial Sales:** Commercial real estate takes a lot more experience and knowledge than residential. Breaking into commercial is difficult unless you start with a commercial firm who can mentor you. Experienced and successful commercial agents can easily make hundreds of thousands of dollars per year.

**REO sales:** REO agents list and manage these houses for the banks. Agents can make a very lucrative living if they work with the right banks. Building up your business can take years, and the supply is determined by the number of foreclosed houses. It is a conflict of interest for REO agents to buy their own listings. Being an REO agent is not a huge advantage for your own investing.

**Short Sales:** Short sales are listed for sale by private sellers who are selling the house for less than they owe the bank. There is a huge market for short sales, and many agents make a great living specializing in this field. Closing a short sale takes a lot of patience and diligence since banks have many requirements and can take months to approve a short sale.

**Broker Price Opinions (BPOs):** A BPO is a one- to three-page report used to determine property values, but it's not an appraisal. Licensed agents can complete BPOs for various clients, including banks. They are usually paid between $30 and $80 per order. Some agents make a living only completing BPOs, and for others, it is a great way to supplement their income while learning the business.

## How can you become a real estate agent?

You must take pre-licensing classes and pass a test in most states. Most of my team got their license through Real Estate Express, which has a great licensing program in most states. Real Estate Express has some of the cheapest prices I have seen, although I have not researched every real estate school. I have many more articles about becoming an agent on InvestFourMore.com. I also wrote a book for real estate agents: *How to Make It Big in Real Estate*.

There are many ways to make money as an agent. Even if you just want to buy or sell a few of your own listings each year, I believe becoming an agent is well worth it.

## Final thoughts on buying below market value

Buying below market value is the key to almost any successful real estate investing strategy. If you want to make money flipping or with rental properties, you will need to buy below market value. While buying below market value is tough when starting out, you can still get a deal without waiving your inspection, without paying cash, and without looking at a house hours after it has been listed. However, getting those deals will be tougher if you cannot act quickly, waive an inspection, or pay cash.

If you are brand new, I don't recommend waiving inspections. Knowing which repairs are needed and knowing how much of a profit margin you need in order to absorb extra costs that may occur takes a lot of experience.

When I buy flips or rentals and waive my inspection, I am assuming that a house will need more work than what can be seen. Houses usually need more repairs than you think they will after you start working on them and uncovering things.

While cash deals are a great enticement to many sellers, some sellers, such as HUD, do not care. HUD does not care if you pay cash or use a loan. All they care about is the net price they are getting on the house. Often, I get a loan on houses, even though I make my offer as cash. I put a clause in the offer that says I have the cash to pay for the house if needed but may use financing from a portfolio lender.

# 7

# How to Finance and Pay for Rental Properties

We have discussed why rental properties are such a great investment, how to buy them below market value, and what makes a good rental property investment. This information will not do you any good though if you do not have money or financing to buy a rental. This chapter covers how much you need to buy a rental, how to buy with financing, and how to buy with less money down.

In the early 2000s, you could get financing on an investment property with as little as 5% down. Those days are gone, and getting financing on investment properties is much tougher. Having said that, obtaining loans on rental properties may not be as difficult as some banks make it out to be. When I was buying rentals, many banks told me I could not get more than four mortgages. That is not true. What they meant is that their bank would not give me more than four mortgages in my name. There is no law or government restriction on how many mortgages you can obtain.

One great way to increase your cash flow and wealth is by using leverage or mortgages to buy rentals. With financing, you can buy more properties with less cash, and if you buy the right properties, you will make more money. This goes against what some people believe: that you will make more money by paying cash for a property. However, I can prove with some simple math why leverage will make you more money.

## Should you pay cash or get a loan on rental properties?

Paying cash for rental properties may seem like a safe bet, but in reality, it can cause you to make less money on rentals. When you get a loan, you can increase your returns substantially.

I am going to use some basic figures to outline the benefits of **leveraging your money**. If you pay cash for a $100,000 house and after all expenses are left with $500 in monthly cash flow, you are making about 6% cash-on-cash returns. If you put 20% down on a $100,000 house, you will have a mortgage payment, but the returns on your cash invested increase because you are using much less cash. If you are paying a 4% interest rate, your principal and interest payment will be about $382. You are only making $118 after subtracting the mortgage payment, but you are making 7% cash-on-cash return due to the lower initial investment.

Even though the cash-on-cash return is 7% you are actually making much more than that in the above scenario. You are also paying down the principal on the loan by at least $118 each month. That $118 equals another 7% return on your money that you would not have on a cash purchase. You have more than doubled your return by getting a mortgage instead of paying cash. This doesn't even take into consideration that over the 30-year life of the loan, your principal paydown will increase each month, which further improves your return.

The exciting part about using leverage is that when you get higher cash flows, the returns increase even more. If you can make $800 per month without a mortgage, you will be making 9.6% cash-on-cash return on the same $100,000 house. With 20% down on the same property, you would cash flow $418 each month after the mortgage payments and make over 25% cash-on-cash return.

The way to make big money in rental properties is to find properties that will give you a lot of cash flow and buy as many as possible. The way you buy as many as you can is by getting mortgages. I make over $500 monthly cash flow on each of my properties with loans in place. Yes, I would make more per property if I paid cash, but I would have fewer properties and less total cash flow.

You can buy three or four houses with $100,000 instead of just one house with all cash. Using the cash flow figures from above and buying three properties instead of one, you would make $1,254 per month instead of $800. Not only does your cash flow increase when you own more properties, but the equity paydown, tax benefits, and appreciation also increase. If you can **purchase a house below market** value every time, your net worth increases as well!

## What are the other advantages of buying multiple properties?

Rental properties have many tax benefits, including depreciation. The IRS allows you to depreciate a percentage of your rental properties every year and write that off as an expense. If you have three houses instead of just one, you can get triple the tax deductions, and if the market appreciates, you have the benefit of triple the appreciation.

It is the same situation if rents go up. The more properties you have, the more money you will make. I never count on **rents to go up or for the houses to appreciate, but it is a nice bonus.** With multiple rental properties, you are also paying down the loans on three properties, which increases your returns as well. When you think of the tax savings, possible appreciation, and equity paydown, the returns shoot through the roof.

## Downside to buying more rental properties with leverage

There is a downside to owning more properties: you will have to spend more **for repairs** and improvements since you own more houses. You will also have multiple rental properties to manage. However, if you can cash flow $400 or more with a mortgage, you will still be way ahead of the game by leveraging your money. You will also have more total cash flow coming in, which can pay for a property manager. We accounted for the repairs and maintenance when we determined the cash flow, so it will not be an added expense with more properties, but managing the properties yourself will involve more work.

Some people think buying with cash is less risky than buying with a loan, but I disagree. Here are some reasons why cash may be riskier than a loan.

- When you buy with cash, you have fewer properties. The fewer properties you have, the fewer income sources you have, and the more loss of income will hurt. If you have one property paid for with cash, it really hurts when it goes vacant. That is your only source of income from rentals. However, if you have three rentals that have loans on them, one may go vacant, but you have two more that are bringing in money.
- When you have multiple rentals, you have more diversification. If you have one rental, you are more susceptible to neighborhood changes, storm damage, etc. With multiple rentals, you have less chance of all your properties being damaged or hurt by other factors.

In my opinion, using other people's money and increasing your returns versus paying cash is better. Some people are very averse to any risk and do not want any debt at all. If the idea of debt makes you sick to your stomach, maybe paying cash is the best route for you. I will continue to get as many loans as I can and to buy as many rental properties as I can because of the incredible benefits rental properties offer.

## How much money do you need to buy a rental property?

The biggest hurdle for most people when purchasing a real estate investment is the money it takes. If you are paying cash for a property, figuring out how much money you'll need is easy. It can be a little tougher to determine what you'll need when you are getting a loan. There are different loan programs and many ways to buy rental properties. Buying an investment property is very expensive. Most banks require at least 20% down. There will be additional costs as well, but there are ways to invest in real estate for less than you think.

Most banks will require 25% down once you have four mortgages in your name. Some banks will stop lending to you all together once you reach ten financed properties. Later, I will get into ways to finance multiple properties.

Depending on house values in your area, 20% down is a lot of money. The houses I buy are usually right around $100,000, which equates to about $20,000 for the down payment. You also need to pay closing costs, which consist of interest, insurance, recording fees, origination fees, tax certificates, appraisals, and more. It is usually safe to assume closing costs will be at least 3% of the purchase price, although you can ask the seller to pay part or all your closing costs. In some cases, I ask the seller to pay part of the closing costs to reduce the amount of cash I have into a property. Remember that asking the seller to pay your closing costs may make your offer less attractive. You also may have to pay for an inspection, which can cost $250 to $500. Some sellers, such as HUD, do not pay for title insurance, which can add another $500 to $1,000 to the purchase costs.

## How much money do you need for repair and carrying costs on a rental property?

Repairs can add a huge chunk to the amount required to buy a rental property. You must wait for the repairs to be completed before it can be rented out, and while you are waiting, you are paying carrying costs (interest, utilities, taxes, and insurance), which also increase the amount needed. In a perfect world, having a professional contractor complete most repairs should only take a week or two, but it always takes longer.

Repairs usually cost more than you think as well. On a house with minimal repairs, I still assume I will spend at least $5,000 before I can rent it out. On a house that needs more repairs and updates, I can easily spend $20,000 or more. The little things always take time, and costs add up quickly. As a rule, I always add $5,000 for unknown costs on any rental or fix and flip that I buy.

Make sure you get bids if you are not an expert at estimating repairs. Estimating repairs can be very difficult, even for experienced investors. Repairs always seem to cost more than the investor thinks they should, and contractors always seem to find more things that need to be repaired.

## How much will you need to buy a rental property?

Here is a breakdown of the costs I would normally have on a $100,000 rental property:

These figures are for a house that needs moderate work. If I had bought this house from the MLS, I would get back about $3,000 in real estate commissions since I'm an agent. I could also ask the seller to pay $3,000 of my closing costs if I thought it would not jeopardize my chances of getting the deal.

If you must put 25% down, the amount you'll need would increase dramatically. Repairs also affect how much you would need. A higher or lower purchase price will also affect the down payment.

Another factor to consider is the bank will want you to have money in reserves when you get an investment-property loan.

## How much in cash reserves will you need for a rental property?

Buying rental properties takes a lot of money, and you must have money in reserve to handle vacancies and maintenance. I have 16 rental properties, and purchasing them has taken a great deal of cash. I also have maintenance and vacancies to consider. I must keep money in reserves for maintenance and vacancies, and the bank also requires me to have money in reserves for my rentals.

You must have money set aside to handle vacant months and repairs. Most repairs are minor and don't cost much, but some repairs—such as replacing a roof—can cost $5,000 or more. Repairs are often done when a house is vacant, which means you will not be receiving rent, and you must pay for repairs.

## How much will a bank require in reserve?

The money you need to keep in reserve depends on many factors. Older houses need more maintenance, and some houses will have more vacancies than others. Most lenders require investors to have at least six months in reserve for all mortgages in an investor's name before they will give them a loan. To figure how much cash you would need, add all your mortgage payments, including your personal residence, and multiply by six.

A bank will require all the minimal costs required on an investor's mortgage to be accounted for when calculating reserves. Taxes, insurance, and mortgage payment will be counted. My monthly mortgage payments, which include taxes and insurance, range from $450 to $650 on my rental properties. I must also account for my personal-residence mortgage payment, which is over $2,000 per month. Of my 16 rentals, two do not have loans against them. In total, I need over $50,000 in cash reserves to show my bank that I am in a good enough financial position to purchase more rental properties.

Reserve needs vary with each investor and the properties they own. A huge factor when considering how much you need is how much cash flow your rental properties are producing. If you have minimal or negative cash flow, you will need much more in reserve. Having to cover part of a mortgage payment on top of paying for vacancies and maintenance can add up quickly. Most banks will also consider the investor's rental-property cash flow when making loans. If you have little to no cash flow, qualifying for more loans will be harder. I suggest buying rentals for cash flow and not appreciation, but if you have negative-cash-flowing properties, you should have more than six months of mortgage payments, taxes, and insurance in reserve.

If you have high cash flow, you should be able to build your reserve quickly. If you find you are short on cash, save the cash flow until you have a decent amount in reserve. Many of the problems investors run into are easily solved if they invest for cash flow!

If you have one personal residence with a mortgage payment of $700 per month and a rental property with a payment of $500 per month, you would only need $7,200 in reserve according to bank requirements. However, that is not much money if you must make major repairs. Roof replacement could wipe out your entire reserve. You better hope the house stays rented and no other repairs come up while you build the reserve. I think an investor should have at least $10,000 in reserve no matter what the bank says you should have. This assumes your rental properties are basic houses that are in decent condition. If you have old properties that need maintenance, you may need to save even more.

When you have a reserve for vacancies and maintenance, that money should not be used for personal items or for buying more rental properties. You never know when you might need to evict someone or make major repairs. If you do not have the money to complete an eviction or make repairs, you could have major problems renting out the house. If you cannot rent it out, you will not be able to bring in more money to cover the expenses. You may find yourself in a heap of trouble and be forced to sell the property.

While purchasing a rental property, making repairs, and covering carrying costs can take over $30,000, so you may need even more in the bank. You should not spend all your cash to buy an investment property, and the bank most likely will not let you spend all your money either. This seems like a huge amount of money, but there are ways to buy with less money down and ways to recoup that money later, so do not get discouraged.

## How to qualify for a loan on an investment property

Qualifying for a loan on an investment property is much more difficult than qualifying for a loan on an owner-occupied house. Many banks consider investor loans riskier than owner-occupied loans. New lending regulations also make it harder for investors to get a loan on rental properties. If you are an investor and want to get a loan on more than four or ten properties, it really gets difficult. Investors can do many things to give themselves a better chance of qualifying.

One of the biggest issues facing investors is qualifying for multiple mortgages when they have a loan on their personal residence and want to finance a rental. Because of this, it is very important not to buy the most expensive house you qualify for. Maxing out your qualification on your personal residence makes qualifying for a loan on an investment property very difficult because it raises your debt-to-income ratio.

## Banks are much tougher on investors than on owner-occupants

Just about every bank will require at least 20% down. In some cases, owner-occupants can avoid the down payment, but banks want investors to put more skin in the game. The origination fees, appraisal, and other loan costs may be more expensive as well depending on what type of investment property you are buying.

Investors must also have more money in the bank than an owner occupant. We saw how much an investor must save to buy a rental, but an owner-occupant may not need any reserves in the bank to get a loan! The reason owner-occupants are favored over investors is the government encourages home ownership. The more people who own houses, the better it is for our economy. They give subsidies and special programs to owner-occupant homeowners, which allow them to buy houses more easily than investors.

Most banks require a higher credit score for investors looking to buy rental properties. After you have four mortgages, conventional lenders will require a score of at least 720, while some owner-occupied loans may allow a credit score under 600. Do not expect to get a loan on an investment property with a credit score under 620.

A common problem with buying rental properties is having a low enough debt-to-income ratio to qualify for a loan. Often, banks will not count rental income after you buy an investment property, which makes it even tougher. The rules regarding rental income vary by the bank and type of loan. My portfolio lender has less-strict guidelines than a bank that follows Fannie Mae guidelines. Many lenders do not count rental income until it shows up on your tax return. Some lenders will only count 75% of rental income, and others are even stricter.

## Is it hard for an investor to get a loan on a house that needs repairs?

Often, houses that need repairs can be bought below market value. However, many lenders will not loan on a house that needs repairs if the repairs affect livability. Whether you are an investor or owner-occupied buyer, repairs can cause a deal to fall apart, which is why cash offers are attractive to sellers who have a house that needs work. If you are an investor or owner-occupied buyer, there are ways to get a loan on a property when it needs repairs, even if they're extensive.

Most lenders use FHA guidelines to decide what condition a house needs to be in to get a loan. That means all major systems such as plumbing, electrical, and heating need to be in working order. The roof needs to be in good condition, and there cannot be any holes in the walls or floors. FHA previously required flooring to be in good condition, but that is no longer the case. All the carpet can be missing and it will still go FHA. The tricky part is that not all lenders follow FHA requirements precisely.

An FHA loan is federally insured by the government and is a big reason owner-occupants can buy houses with little money down. Conventional loans are not federally insured or sponsored by any government agency (in most cases). There are many types of conventional loans and many different requirements depending on the lender. Some conventional loans require a house to be in the same condition as FHA loans require. If a conventional lender will not offer a loan, that does not mean another conventional lender will have the same guidelines. If you can find a portfolio lender, their guidelines may be less strict.

The government also sponsors other loans, such as VA and USDA. Different states also have loan programs that have varying requirements. Most government-lending programs have the same or even stricter requirements than FHA. Remember those low-down payment loans are only available to owner occupants.

## How do you get a loan on a house that needs repairs?

There are many options for working through lender-required repairs. Your choices will differ depending on whether you are an owner-occupant or an investor. The first strategy is to ask the seller to make repairs so house is in livable condition. Which situations allow the seller to make repairs?

- **Traditional seller**: If an owner is selling a house for retail value, they usually expect to make repairs (if required by the lender). To get top dollar, the house must be in livable condition. Those of us who want a great deal usually deal with sellers who want to sell quickly without doing any repairs. The better the deal, the lower the chance the seller will make any repairs.
- **REO properties**: Some REO sellers make repairs and some do not. The decision to repair or not is usually made on a case-by-case basis depending on how much work is needed. REO homes listed in as-is condition indicate that the seller will not make repairs. However, some REO sellers will still make repairs if required to do so by the buyer's lender.
- **HUD Homes**: HUD does not make any repairs under any circumstance for lender-required items. HUD does have a program to allow FHA buyers to make repairs after closing. If you are an investor and your lender requires repairs to be made before closing, you will have to cancel the contract or find a new lender.
- **Short sales**: Most short-sale sellers do not have a lot of money. If you know a short sale needs work and your lender requires repairs to be made before closing, there is a good chance the work will not be done. The sellers are not receiving any money in most short sales, and they do not want to spend any more money on the house.
- **Auctions sales**: Do not expect any repairs on auction properties. Properties that are sold at auction are usually sold as-is and will not be repaired.
- **Wholesale deals**: There is almost no chance you will get any repairs on a house you buy through a wholesaler.

## Know who you are dealing with before you write a contract

When shopping for a house, you should have already talked to a lender, and you should know condition the lender requires of the house. If you are using a conventional loan on a HUD home and the water cannot be turned on but your lender requires this, guess what will happen: the contract will fail. If a short sale needs $10,000 in work for you to get a loan, the deal will probably never go through. On REO or traditional sales, the seller may or may not make repairs. Do not expect HUD or an REO seller to make repairs just because your lender requires it.

If an owner-occupant wants to get a loan on a house that needs repairs, but the seller will not repair the house, the deal is not always over. HUD offers a program for FHA buyers which allows them to escrow for repairs and add the repair costs to the loan. HUD's program is the FHA 203b loan, which can only be used on HUD homes with repairs costing less than $5,000. This escrow cannot be used on any other type of loan, such as VA or conventional. For repairs over $5,000, an FHA 203k loan can be used on any house. This loan can have an unlimited number of repairs but will take more time to close and will have more fees. FHA loans are only available for owner occupants.

An FHA 203k rehab loan is not available to investors, which makes it harder for an investor to deal with houses that need repairs. That does not mean investors are out of luck. I buy houses that need a lot of work all the time, and I get loans on almost all of them.

I use a portfolio lender that does not have any repair requirements. I can buy houses with bad roofs and bad heating, and my lender does not even require me to turn on the utilities. Not all portfolio lenders have the same requirements, but many will work with investors much more than the big banks will. My portfolio lender has saved many deals for investors and owner occupants whose original lenders would not loan on a house because it needed too much work.

Escrowing repairs is sometimes impossible. In some cases, an investor can escrow repairs so they are done after closing. Usually, the lender will escrow for minor repairs but may be hesitant to escrow for major one.

Investors can use a Homestyle Fannie Mae Renovation loan to repair houses after closing. This loan is like the FHA 203k loan but is meant for investors.

If your lender will not loan on a house that needs repairs and the seller will not make repairs, do not give up. Ask them about the Homestyle renovation loan; ask about escrowing repairs; or search for a local portfolio lender who might have different guidelines and will give you a loan.

Another option for investors is hard-money lenders. Hard-money lenders are much more expensive than conventional lenders and only offer short-term loans. Hard money usually works better for fix-and-flips because of the short loan term, but it can be used for rentals as well. Hard-money lenders may be a decent short-term solution for rental properties, but you will have to refinance the loan very quickly. I will discuss hard money in more detail shortly.

## How to lower debt-to-income ratios

High debt-to-income (DTI) ratios cause some of the most problems when people try to qualify for a mortgage or investment-property loan. Most lenders want to see a debt-to-income ratio of 45% or lower. If your debt-to-income ratio is higher, qualifying for a loan will be very difficult. Investors always ask me how to get around high DTI ratios. Even my portfolio lender, who is very lenient with lending requirements, will not loan to people with high DTI ratios. The two options for reducing your DTI ratio are to make more money or pay off debt.

### What is debt-to-income ratio, and how is it calculated?

DTI ratio is calculated by taking your monthly debt payments and dividing them by your gross income. If you have $2,000 in monthly debt and $5,000 in gross income, you have a DTI ratio of 40% ($2,000/$5,000 = 40%). It is a very simple equation, but coming up with the monthly debt and income figures is not always simple, especially if you own rental properties.

You must count the new mortgage payment against your DTI ratio. Even though your debt-to-income ratio may be 35%, a new mortgage payment may push that number to 45%, and you may not qualify. The highest payment you can qualify for on a new mortgage is the payment that pushes you to the maximum DTI ratio a lender will allow. If a lender will allow a 40% DTI ratio and a $1,000 house payment pushes you to 40%, that is the highest payment you could qualify for (notice I am using different maximum DTI ratios because different lenders and programs allow different DTI ratios).

Banks pay attention to your monthly debt payments and monthly income...not total balances. You may not think having a $2,000 credit card balance would affect your ability to qualify for a loan. However, if the monthly payments are $200, they would have a huge impact on how high your mortgage could be. A $200 monthly difference in mortgage payments can reduce the amount you qualify for by as much as $40,000!

## What expenses and income are included in DTI ratios?

Everyone on the loan will have to include these debt figures:

- Minimum credit card payments
- Auto loans
- Student loans
- Consumer loans
- Other financial obligations, including child support and alimony
- If you are keeping your house, count the housing payments. If you are selling your house before you buy the new one, do not count the housing payments.
- Estimated future housing expenses, including principal, interest, taxes, insurance, and HOA fees

**To calculate your income, you use:**

- Your gross monthly salary before taxes, including overtime and bonuses.

Include any alimony or child support received that you choose to have considered for repayment of the loan.
· Any additional income, such as rental property profits. This is tricky because some lenders will not count rental income until it shows up on your taxes. Other lenders will count 75% of your rental income if you are an experienced investor or if the house has been leased for an extended period.

Calculating your DTI ratio is usually a little tricky because different banks calculate things differently. It is best to let your lender calculate the DTI ratio for you. If the bank comes up with a DTI ratio that seems very high, double-check their calculation method to see if they are doing something strange or if they put a wrong number somewhere. Some banks count depreciation of investment properties against you, even though that depreciation is not a monthly expense.

Different banks and loan programs use different DTI ratios. VA and FHA typically limit borrowers to 52% DTI ratio, but in some circumstances, they may slightly increase that percentage. Fannie Mae allows up to a 45% DTI ratio on some loans, but you must have great credit. With credit scores under 700, your DTI ratio should typically be under 36% (these numbers are constantly changing).

As you can see, figuring this all out yourself can be very confusing. The best thing to do is to talk to a lender and work on lowering your DTI ratio if it is too high.

## How can you lower your DTI ratio?

The best way to lower a debt-to-income ratio is to make more money. The more gross income you have, the higher your DTI ratio will be. Lenders look at other things besides DTI ratio. Making more money isn't easy, but many investors, self-employed individuals, or business owners claim very little income on their taxes. Claiming little income is great if you do not want to pay too much in taxes. However, claiming little income can make qualifying for a loan nearly impossible. You may be making $10,000 per month, but if your taxes show you making $2,000 per month, the bank will only count what is on your taxes. Claiming more income on your taxes will mean you must pay the IRS more, but being able to buy a house may make that worth it.

Reducing debt is another way to improve your DTI ratio. DTI ratios take into consideration all monthly debts that show up on your credit report. Usually, the shortest-term debts hurt you the most because they have the highest payments. Even though you think you are doing the smart thing by getting a 15- instead of a 30-year loan on your primary house, it actually will hurt your DTI ratio. A three-year car loan will make your DTI ratio higher than a six-year loan. I am not saying you should always get the longest term possible, but the lower your minimum payments are, the lower your DTI ratio will be. You can always make extra payments if you want to pay off your loans faster. What kind of situations ruin your DTI ratio?

- **Minimum credit card payments**: Credit cards typically have very high interest and very high monthly payments. Paying off the entire balance will greatly improve your DTI ratio.
- **Auto loans:** Car loans can destroy a DTI ratio! A $600 car payment is equivalent to a $120,000 mortgage, and it will reduce your ability to qualify for a mortgage by $600 per month. Do you need to have a new car every three years if it means you cannot buy a house?
- **Student loans:** Student loans may have low interest and low payments, but they still hurt DTI ratios.
- **Consumer loans:** Do you have a loan for a TV, furniture, home equity line of credit, or any other monthly payments that show up on your credit? Even a home equity line of credit that you are not using can count against your DTI ratio.

If you do not have the money to pay off your debt, you may be able to consolidate it with a larger loan against your house that would have a lower interest rate and lower monthly payment.

## What is the best way to pay off debt?

If you have a lot of credit card debt, car loans, and consumer debt, it is best to pay off one at a time as quickly as possible. The payments will stop affecting your DTI ratio once they disappear from your credit. Paying off one debt at a time will improve your DTI ratio more quickly.

When you pay off one debt, you can use the money you were spending on those payments to pay off the next debt sooner. Pick the debt with the lowest balance compared to the highest payment to pay off first. If you have a $2,000 debt with $200 payments, pay that off before you pay off a $5,000 debt with $300 payments. You will pay off the $2,000 faster and be able to use that extra $200 to pay off the next debt.

If you have a huge car payment, do not be afraid to sell the car and buy a less-expensive one. My daily driver for ten years was a 1991 Mustang that I bought with cash. I never had a car loan until I was 28 and earning good income.

There is no secret way to reduce your DTI ratio. It takes making more money or lowering your monthly debt payments. A few lenders do not consider DTI ratio, but they are usually lending high dollar amounts on large investment properties or many investment properties at once. If you find yourself with a high DTI ratio, talk to your lender, make sure they are calculating everything correctly, and concentrate on reducing your monthly debt payments.

## Should you get a 15- or 30-year mortgage?

15-year loans appear to be cheaper than 30-year loans because they have a lower interest rate. However, I would much rather have the flexibility of a 30-year loan. I use 30-year loans to buy rental properties because I get more cash flow, lower DTI ratio, and I have more flexibility with the extra money.

## What are the advantages of a 15-year loan versus a 30-year loan?

The biggest advantage of a 15-year mortgage is the interest rate. The difference in rates changes daily and varies with different banks, but the interest rate on a 15-year loan is usually about .5% less than on a 30-year fixed mortgage.

Some people think the biggest advantage of 15-year loans is the earlier payoff. However, I do not agree because you can pay a 30-year loan off early if you want to. If you get a 15-year, $100,000 loan with a 4% interest rate, the payments will be $740 per month (check out Bankrate.com's mortgage calculator for calculating mortgage payments). Over 15 years, you will pay $33,143 in interest. With a 30-year loan at 4.5% interest, the total interest will be $82,406.

On the surface, it looks like you are saving almost $50,000 by getting a 15-year loan. However, you are paying interest over 30 years on one loan and over 15 years on the other. The monthly payment on a 30-year loan is only $507, which is $233 less than on the 15-year loan. If you were to take that $233 and put it back into the 30-year loan each month, the 30-year loan interest would total $39,754, and you would pay it off in less than 17 years. The higher interest rate definitely costs you a little more, but over 15 years, that is only $550 extra each year.

## Why would a 30-year loan be better than a 15-year loan?

You will pay less interest with a 15-year loan. However, your monthly payment is higher. If you add up the payment savings with the 30-year loan, you save $2,796 each year and $41,940 over 15 years.

That extra money can be used for many things that will make you much more money than the $6,000 you save over 15 years. You can buy more rental properties. You can use the money to build an emergency fund. You could also pay off the mortgage early in the beginning, and if you ever need the extra money later, you can stop putting extra money toward the mortgage.

Another huge factor when considering whether to use a 15- or 30-year loan is being able to qualify for more properties. Banks look at debt-to-income ratios when qualifying an investor. A 15-year loan has a higher payment and increases your monthly debt-payment number. The higher your loan payments, the less cash flow you have, and the harder qualifying for new loans will be.

## Using a 30-year ARM (adjustable rate mortgage) versus a 15-year fixed loan

I use 30-year ARMs to finance my rental properties. An ARM is an adjustable rate mortgage that has a fixed interest rate for a certain amount of time. The interest rate can go up or down after the fixed period is up. My portfolio lender offers 5- and 7-year ARMs with a 30-year amortization. The rate will stay the same for the five or seven years but can change after that term is up. There are limits to how much the rate can change each year, and the rate can never exceed a certain ceiling. The great thing about ARMs is the rate is lower than a 30-year or even a 15-year fixed rate loan.

If you get an ARM for your rental properties, you will have an even lower payment than with the 30-year fixed-rate loan, and you will save even more interest over a 15-year fixed-rate loan. It is the best of both worlds.

## Are ARMs good loans?

I use ARMs on my rental properties for many reasons. I can get more than four loans on a property. The rates are lower, and an ARM is one of the only loans I can get because I have so many loans.

ARMs have gotten a bad rap from the housing market crisis. A 5/30-year ARM is a 30-year loan with an initial five-year fixed rate that can go up in year six. ARM interest rates are tied to market rates

ARMs have very low-interest rates that are locked in for a guaranteed period. ARMs can offer rates that are 1% or less than a 30-year fixed-rate loan. You may have heard horror stories about ARMs as some people used them carelessly. You used to be able to get six-month or one-year ARMs with very low rates that would then jump to very high rates. Often, buyers could not qualify for normal 30-year fixed-rate loans, but they could qualify for the lower payment the ARM offered. I would not suggest using an ARM if you cannot qualify for a 30-year fixed-rate mortgage. If things are that tight, reconsider your financial plan!

Another reason I use an adjustable rate mortgage is they are one of the few options available from my local lender. I use a portfolio lender who loans their own money and does not sell their loans to investors. My portfolio lender offers a 5- and 7-year ARM as well as a 15-year fixed loan. The 5/30-year ARM has the lowest payment, lowest interest rate, and works perfectly for my cash-flow strategy. The reason I use a portfolio lender is many lenders will not loan to investors when they have more than four mortgages. My portfolio lender will lend on as many loans as I can qualify for, but I must use their limited loan options. If you can get a 30-year fixed loan with a similar rate to an ARM, I would definitely consider it based on your goals.

ARMs have gotten a bad name the last decade due to the high number of loans that were foreclosed on during the housing crisis. With rental properties, you need to make sure you can qualify for the loan and that you will still have a cash-flowing property if the rate on your loan increases over time.

## An ARM may be cheaper than a fixed-rate loan

The interest rate on an ARM is lower in the beginning than a fixed rate loan, but the rate can go up after the fixed-rate period. Even though the rate can increase, an ARM can be cheaper than a fixed-rate loan depending on how long you have it. During the five years that the ARM is at its lowest rate, you are saving money every month over the fixed-rate loan. Even if you do not pay off that ARM and the rate change, it would still take years for the total cost of the ARM to catch up to the fixed-rate loan. If you reinvest the money you are saving from the ARM and make a higher return on that investment than the interest rate on the loans, you will make even more money. In my calculations, it would take until about year eight before you spend more money on interest on a 5-year ARM than on a 30-year fixed-rate loan. Another thing to consider is that money will be worth less in the future due to inflation. Saving money now and paying more in the future is usually a good thing.

Some lenders will offer balloon payments on their loans. A balloon payment means the loan must be paid off within 5 or 10 years. My loans do not have balloon payments, but be careful with loans that do. If you buy houses below market value with a lot of equity, you should be able to refinance or sell the house when a balloon payment comes due.

ARMs are great loans, especially when you have few other options. Be smart when deciding to use an ARM. The biggest mistake you can make is not being prepared for a payment increase if you are not able to pay off the loan or refinance. If you are prepared to hold the loan, you should be just fine.

## How to finance more than four mortgages

Some banks may tell you that getting more than four mortgages in your name is impossible, but some banks will loan on 10, 20, or even 100 properties. If you know where to look, you can find traditional banks and portfolio lenders that will finance more than four properties.

When I bought my first rental property, I used a mortgage broker to fund my deal. He did a great job of finding the right bank for my needs. However, the lender still required me to jump through multiple hoops, send in every financial detail of my life, and justify any deposit over $1,000 over the last year. As an agent, I make many deposits over $1,000, and I spent hours and hours hunting down each deposit and explaining exactly what it was. After bending over backwards, I still had to put 25% down to get a decent interest rate. The sad part was I did not have four mortgaged properties at that time...I only had two.

Technically, Fannie Mae guidelines say investors should be able to get a loan for up to ten properties. Even with these guidelines in place, many lenders still will not finance more than four properties because it is too risky for their investors. If you are diligent and make enough calls, you should be able to find a lender who will loan on up to ten properties. If you want to try an easier route, call a mortgage broker who can help you find a lender who can get it done. These are the requirements for most conventional lenders who will finance from five to ten properties.

- Own five to ten residential properties with financing attached
- A 25% down payment (30% for 2-4 unit)
- Minimum credit score of 720
- No late payments on any mortgage within the last twelve months
- No bankruptcies or foreclosures in the last seven years
- Two years of tax returns showing rental income from all rental properties
- Six months of PITI reserves on each of the financed properties

Most banks will only allow a 70% loan-to-value ratio if you already have four mortgages and want to refinance any of your properties. They also will not allow you to take out any cash with the refinance. I use cash-out refinances all the time to take out money for more rental properties. Lenders say it is too risky to do a cash-out refinance for investors with more than four mortgages. In my opinion, if an investor has the 20% down and the cash reserves needed, they are less of a risk than a first-time homebuyer putting down 3.5% or less.

## A portfolio lender will finance more than four mortgages...and possibly many more

Another (and my favorite) option for investors is local lenders that offer portfolio financing. Finding a portfolio lender can take some research, time, and networking, but they have much looser lending guidelines. Portfolio lenders use their own money to fund deals and do not have to adhere to Fannie Mae guidelines. My portfolio lender has no limits on how many loans they will give investors as long as they have the cash, reserves, and income to support the mortgages. They allow 20% down on those properties and do not require your life history to give you the loan.

There are some drawbacks to using a portfolio lender. My local bank does not offer a 30-year fixed mortgage. They offer 15-year fixed and 5/30 and 7/30 ARMs. The local bank charges slightly higher rates and origination fees, but not by much. My last loan on my tenth mortgage was a 5/30 ARM at 4.5%. This interest rate was .5% higher than my other loans because I have more than ten mortgages. The local bank may require you to move all your accounts over to them, but that is a small price to pay for investor loans.

## How to find a portfolio lender who will finance more than four properties

A portfolio lender is crucial to many investors' strategies because they often loan on multiple rentals and flips. They often have less-strict lending requirements than large national banks, making it easier for investors to get loans. These loans are often called commercial products. If you are having a hard time communicating with a bank about portfolio loans, ask to talk to their commercial loan department.

A portfolio lender is a local bank that loans their own money, so they do not have to meet Fannie Mae lending guidelines. This allows the portfolio lender more flexibility, but they may not have as many loan programs as large banks. Each portfolio lender has different terms and loan programs. Some portfolio lenders will not offer 30-year amortizations, may have balloon payments, or may have other restrictions on their loans.

A portfolio lender will also prefer that you have all your accounts and money in their bank. This is usually not a big issue for most people since a portfolio lender will have very competitive programs and products. The better relationship you build with a portfolio lender, the better loans you will get.

I found my lender through word of mouth. I heard real estate agents say my portfolio lender was the best bank for investors. After I ran into problems financing my fifth rental property with my previous mortgage broker, I contacted my current portfolio lender. They had the perfect loans for my investment properties. Moving my accounts to their bank so I could easily finance new rentals took me about a week.

The first way to find a portfolio lender is to ask everyone you know. Some people may not know what a portfolio lender is, so ask them if they know a lender that likes to loan to investors. Whom can you ask?

- Real estate agents know many lenders and may be your best source.
- If a lender cannot do a loan for you, they may be able to refer you to a portfolio lender.
- Investors will know portfolio lenders. Real estate investor meetings are a great place to meet investors and get local information.
- Ask your local bank whether they are a portfolio lender and what types of investor-lending programs they offer.
- Ask title companies who local investors use to finance their rental properties.
- Ask your chamber of commerce who the most investor-friendly banks in town are.

Searching the internet is the easiest way to start. Simply search for a portfolio lender in your state. I have tried this a couple of times for people in different states, and I always get results. Once you find a bank that mentions portfolio lending in your state, call them and ask what type of investor programs they offer.

If none of the options above are working and you cannot find a portfolio lender, you may have to resort to calling local banks in your area that are not national chains and see what type of investor loans they offer. If they do not have what you are looking for, ask them if they know which bank might. Keep trying until you have called all the local banks you can find.

## What questions should you ask when calling a bank?

Many banks do not advertise that they are portfolio lenders, and many people working at the bank may not even know what a portfolio lender is. If a bank says they are not a portfolio lender, do not give up! Ask to talk to a commercial loan officer or the business-banking department. Ask specific questions about what type of investor programs they offer. Here are some good questions to ask:

- Do you loan to investors who already have four mortgages?
- Do you have a commercial loan or business-loan department?
- Do you sell your loans or keep them in-house?
- Do you allow investors with four or more mortgages to do a cash-out refinance?
- What terms and loan programs do you offer investors? ARM, 15- or 30-year fixed, balloon?
- What interest rates do you charge and what are the initial costs for your loans?
- What loan-to-value ratios do you offer investors for new purchases and refinances?
- What are your seasoning requirements for refinances?

Finding a portfolio lender is not easy, but it makes investing a lot easier. My portfolio lender has been awesome with financing both my rental properties and fix and flips.

# How do you find a national portfolio lender?

If you cannot find a local lender who will loan on multiple rental properties, a national portfolio lender might be able to help. In the past, investors looking to finance more than ten properties had to rely on local portfolio lenders, but there are now nationwide companies offering commercial products for investors looking to finance multiple properties. I am in the process myself of deciding if I want to refinance eight of my rentals with one of these lenders. Hedge funds primarily fund the national companies. They tend to loan based on the properties and not the borrower.

## What type of loans do national portfolio lenders offer?

National lenders offer many types of loans, from 5- and 10-year ARMs to 30-year fixed-rate loans. Amortizations, rates, and terms differ based on the company and the properties that are being used as collateral. Many of these funds offer hard-money loans for fix-and-flips as well.

With rental property loans, the interest rates are higher (6 to 8%), and there may be more fees. National lenders tend to be more willing to loan more and offer blanket loans that cover more than one property. Some local lenders will be hesitant to loan too much to one investor, where the larger lenders are more flexible.

## What is a balloon payment, and how does it affect rental properties?

Some national—and even some local—lenders have balloon payments on their loans, requiring you to repay the loan after 5 or 10 years. If you choose a loan with a balloon payment, you must have an exit strategy. Many lenders say they will work with investors and figure out a way to offer them financing again in 5 or 10 years, but there is no guarantee. Commercial loans with a balloon payment can be very risky. We also do not know what interest rates will be in five years, and refinancing in 5 or 10 years if rates rise significantly may not make sense or even be possible.

An investor must have a backup strategy to pay off these loans when the term is over. Using cash flow to pay down the loan may be an option. Investing cash in other high-yield investments may be another option. You could also keep a portion of your property portfolio without loans. In the worst-case scenario, you could sell houses to pay off the loan at the end of the term.

## How do the national lenders determine how much someone can borrow?

National lenders have different guidelines than many lenders. Many national rental property lenders will not care about DTI ratios as much as they will cash flow. They tend to loan 75% of the value of houses, but they must have decent cash flow.

- The loan to-value ratio is calculated from appraisals on each house, which the investor must pay for.
- There could be prepayment fees on the loans if you pay them off before the term is over.
- Debt Service Coverage Ratio (DSCR) must be 1.2 times the mortgage payment. The DSCR is determined differently on each property, but it is based on rent minus taxes, insurance, vacancy, maintenance, HOA fees, and any other costs.
- Recourse and non-recourse loans are available. A recourse loan means the bank can come after your personal assets if you default on a loan. Almost all residential and most small commercial loans are recourse loans. Some large commercial loans are non-recourse, which enables limited partners to invest in a large property without fear of losing their personal assets as well as their investment.
- There may or may not be seasoning periods for refinancing properties and taking cash out.

A few large companies offer portfolio loans to residential property owners. Please visit my site at https://investfourmore.com/resources/#financing to see an updated list of national portfolio lenders.

## What is the best option for investors looking to finance more than ten rental properties?

I love my local portfolio lender. I think local portfolio lenders are your number one option if you can find one in your area. If you cannot find one or you want to refinance numerous properties, larger portfolio lenders may be a better option.

## Should you put rental properties in an LLC?

This may seem like a weird topic for the financing chapter, but LLCs can have a huge effect on your ability to finance properties. Many conventional lenders will not loan to an LLC, but some portfolio lenders will. Before you put all your properties into an LLC, make sure you have your financing figured out.

LLCs can be a powerful tool and can protect investors from liability on rental properties. I have a separate LLC for each of my 16 rental properties, but an LLC is not the right choice for everyone. I put my rentals in an LLC mainly to protect myself from liability. However, there are many things to consider when deciding to use an LLC. LLCs can affect financing, increase costs, and have many negative consequences. I am not a lawyer, nor am I providing legal advice. If you have legal questions, please consult an attorney.

I have always put my rental properties into a separate LLC for each property. I do this because of the liability risk that comes with owning rental properties. If you own a rental property in your own name, someone can sue you personally and attack your assets. That lawsuit may not only affect your rental property but your personal assets as well. If you have your rental property in an LLC with a separate checking account, there is a better chance that only that rental property will be affected by a lawsuit.

In Colorado, creating an LLC isn't very difficult. My assistant creates the paperwork and submits the documents to the Secretary of State. Each state has different requirements and rules for creating an LLC. Check out your state's requirements before you take this on yourself. I learned how to create and submit the paperwork by looking at documents a lawyer created for other LLCs.

In Colorado, setting up an LLC costs $50 if you create the documents and file yourself. Every year, there is a $10 filing fee to keep the LLC active. Most states charge much more.

Hiring a lawyer to create the LLC can cost hundreds and possibly thousands of dollars. When I asked a lawyer to create an LLC for me, he wanted $850. You must consider the cost when deciding whether to use LLCs. If it costs you $1,000 to create and $500 per year to maintain the LLC, it may not be worth it. On the other hand, you may want to use one LLC for all your properties. The fewer LLCs you use, the less protection you will have. You could also hire a lawyer to create the first LLC for you and then create the next LLCs yourself.

## Why do you need an LLC for each rental property?

I put all my rentals in their own LLC. I do this to protect myself from liability. According to my lawyers, if one rental property is affected by a lawsuit, all the properties in the same LLC can be affected. Likewise, if you have separate LLCs but have one bank account for all the properties, it can be argued that the rental properties are not separate entities, and they all could be affected by the lawsuit.

You could also use one LLC for two or three rental properties to reduce your costs, but again, all the properties in that LLC could be affected by a lawsuit. It is always best to talk to a lawyer in your area to see what they suggest the best protection is.

LLCs can help project your rental properties from liability, but LLCs can also create problems. Many banks will not loan to an LLC; they will only loan to an individual person. Buying a property in your own name, getting a loan, and transferring the property to the LLC is possible. The problem with this strategy is the bank may have a due-on-sale clause, meaning if the property is sold, the bank can call the loan due immediately. Transferring a property from an individual person to an LLC is considered a sale, even if the individual selling the house owns the LLC.

Most people will tell you the chances of a bank calling a loan due because you sold the property to your LLC are very small. However, it can happen. If they call the loan due, you will have to pay it off by selling or refinancing the property quickly.

I use a portfolio lender who will loan to an LLC, so I have no problem putting all my properties into LLCs. My portfolio lender will refinance my properties that are in LLCs and let me buy new houses with an LLC or transfer my properties into an LLC. If your bank does not loan to LLCs, you may not be able to refinance or purchase properties with an LLC. Remember, many national lenders who we just talked about will not care if your properties are in an LLC.

## Additional ways to protect yourself from liability

If you decide to forego an LLC or want more ways to protect yourself, here are some tips.

- Do not be a lazy property owner! Make sure your houses are safe, with working smoke and carbon monoxide detectors. Most lawsuits come from a tenant getting hurt...or worse.
- Get liability insurance. Property owners can also get an umbrella policy that will cover all their properties and protect against lawsuits. Talk to your insurance agent about your options.
- Land trusts may provide another source of protection if used correctly. I am not an expert on land trusts and do not use them myself.

An LLC offers protection from lawsuits against a rental property. However, you will have to decide if that extra protection is worth the cost and the possibility of not being able to refinance houses or your loans being called due. Always talk to your bank before you use LLCs to make sure they are okay with it. Always consult your attorney about using an LLC, and make sure it is set up to correctly protect you.

## Conclusion

Financing rental properties is one of the most important things you can do as an investor. Using leverage will increase your returns and make you more money in the end. Financing properties is not always easy, and you should never assume you would be able to get a loan for rentals.

One of the first things any investor should do is talk to a lender. If there is a problem with your credit, your DTI ratio, or something else, the sooner you know about it, the better. If you can start fixing those problems right away, you can buy rentals properties sooner and make more money in the end. If you wait until you are ready to buy a property to talk to a lender or figure out financing, you may be in for a rude awakening if the lender says, "Sorry, we just cannot loan to you right now." You do not want to miss deals or delay your investing because you assumed everything would be okay. If you know you have bad credit or another issue, a lender can help you get it solved much faster than you can on your own.

# 8

# How to Invest in Rental Properties with Less Cash

There are about 1,000 advertised strategies for investing in real estate with little or no money down. Some of the strategies are great and some are horrible...or even illegal. Real estate is expensive, and many people use the allure of using no money to get rich by selling programs or properties.

The truth is that you can buy with less cash, and in some cases, less money down. However, there is no secret recipe or easy way to do it. Buying rentals, finding great deals, building cash flow, and buying with less of your own money will take sacrifice and hard work.

It is also important to realize that buying with little or no money down is not always a good thing. There are many deals out there where you can buy with less money down, but the properties will not generate any money. Buying properties with none of your own money will not do you any good to if they never make you any money. When using these strategies to buy with less cash, always be certain you are not sacrificing all your cash flow or betting on appreciation to make your money.

Many people do not have the 20% down payment that most banks require when buying an investment property. The easiest way to buy an investment property with less than 20% down is to buy as an owner-occupant and later rent out the house, but there are other options for investors as well.

Lines of credit, refinancing, and even credit cards can provide ways to buy investment properties for less money. Seller financing is a great way to put less money down on a rental property if you can find willing sellers. A more advanced technique is to use hard-money financing and refinance to a conventional loan. However you choose to buy a rental property, always research the method to make sure it is legal in your state, is okay with your lender, and that you are not stretching your finances too thin.

## How to buy an investment property as an owner-occupant with little money down

The easiest way to buy an investment property with less money down is to buy as an owner-occupant and keep the property as an investment after you have satisfied your loan requirements. Most owner-occupant loans require the buyer to occupy the house for at least one year. However, once that year is up, the house can be rented out and used as an investment property. Down payments for owner-occupied loans range from no money down to 20% or more. USDA and VA have great no-money-down programs, which I discuss later in this chapter. Those programs also have little to no mortgage insurance, which will save an investor a lot of money each month. Mortgage insurance is typical on most loans that have a loan-to-value ratio of more than 80%. Mortgage insurance can add hundreds of dollars to your mortgage payment and eat away at your cash flow. The process for buying as an owner-occupant and turning the house into an investment property is as follows:

- Buy a house as an owner-occupant that will cash flow when you rent it out.
- Move into the house and live there for at least a year.
- After one year, buy another house as an owner-occupant that will cash flow.
- Move into the new house, rent out the first house, and repeat the process every year!

Eventually, you will build up equity and extra cash flow that will enable you to buy properties with a 20% down payment. If you could repeat this process ten times, that would be an excellent way to get started, but no one wants to move ten times in ten years. Convincing your family to live in a house that would also be a great rental can also be tough. As we talked about earlier, you may run into problems qualifying for new houses if your DTI ratio gets too high.

## Which loan types allow for investing with little money down?

How do you get a loan that will allow you to buy properties with a lower down payment? This section covers the different loan options available for owner-occupants who are looking to live in a house and then turn it into an investment property.

### How I would buy an investment property with little money down if I had to start over

If I were to start over, I would drastically change the way I did things. When I bought my first house in 2002, I put a little work into it, lived there seven years, and then sold it. I did not make much money, and although it was a great house to live in, it did not provide any financial benefit. With what I know now, I could do so much better! I would buy houses as an owner-occupant, live in them one year, and then rent them out after I had satisfied the owner-occupant requirements. I would make sure I bought below market value, and I would buy houses that would provide plenty of cash flow when I was ready to rent them out.

I am not advising that an investor pretend to be an owner-occupant. There are serious penalties for pretending to be an owner-occupant, especially on HUD homes (up to two years in prison and $250,000 fine).

## FHA loans

FHA loans are government-insured and can be obtained with as little as 3.5% down. You can only have one FHA loan at a time unless you have extenuating circumstances such as job relocation. You do have to pay mortgage insurance, which I will discuss later. There are limits to the amount an FHA mortgage can be, and those limits vary by state and even by city.

## USDA loans

USDA loans can be used in rural areas and small towns. These loans most likely cannot be used in medium-sized towns or large towns/metro areas. This loan is fantastic for those who qualify and want to buy a house in the designated areas. USDA loans can be obtained with no money down but also have mortgage insurance.

## VA loans

The United States Veterans Administration administers VA loans. You must be a veteran, active duty, or certain honorably discharged military, but this loan can be obtained with no money down and no mortgage insurance! VA is a great option for those who qualify because the costs are so much less without mortgage insurance.

## Down payment assistance programs

Many states have down payment assistance programs. In Colorado, we have a program called CHFA. The program helps buyers get into owner-occupied houses with very little money down. CHFA actually uses an FHA loan but allows for a down payment of less than 3.5%. Check with lenders in your state to see if they have any down payment assistance programs.

## Conventional mortgages

Conventional mortgages offer owner-occupants down payments as low as 3%. You will most certainly have to pay mortgage insurance with any conventional loan that requires less than 20% down. Unlike some of the other loan options available, owner-occupants can have as many conventional mortgages in their name as they want.

## FHA 203K Rehab loan

A FHA 203K rehab loan allows the borrower to finance the house and the repairs. This is a great loan if a house needs work but the buyer has limited funds to repair the house. There are more upfront costs associated with this loan because two appraisals are needed and lenders have higher fees for them. The same down payments and mortgage insurance will be needed as with a regular FHA loan. The borrower must be able to qualify for the loan amount after the work is done.

## Besides the down payment, which loan costs does a buyer need to consider?

On almost any loan, you will have more costs than just the down payment. The lender charges an origination fee, appraisal fee, prepaid interest, prepaid insurance, and possibly prepaid mortgage insurance. In addition, the title company may charge a closing fee, recording fees, and possibly, title insurance. In most cases, the seller pays for title insurance, but with HUD and VA foreclosures, the buyer must pay for it. These costs can add up to another 2 to 4% of the mortgage amount...or sometimes more. A lender can give you an estimate of these costs before you get your loan.

The lender and title company charge more fees than just the down payment, but that does not mean that you must pay them up front. You can ask the seller to pay closing costs. You can obtain loans with no out-of-pocket cash, such as VA and USDA, if you can get the seller to pay closing costs. You may still have to put down an earnest money deposit, but that can be refunded at closing in some cases. When you ask the seller to pay closing costs, it reduces the amount of money they are getting from the sale, so you might actually pay more for the house than if you did not ask for closing costs. However, in my mind, paying a little more for the house and financing those costs to save cash is better than paying more money out-of-pocket for a little cheaper house.

## What is mortgage insurance?

Consumers must pay mortgage insurance when they put less than 20% down. Lenders charge mortgage insurance to help mitigate risk because the less money someone puts down, the riskier the loan is. There are many different types of mortgage insurance, and a few loans do not charge mortgage insurance, but they are rare. Some mortgage insurance can be removed after a certain amount of time, and some cannot. The cost of mortgage insurance also varies greatly depending on the loan program you use

During the great depression in 1934, the Federal Housing Authority (FHA) was created to help the economy. Prior to FHA, everyone, for the most part, had to put 20% down to get a loan. Most banks thought 20% down payments would show consumers they could afford a house. The practice of putting 20% down made the housing market much more stable, but it also meant fewer people could own a house.

Usually, the more people who own a house and the more houses that are bought and sold, the better our economy does. That is why there are huge tax incentives when buying a house as an owner-occupant or as an investor. The government encourages homeowners to buy houses with less than 20% down by offering FHA-insured loans. FHA was not meant to finance houses but to create insurance for banks who gave consumers loans with less than 20% down. Many private mortgage insurance companies work with conventional loans to offer less than 20% down as well.

Once banks started lending with less than 20% down, the risk of default increased greatly, and it was not worth it. To help mitigate that risk, lenders charge the borrower mortgage insurance, which can be .5 to 1% the loan each year. The mortgage insurance allows banks to loan to borrowers who cannot put 20% down because the insurance will reduce the losses the banks incur in a default.

Although the bank requires mortgage insurance on properties with less than 20% down, the bank does not keep the money paid for mortgage insurance. On conventional loans, private mortgage insurance companies take the premiums if the borrower defaults. The mortgage insurance company will either take the property or pay off the bank for the amount insured.

With FHA loans, the mortgage insurance is paid to the federal government, who insures the loans for the banks. FHA homes that are foreclosed on and repossessed by the government become HUD homes.

## How much is mortgage insurance on residential properties?

FHA has set guidelines for how much is charged for mortgage insurance. The current cost is 1.75% up front, and the monthly fee varies based on the amount of the loan. The amount FHA charges changes frequently since FHA must keep 2% of its total liability as cash. Due to the housing crisis, the fund dropped to well below 2%, which caused FHA to increase mortgage insurance.

Upfront mortgage insurance is paid when the buyers close and the monthly payments are made as long as the loan exists. The payment on a $100,000 loan would be $506 (without taxes and insurance) based on a 4.5% interest rate. The payment increases to $574 after FHA mortgage insurance is added. The upfront mortgage insurance cost would be about $1,700, which can be financed into the loan.

Private mortgage insurance (PMI) varies with different banks and loan programs. Private mortgage insurance typically costs from 0.5 to 1% of the entire loan amount each year. On a $100,000 loan, the homeowner would pay $83.33 per month or $1,000 per year with a 1% fee.

FHA mortgage insurance must be maintained for the life of the loan.

However, some types of PMI can be eliminated after a certain amount of time and equity build up. Some PMI programs can be removed after two years if the loan is 80% or less than the value of the house. If your house goes up in value or you pay off some of your loan balance, you may be able to get the PMI removed. The lender may require an appraisal or a simple BPO to determine the value of the property. Not all conventional loans will allow the borrower to remove the PMI, so ask your lender when applying.

Another option to put less money down is to use a 20% down first loan and a second loan that covers part or the rest of the down payment. The first loan is for 80% of the value of the house, and the second loan could be 10 or 15% of the value. These loans were more common before the housing crisis but are still available. The second loans that are available now are for owner-occupants only and tend to have much higher interest rates than first loans. The actual savings of getting a first and a second is not minimal over getting a first loan with mortgage insurance.

## How does mortgage insurance affect real estate investors?

Mortgage insurance does not affect most real estate investors because they do not put less than 20% down. However, investors put less money down by buying as an owner-occupant and then renting out the house after they have satisfied the owner-occupant requirement. When an investor buys as an owner-occupant with less than 20% down, they most likely will have to factor in the mortgage insurance expense. If they use PMI, they may be able to get the mortgage insurance removed—but not on an FHA loan. Make sure to account for that extra expense when determining the cash flow on a property.

There are some 15%-down options for investors, but the cost of mortgage insurance usually makes putting 20% down much more advantageous.

## How will loans with less money down affect cash flow?

Whenever you get a loan with less than 20% down, you are going to raise your monthly payment. Not only does your payment increase because the loan amount increases, but the mortgage insurance will also add even more to your mortgage payment. Often, the difference between a 20%-down loan and a 5%-down loan can be hundreds of dollars per month.

Running the numbers on any house you eventually plan to rent out to make sure the house cash flows after all expenses, including vacancies and maintenance, is very important. Buying these houses below market value to leave yourself enough room to cash flow and sell the house if needed is vitally important. When you have little money available for down payments and repairs, it usually means you have little money for vacancies and maintenance when the house is rented out. In the worst-case scenario, if you bought it below market value and you cannot rent it out—or if you lose your job—you will be able to sell the house and make a profit.

I believe the sooner you start investing, the better. When you buy an owner-occupied property that you plan to turn into a rental, make sure you have a backup plan if things do not go as planned. Could you sell the house after a year if needed? Are you willing to live in the house longer than a year if things do not go as planned?

## How to use house hacking to buy with less money down

House hacking is buying a multifamily property, living in one unit, and renting out the other units. House hacking can be a great way to start investing in rental properties because you can buy with low-money-down owner-occupant loans and still collect rent right away.

When you buy a single-family house as an owner-occupant, you cannot rent out the house for one year (because you are living in it), which can make it harder to buy multiple properties. When you buy a multifamily property as an owner-occupant (which is legal as long as it has 2-4 units), you can live in one unit and collect rent on the other units right away.

House hacking helps you build a rental history and be able to qualify for more rentals sooner than if you bought a single-family property. Most banks will not let you count rents collected as income until they show up on your taxes. This makes qualifying for new loans difficult because you already own a rental property but do not have a long rental history.

## What are the disadvantages of house hacking?

House hacking is a great way to start with rentals, but it takes some sacrifice. When you buy as an owner-occupant, you must live in the house for at least one year in most cases. If you are buying a multifamily house, you will have to live in one unit of the properties for at least one year.

Depending on the stage of life you are in, living in an apartment can be fine...or a challenge. If you are a single college student, you are probably used to living in apartments. However, if you have a family and kids, you may be used to living in a nice single-family house. Living in a multifamily property may be very difficult if you are used to something nicer. For some people, house hacking is worth it, but for others, the sacrifice and family stress it would cause are not.

After that year is up, you can sell or rent the property out. If you live in one unit of a multifamily house, you can rent out that unit. You must live in the property more than 50% of the time to be considered an owner-occupant. You cannot leave one unit vacant and pretend to live there.

After renting out the unit you were living in, you could buy another rental as an owner occupant and repeat the process. As I have already discussed, qualifying for more loans is easier when you have a longer rental history. House hacking makes buying multifamily properties easier than single-family houses if you need the rent to count as income.

If you buy the right multifamily property, you should be able to live there for free or even make money while you are living in one unit. Here is how it would work:

- Buy a three-unit property (does not have to be 3) with 3-bedroom, 1-bath units renting out for $800 per unit.
- Assume property cost of $150,000. With 3% down, the payments would be $900 per month (including mortgage insurance).
- With taxes, insurance, maintenance, and vacancy costs, the total monthly expenses would be about $1,450 to $1,550 depending on taxes in your area.
- You would bring in $1,600 per month in rent, which is less than your monthly expenses, and you get to live in the property for free. When you move out, your cash flow would increase even more because you could rent out the unit you were living in.

This kind of deal is not available in all markets, but they are out there. I still prefer single-family rentals, but house hacking is a great option to get started, especially if multifamily properties have good rent-to-value ratios in your area.

## How to buy rental properties with no money down using hard money or private money

Many investors use hard money as a short-term solution for funding real estate deals. Hard money can be used to fund fix-and-flips or buy rental properties until long-term financing can be put in place. I fix and flip houses and invest in long-term rentals, but I do not use hard money. Hard money is more expensive than traditional financing, and I have other short-term financing in place.

Hard money is used to finance properties for six months or a year. Hard-money lenders use much different terms than a traditional bank. They charge very high interest rates—from 10 to 16% plus points. Points are a percentage of the total loan and can add up quickly when a hard-money lender is charging 2, 3, or even 4 points on a loan.

The advantage of a hard-money lender is they may loan the entire amount you will need to complete a deal. Most hard-money lenders base the amount of the loan on the after repaired value (ARV), which is how much the house will be worth after repairs. They will loan 65 or 70% of ARV.

Here is an example of how one hard-money lender structures a deal. You buy a house for $60,000 with an ARV of $130,000. The hard-money lender will loan up to 70% ARV, or $91,000. They will need bids or estimates for repairs and will pay for repairs the same way as a construction loan. They will pay for 25% of the repairs needed at closing, and the other payments will come in 25% increments as the repairs are completed. The lender does not charge any interest or points until you sell the house, at which point you pay them the loan principal, interest, and points. This particular hard-money lender charges 15% interest and 4 points, but they will reduce the points paid after you do a few deals with them.

On this deal, if you use the money for six months, the interest will be $6,825 and the points will be $3,640. Some hard-money lenders charge lower interest and points but will want to split your profits or require more money down. I do not use hard-money lenders myself because of how much they charge, but for investors who have no other options, they can work out well.

## Where can you find hard-money lenders?

There are many hard-money lenders, but most only loan in specific states. The best way to find one is to search for one in your state using any search engine. I have a list of national hard-money lenders here: https://investfourmore.com/resources/#financing

## What is private money?

Private money is money that comes from a private person. The person loaning the money is not a bank, mortgage company, hard-money lender, or portfolio lender...they are just a person. Regular people will loan for real estate because interest rates on other secured investments are low right now. Have you looked at current CD rates? For a five-year CD, the average is less than 1%! You cannot even come close to keeping up with inflation with that rate. Many wealthy people are looking for a higher-yield, secured investment. Loaning for real estate may be the perfect answer for them to increase returns while creating great opportunities for investors.

## How do you find private money?

The biggest problem with private money is finding someone to loan it to you! Many websites claim to have private-money lenders they can connect you with for a small fee. In my experience, those websites take your money and connect you with a hard-money lender at best. A real private-money lender wants to loan their money to someone they know and trust. They do not want to loan to a complete stranger who may be untrustworthy or won't have a clue what they are doing. I use private money from my sister, who wants a better return on her son's college money. She trusts me; she knows I know how to make money; and she is willing to loan her money at a very reasonable rate: 7% with no points. This is a higher rate than she could get with a CD or other secured investment. It is cheaper for me than financing with hard money.

## How to buy a rental property with no money down using hard or private money

According to Fannie Mae guidelines, you can refinance a loan with no seasoning period. Fannie Mae guidelines do not allow a cash-out refinance without a seasoning period, but if you finance the repairs and purchase price, you still might get all your cash back out. You can get a long-term loan to replace the hard-money loan without waiting a year like you would with a cash-out refinance that requires a seasoning period.

For example, if you buy a house for $100,000 with 100% of the purchase price financed in hard money and $35,000 financed in repairs, the total loan would be $135,000. You fix up the house and refinance using a Fannie Mae loan, which will cover up to 75% of the new appraised value. If the appraisal comes in at $185,000, you could finance up to $135,000. If the appraisal comes in at $190,000, you could only refinance $135,000 because you cannot take any cash out. This technique can be rather expensive because you must pay the higher interest rate on the hard-money loan, the initial points, and the refinance costs with Fannie Mae. However, you just bought a long-term rental and fixed it up with almost no out-of-pocket costs!

If you use private money, you would structure the deal the same way by getting a loan with the private-money lender and then refinancing after the house is repaired.

## How to buy a property with little money down using a turn-key rental property provider

Investing in turn-key rental properties that are purchased, repaired, rented out, and managed by a turn-key provider is a new trend in the U.S. Turn-key properties present a great opportunity for investors to buy rental properties out-of-state when houses are too expensive in their own area. There are turn-key providers who offer as little as 5% down for investors, but they tend to have very high interest rates. With most turn-key properties, you will not have to make any repairs, which reduces the amount of money you need. However, because they are rented, managed, and repaired, many turn-key properties are priced at a premium. Getting a great deal on a turn-key rental is tough. There will be much more on turn-key properties later in the book.

## How to use seller financing to buy investment properties with little money down

Some sellers may be willing to carry the loan on a house or finance a second loan to allow a buyer to put less than 20% down. If your bank is willing to offer 80% loan-to-value, the seller may loan the other 20%, which would equal no money down for the buyer. The seller may also offer many other loan-to-value percentages that can help a buyer get into to a house for less than 20% down.

Finding seller-financed properties is not easy. Most sellers are not looking to finance a loan when they sell. To find seller-financed listings, look for houses that have no loans against them and an MLS listing description stating seller financing is available. The seller's terms can vary greatly depending on how desperate they are to sell and what exactly they want out of the deal. Do not expect to pay 4% interest on a seller-financed loan; they will want a premium on any money they lend. It is also harder to find great deals with seller financing, which is a key to my strategy. There are many new restrictions on seller financing thanks to the recent Dodd-Frank Act. Be sure to check with an attorney regarding the legality of seller financing.

## How to partner with another investor to buy investment property with little money down

The biggest problem facing most investors is finding the money to flip or the down payment for rentals. In some cases, an investor has a lot of money but no time to find deals, renovate houses, or perform other tasks. In other cases, an investor may have the knowledge and time to invest but no money. If done right, a partnership can be a mutually beneficial way to invest in real estate.

I do not have a partner in my business, but I used to partner with my father. Flipping houses or selling real estate without a partner to help with financing and mentoring would have been tough for me. However, in some ways, I think having a partner held me back by providing a comfort zone that allowed to me to relax more than I should have. Having a partner for real estate deals can be a great way to get started, but if you do not set things up correctly, it can be a disaster and destroy relationships.

## How does a partnership in rental properties work?

Rental-property partnerships can be even riskier than fix-and-flip partnerships. The tough part is predicting how the partnership will progress with time. One partner may want to cash out in five years, and the other may want to hold the properties for thirty years.

Determining what the returns will be on rental properties is also a bit tough. You know what the profit is after a flip is completed. With rentals, you have equity paydown, tax advantages, appreciation, and cash flow. Some of these returns, such as cash flow, are in the form of cash in your pocket. Others, such as appreciation and equity paydown, are not realized until the house is sold or refinanced. Not only do you have to come up with a percentage of the actual profits (cash flow) that will be split, but you also must come up with a percentage of the equity that will be split if the properties are sold or if one partner wants to sell out and the other partner wants to keep the properties.

Things to consider when collaborating on rental properties:

- **Who does the work?** Will both partners work to find properties, or will one do all the work? How will repairs and maintenance be handled? Who will screen tenants? Will a property manager be used?
- **How much money will each partner contribute?** Will one partner put in all the money and the other do all the work, or will it be a mix?
- **What percentage of the profits will each partner take?** Calculating profits from rentals can be tough. You will have different amounts of cash flow every month, and houses can be depreciated. With depreciation, tax returns will show less profit than you actually make. You also need to have reserves in place for maintenance and vacancies. You must decide what each partner's role is worth and how profits will be split.
- **What percentage of the equity will each partner get?** The equity will

slowly increase as mortgage payments are made, and the property might appreciate as well. If you bought the property below market value, your equity might also increase. The equity is not realized until you sell or refinance, but you need to decide what percentage each partner will get if you do sell or refinance.

- **What happens if one partner wants out**? The biggest challenge facing rental properties and partnerships is ending the relationship. How long do you plan to own the property together? What if one partner needs money and wants out? What if the house does not make as much money as you thought and one partner wants out? Before the partnership begins, you must figure out how to end the relationship if one partner wants out.

As you can see, handling a partnership with rental properties can be very complex. Determining the amount of work each person is responsible for, an exit strategy, what percentages each investor gets, and when to end the partnership is tough.

## Why does everything need to be in writing with a real estate partnership?

If you decide to enter into a partnership, get everything in writing. I do not care if your partner is your brother or best friend: it should be in writing. There are multiple reasons why everything should be in writing.

- **People forget things**: You would think that a person would never forget the details of a partnership that involves thousands of dollars, but it happens. I wrote an article about private money a while back and mentioned I pay my sister 6% interest. She read it and was quick to remind me I pay her 7%! We have everything in writing so there are no mistakes or fall outs from simply forgetting the terms.
- **Partners need to know roles**: If you are doing a flip with a partner and decide to share the work, how much time will each person put in? One

partner may have a family emergency or may have to work overtime. How many hours will each person put in and what are the consequences if they do not pull their weight? One of the biggest problems is one partner thinks he does all the work while the other collects the profit without doing anything.

· **Exit strategies**: With rental properties, you must determine what happens if one partner wants to be bought out or must sell. How is market value determined; how will costs be split; etc.? With a flip, you must determine what happens if you decide not to flip the house because the market has changed.

· **Use of professional services**: If one partner is a contractor or real estate agent, how will they be paid for their services? Will they get a higher percentage of the profits for their expertise or for the money saved on commissions? Will the contractor or agent be paid as they would any other job?

· **Rates, terms, payoffs**: If you are borrowing money from a partner, all the loan terms or agreements need to be in writing. Some agreements are a pure profit split, but others might involve private-money lending with interest rates, length of the note, etc.

· **Decision making:** Who has the final say on how much money to spend, how to repair a house, what properties to buy etc.? What happens if the partners do not agree? Decision making is another big issue that can cause problems if not in writing.

A huge issue with partnerships is when one side either forgets or does not live up to their agreed-upon obligations. Detailing in writing the obligations and what happens if those obligations are not met will make the partnership much more successful. The partners will have more motivation to work hard, and handling problems when they come up will be easier.

## Do you need a partner to invest in real estate?

Many people ask me how to structure a partnership when they collaborate on rental properties. One question is, "We have the money and knowledge to buy rentals, but we have the opportunity to partner with another investor, so how do we structure it?"

My answer is, "Why do you need a partner? Why bring someone in to share the profits on a deal when you have the money and know-how? You will make much more money on real estate deals when you do not have a partner. The purpose of a partner is to provide something that you cannot or do not want to provide. You give up some of the profits to spend less of your own money, use someone's time or their expertise. If you do not need any of those things, do not give up your profits!"

## Do you have anything to offer a partner?

I also see many people looking for a partner or mentor to help them start investing. They want someone to show them how to buy houses, fix them up, find great deals, and make a ton of money, but they have nothing to offer except a willingness to work hard.

People repeatedly propose that scenario to me, and almost every time, there are huge problems on my side of the deal.

- When I ask the person what they can offer me in return, they say determination, hard work, etc., but they list no specific skills. What can you do that will help me become more successful or help the deal be more successful? Are you good with computers? Do you have carpentry skills? Are you an expert marketer? Willingness to learn and work hard is not a skill. Everyone says that they are motivated and will work hard, but words are easy to say. If you want to impress people, be as specific as possible about how you will help them make more money.
- Most successful investors do not have time to teach someone the entire process of investing. They also may not want to train someone to

compete against him or her! Do not be put off if an investor does not want to mentor someone; it is a very involved process that takes time. Paying for knowledge and experience is also an option and shows you are serious. Most people who want free help and have nothing to offer in return will not even use that help if they get it, and it is a giant waste of time for everyone. Successful people will charge money for their expertise. Nothing is more frustrating to successful people than wasting time. If they know someone has a financial stake to learn, they know that person has a better chance of listening and learning.

· Many aspiring investors looking for a mentor want someone to tell them how to do everything. I have had people come to me asking how I make money by flipping houses. Well, I could write a book on that and still not answer all your questions (actually, I did write a book on flipping). I point out articles for people to read or point them toward my book, and they do not want to take the time to read the articles or pay $10 for a book. They want everything done for them without doing any work. If you want to impress a potential partner or mentor, do your research, and learn as much as you possibly can. The more knowledge you have, the better chance you have of impressing someone enough to help you.

If you want to be a partner in a real estate deal, you must have something to offer. You need to bring money, expertise, skills, or pay for the opportunity. There are no shortcuts to becoming a successful real estate investor.

## Why did I end my real estate partnership with my father?

I partnered with my father on flips and on our real estate team before I bought him out in 2013. The partnership was great for helping me get started after I graduated college in 2001. I would not have been able to flip houses right out of college because I had no money and no way to finance a deal. In return for knowledge and money to flip, I gave up most of the profits. For a while, I was even doing the painting, and on one house, most of the repair work. When I did the work myself, I did not get a higher percentage—I was paid

BUILD A RENTAL PROPERTY EMPIRE

hourly. Flipping with a partner was great in the beginning, but at the end, I was doing almost all the work and did not have the final decision on what to buy.

On our real estate team, my father paid the staff, took care of most expenses, and took a big chunk of my commissions. Not having to worry about payroll and everything else was nice, but I also sold most of the houses on the team, and I was giving up a lot of profit by having a partner. My father also was tired of running the team and managing all the people.

I wanted to take over everything for a while, but I was worried about the time it would take to manage it all and what my father would think. I approached him about it, and my parents said they were waiting for me to take over because they were ready to retire! A good friend who could help with the transition was joining the team, and I had a good relationship with my portfolio lender, so I could finance the flips. I ended up buying out my parents and taking over the entire business. I love having complete control and keeping the profits!

Partnerships can be a great way to get started if you need help. Partnerships can also be a nightmare if you do not have roles clearly defined and everything in writing. Partnerships evolve, and you may have to be flexible as people's priorities in life change. My partnership with my father changed over the years until I ended up buying him out. We had everything in writing when we made changes, and that helped things go smoothly.

If you enter a partnership, make sure you take the time to set it up correctly. If you do not need a partner, having complete control and keeping all the profits sure is nice.

# How to use credit cards to purchase rental property with little money down

Most of us have access to cash, but it is expensive and should be reserved for people looking to do a quick flip. If you have a killer deal that you cannot pass up, you may consider these options, but I do not recommend them unless it is necessary. Many successful investors I've featured on my podcast got started by using credit cards.

The easiest way to get quick cash is with credit cards. You can get a cash advance or pay for repairs. If you use a credit card to finance your down payment or repairs and cannot pay it off right away, do not pay the 17% interest rate. Try your best to get another card that will allow a balance transfer. Often, you can transfer the entire balance and pay little to no interest for up to a year. Hopefully, that will give you enough time to pay off the card and not be stuck with a high interest rate that eats all your profits. I also suggest using a rewards card for repairs on your investment properties. This is a great way to make a little extra money if you pay it off every month. I have credit cards that offer a 2% cash back program on everything I buy. As long as I pay off the cards every month, I don't pay interest and get 2% cash back. That 2% adds up very quickly when you are buying all your materials on credit cards.

# How to buy an investment property with no money down using a 401k

Some retirement plans allow an investor to take out a loan against their 401k. The loan must usually be paid back relatively quickly, and you will have to pay interest. You should be very careful when borrowing from a 401k because the money you borrow is no longer earning interest or growing in your retirement fund. If you lose your job, you may also be required to pay back the loan within 60 days or pay a 10% penalty and income tax on the loan.

You can also borrow against some life insurance policies. They are a great option for buying with less money if you already have the policy. I am not a huge fan of investing in insurance policies in order to borrow from them at a later date.

## How to buy a house with little money down using subject-to loans

Subject-to means buying a house without paying off the previous owner's mortgage. This is another tricky situation, so use caution. Almost no bank loans are assumable, which means when a house is sold, the loan must be paid off. The bank will most likely have a due-on-sale clause stating that the loans must be paid in full once ownership is transferred. Subject-to is buying a house subject-to an old mortgage and not paying off the loan. There is a chance that the bank will require the loan to be paid off if they find out the house was sold.

Investors buy houses subject-to a mortgage so that they do not have to get a new loan. It may be hard for the investor to qualify for a mortgage, or they may be maxed out and unable to get new loans. If you buy a house for $80,000 that has a $75,000 mortgage in place, the investor would only need $5,000 to buy the house instead of the normal 20% or more.

When you leave the loan in place, the person who originally borrowed the money is still responsible for the loan.

## How to use a cash-out refinance to get more money for rentals

A cash-out refinance is one of the best tools an investor can use to get money out of their rental properties. When I purchased my first long-term rental, I was able to buy the property from proceeds from a cash-out refinance on my personal residence. I took out $40,000 in equity from my house just one year after I bought it. I have also refinanced 7 rental properties, which has allowed me to buy even more rentals.

## How do increasing values make getting a cash-out refinance on rental properties easier?

Values are going up across the country, and that has created an opportunity for homeowners to complete cash-out refinances. Most banks are using stricter guidelines for qualifications and lower loan-to-value ratios than they did ten years ago. However, if you purchased your house at a great price, or if you have owned it for a while, you still may be able to do a cash-out refinance. Many banks require an 80% or lower loan-to-value ratio when refinancing a rental property, and they will use an appraisal to determine that value. It is imperative that you have a lot of equity in your property if you want to complete a cash-out refinance with an investment property. If you are refinancing an owner-occupied house, you may be able to refinance up to 95% of the value.

## What are the risks of a cash-out refinance on a rental property?

A cash-out refinance increases the loan amount on your rental property. For some people who are averse to risk, paying off their house is a great option, and they may not want more debt. However, I am not averse to risk, and I want to maximize my returns. Debt can be a very bad thing if it is used for the wrong things, but if you use debt to buy cash-producing investments correctly, it can be a good thing.

In my market, I can get a cash-on-cash return of 15% or higher on rental properties, whereas interest rates are less than 5%. It makes more sense to refinance for 5% and use that money to buy properties that will give me over a 15% cash-on-cash return.

Values could possibly go down, and a cash-out refinance would reduce the equity. But if you do not need to sell, the amount of equity you have won't matter. If refinancing the property creates a negative or break-even cash flow situation, you could get yourself in trouble. When I refinance my rentals, I am still getting monthly cash flow of at least $400. I am able to do that because rents have increased since I bought the properties.

Another problem with taking on more debt is you may be decreasing the amount you can qualify for on future houses. If you are close to reaching your maximum debt-to-income ratio with your lender, a refinance could make buying new rentals tough. Make sure you talk to your lender about your debt-to-income ratio and how the refinance will affect future purchases.

Refinance costs are similar to new loan costs. You may have to pay 2 to 3% in closing costs, which can add up to a lot of money on higher-valued loans. Make sure paying those costs is worth it.

## How does a cash-out refinance work on rental properties?

I did a cash-out refinance on one of my rentals in 2012, one in 2013, two in 2015, and three in 2016. On one of my refinances, I was able to pull out about $26,000, and my monthly payment only went up $136. The terms are usually more restrictive, and refinancing can be difficult if you have more than four mortgaged properties with conventional lenders. I was able to do a cash-out refinance with more than four mortgages because I used a portfolio lender.

When I did a cash-out refinance on my investment property, the max they would loan me was 75% of the value of the house.

I purchased one of my properties for $92,000 in October 2011. I put about $18,000 into it for repairs. I was able to turn it into a 5-bed, 2-bath house and rented it out for $1,100 (which was low because it was rented to my brother-in-law). I had to wait a year to do a cash-out refinance, and the current value was determined by an appraisal. The appraisal came in at $140,000, which I thought was low, but I had to go with it. After all the lender fees, interest, and miscellaneous costs of the cash-out refinance, I was able to take out over $26,000. My payment went up $136 per month, and I took out more than enough money for a down payment on another rental property. *In 2016, the house is rented out for $1,500 per month.*

On the rental properties I refinanced in 2015, I was able to take out almost $50,000 in cash on each property. This was due to buying below market value, making repairs, and appreciation in my area.

The more properties you can buy, the more cash flow builds up and the more wealth you can create. A cash-out refinance can help you purchase more properties and increase your wealth. Make sure you purchase houses below market value because it will make a future cash-out refinance much easier.

## Which is better, a cash-out refinance or a line of credit?

A cash-out refinance can allow you to take cash out of your house with a long-term mortgage. A home equity line of credit (HELOC) allows a homeowner to take money out with a short-term loan. A HELOC gives you more flexibility on when and how much you can take out, but the line can have shorter terms and higher rates. I have used both a cash-out refinance and a HELOC, and I will detail the advantages and disadvantages of each.

When you take out a line of credit, you do not have to use the money right away...or ever. You can use as much of the money as you want and pay it back when you like. You can even borrow the money again after you pay back the line.

A HELOC will have closing costs, but they will often be less than a cash-out refinance. The terms and fees will differ depending on whether you are getting a line on an investment property or a personal residence. The term of the HELOC could be two years, five years, or longer, but not 30 years like on a refinance.

I paid off my first rental property in 2014. I was able to get a HELOC on that property shortly after paying it off. Since this was an investment property, my portfolio lender charged me a 1% origination fee and had an appraisal done to determine the amount of the line of credit.

The appraisal came in at $160,000. My lender allows 75% loan-to-value on investment-property lines of credit (on a personal residence, they will go up to 90%). I was able to get a line for $120,000.

The line of credit has been awesome for my flipping business. With up to 20 fix and flips going, I do not always have the cash available to buy more flips. I use my portfolio lender to finance my flips, but they cannot always close as quickly as I need them to. When I must close quickly, I use cash and my lines of credit and refinance the flips with my portfolio lender.

## When is a HELOC better than a cash-out refinance?

A HELOC has many advantages over a cash-out refinance. With a HELOC, you do not have to take out the full amount of the loan as you do with a refinance. This gives you the option of taking out the money at some future point if you do not need it now. You can also pay back the money from a HELOC at any time and then take it out again at any time. With a refinance, once you pay back part or the entire loan, you cannot take that money back out of the loan without completing another refinance.

If you have a loan on a house with a lot of equity, you can get a line of credit without paying off the loan. The HELOC can be placed in second position, and the first loan can stay in first position. When you refinance, you must usually refinance any loans on the house as well (this makes the loan amount higher and can increase the closing costs).

If you think you may need money for your business or rental properties, but you will not need the money long-term, a HELOC may be perfect. If you need long-term money for financing rental property down payments, a cash-out refinance may be the better option.

Both a cash-out refinance and HELOC can offer great opportunities to real estate investors. Often, a real estate investor's biggest challenge is finding enough money to fund deals. Both a HELOC and cash out refinance can help provide funds which allow investors to buy more properties and make more money.

## Conclusion

Buying with little money down can take some work and sacrifice when you first start out. The more rentals you buy below market value and the longer you own those rentals, the easier it gets to buy more. Buying your first and second properties can take time, but when you have multiple properties, your momentum grows, and the process gets easier and easier.

# 9

# How to Repair and Maintain Rental Properties

Once you have purchased and financed a rental property, you may need to do some work on it. In fact, many of the properties I buy need a lot of work. The more work a property needs, the better deal you can usually get. However, you must be careful when buying houses that need work because the deal must be good enough to compensate for the time and money all that work requires!

When you buy a rental property that needs work, you want more than the discount that the work will cost you because making repairs takes time and cash. Some lenders will finance repairs, but those lenders are tough to find, especially for an investor. My lender loans me 80% of the purchase price, but they will not loan on any of the repairs. I must pay cash for any repairs I make, and recouping that money takes time unless I refinance.

Because making repairs takes cash, you must be very cognizant of the amount you spend on repairs. The cash-on-cash returns that we talked about earlier are greatly affected by the cash you invest. Even though a house may cost more if it needs less work, the cash-on-cash returns may actually be higher on a house that needs less work than a house that is cheaper but needs more repairs.

Here is an example:

## House 1

Purchased for $150,000

Rents for $1,500 per month

Needs $5,000 in repairs

20% down

3% closing costs

Cash flow is $338 per month*

*Cash-on-cash return is 10%*

Cash needed: $40,000

## House 2

Purchased for $130,000

Rents for $1,500 per month

Needs $20,000 in repairs

20% down

3% closing costs

Cash flow is $420 per month*

*Cash-on-cash return is 10%*

Cash needed: over $50,000

*(includes property management, maintenance, and vacancies)*

As you can see, the cash-on-cash return is about the same for both houses, but the cash needed to buy the second house is much more. While you are buying the house for $20,000 less than the first house, you are spending much more of your cash and getting the same return.

I would not like either of these deals very much because the cash-on-cash return is not 15% or higher, but I have very strict buying criteria. If I had to choose between the two, I would pick the first house because buying it took less of my cash. I would like to see the second house priced at $110,000, and then it would be worth it for me to make the repairs and spend the extra cash.

Whenever you analyze properties, you need to look at the numbers and your personal goals to see if they make sense. Do not buy a house just because it is cheap. If the house needs $50,000 in work, and you can buy the equivalent of that house for $50,000 more that does not need work, buying the cheap house doesn't make any sense. Now if you can buy the cheap house for $80,000 less than the fixed-up house, it might start to make sense.

Having said that, I cannot tell you what is or isn't a good deal. You must figure that out. Some people are happy with 5% returns, and others want 25% returns.

## How do you decide what to repair on a rental property?

What I do and do not repair is very important. I have 16 long-term rental properties, and I fix and flip 15 to 30 houses per year. I have a completely different strategy for repairing fix-and-flips versus rental properties.

Keeping repair costs as low as possible while still making houses look great is key to my long-term rental strategy. I tend to make fewer repairs with my long-term rentals than with my fix-and-flips. I make the rental properties look very nice and make sure they are safe, but they don't have to be perfect. I do not fix as much on a rental property because renters are not nearly as fussy as buyers. Most renters do not think of a house they rent as their property, so they are not as concerned with the age of the mechanical systems or the finish details. If something breaks, the tenant knows the property owner will fix it...or at least should fix it. I have found renters to be very nonchalant about light fixtures and paint color, where buyers are very meticulous about these items. In one of my rental properties, I left brass fixtures in the house as an experiment to see if it would be hard to rent out (we usually put in oil rubbed bronze). It rented right away, and the renters did not even seem to notice the fixtures.

### How I decide what to repair on my fix and flips

In a flip, we almost always repair and update everything. A buyer will hire an inspector to go through the entire house. That inspector will find most things that are wrong, and an inspection that finds many things wrong will often scare off buyers. We try to have as few items mentioned on the inspection as possible.

We also have an inspection done on our flips before the work is done so that we know everything that must be fixed. We do another inspection after the house is fixed up to show the buyers that it is in great shape.

## What repairs need to be done in both a rental and a flip?

Paint color can make a huge difference in how a house feels. Dark paint can make a house feel small, while white paint can make a house feel stark and boring. Many people love to paint rooms different colors to show their style and personality. The problem is that everyone has a different style and personality. Pleasing everyone is impossible, so a nice neutral color is the best choice. We use beige or grey paint in all our rentals and flips. If the house has white trim, we use Kwal Paint's Sawyer's Fence color. For oak trim, we use a color called Millet. Paint colors definitely look different in different houses due to the trim colors and carpet colors. If you are trying out new colors, use paint samples on the wall to see how they look before you paint the entire house.

We sold a flip recently that had brand new paint throughout the entire house. At the closing, the buyers informed me the first thing they were going to do was repaint almost the entire house. It may seem like a waste, but the buyers let me know the paint we picked looked good—it just wasn't what they wanted. We could have just as easily had buyers that would have kept the paint we used for five years. We still sold the house by choosing a neutral color, but if we would have tried to pick trendy colors in multiple rooms, it could have thrown off the feel of the house and scared the buyers away.

Just like paint, if you want to sell your house quickly and for a lot of money, other designs should be neutral. Carpet color can range from dark to light, but once again, too dark a color makes a house feel dark and small. If the carpet is too light, people worry about stains and visible wear and tear. We always put in new carpet or refinish hardwood floors in all our fix and flips and long-term holds.

For a few years, we put in brushed bronze fixtures for all our properties. Brushed bronze is bronze covered in black paint. After a bit of use, the black wears off to show the bronze color, which I think is very cool. My wife recently told me nickel fixtures may be coming back as the "in-style" again. I still prefer the dark fixtures with light paint, because I think it creates a nice contrast. Nickel fixtures are not bad if you want to save a little money, but I would stay away from brass. Brass fixtures really date a house and can take away from the other new features.

The cost to replace all fixtures in a house can add up quickly and can easily amount to $700 to $1200 in just materials for basic fixtures from a box store. We usually replace fixtures on all our flips, but if they are in decent shape, we may keep the current fixtures on our rentals.

When you repair investment properties, the biggest decision can be how much to update and upgrade. Many of the houses I buy are very dated, and that is why I get a great deal on them. The most expensive work usually comes from replacing kitchens and baths. I try to avoid replacing kitchens if possible, especially in my rentals. I also like to avoid replacing bathrooms because of the price to replace tubs, sinks, toilets, and the labor. I make sure all the mechanicals are working well because I do not want a plumbing leak destroying all the work I just completed.

On my flips, I tend to replace kitchens more often because I will be getting that money back right away when I sell. On a rental property, a brand-new kitchen might help it rent for slightly more, but making back that investment will take years. I try my best to save the kitchens in my rental properties and keep costs down

We always put stainless-steel appliances in our kitchens. They are a little more expensive than black or white appliances, and most buyers love them, which helps the house sell more quickly. We usually replace the countertops as well. The countertops in houses I buy are usually pretty beat up, and you can put in nice laminate counters fairly cheaply. Depending on the price of the house, we may put in granite counters to spice things up. Nice laminate counters are around $500-$1000, and granite slab counters are around $1,500-$2,500 depending on how many square feet we must install. For houses under $150,000, we usually use laminate counters, and for houses over $150,000, we use granite. What you do would depend on what is common in your market. Replacing cabinets is trickier because there are so many different types of cabinets in varying condition. Once again, the price of the house will dictate if we try to save cabinets or not. If the cabinets look solid and are in good condition, we may paint them white.

I try to save cabinets in my rentals and low-range flips. If the cabinets are broken at all, I usually replace the kitchen. We can replace all the cabinets in a basic kitchen for $3,000 or less from a box store. Box store cabinets are not top of the line, but they offer many styles and work great for us. I am particular to maple cabinets as I think oak has too much grain and makes houses look dated. Cherry is nice too but can be too dark. The knotty pine look used to bug me until I bought a house with those cabinets. After a few years, it really grew on me. The problem was that it took a few years for me to like them, and when selling a house, you do not have that much time. I think knotty pine is an acquired taste, and when you repair investment properties, you want to appeal to as many people as possible. We always stick to a light- to mid color stain and basic maple cabinets.

## Additions or large remodel jobs

My general rule of thumb is to never put on an addition. In my area, land is not valuable enough to call for an addition, and I will almost never get my money back. Remodeling or moving rooms around in an existing structure may make sense in certain circumstances, but I am usually not in favor of moving kitchens, baths, or other major components. Making major changes is too expensive and usually not worth the cost. In my rental properties, I will add a bedroom if it is easy because it adds value and I can charge higher rent. I may have to move a wall or finish a room in the basement to complete a bedroom, but it is usually worth the cost. Many times, I can turn a four-bedroom house into a five-bedroom one for $1,500 or $2,000. If you already have five bedrooms in a single-family property, adding a sixth probably isn't worth it. In my market, there is a big price difference in rent between

2-, 3-, 4-, and 5-bedroom houses. When you get to six or more bedrooms, it does not make nearly as big of a difference, and you are inviting more wear and tear with more people living in the house.

The more expensive the house, the more expensive the repairs will be. This is a key point to remember when you sell. The more expensive the house, the nicer the house will need to be for buyers. Buyers will want upgraded appliances, kitchens, baths, and they'll want everything to be perfect. In the lower price ranges, you can usually get away with fewer upgrades. On our more expensive flips, we usually make less money percentage wise than our lower priced flips, especially if they need many repairs. High-end repairs and upgrades really add up and eat away at profits.

Landscaping can be another tricky item, and much of what I do depends on the time of the year. I love completing flips in the winter because I do not have to worry if the yard is dead or not. In the summer, a nice green lawn can really make a house look great. We try to make sure our flips have nice yards and great curb appeal. We will sometimes add mulch or other landscaping material to make the house look as good as possible. First impressions make a big impression on buyers.

On my rentals, I make sure every house has a sprinkler system on a timer. I set the sprinklers for the tenants and do not have to worry about the yard dying. I do various degrees of yard work depending on the season and what the tenants want. I make sure the front yard is nice, but often, the tenants do not care about the back yard.

When we repair investment properties, we always make sure the mechanicals are working properly. Much of our repair costs go into new hot-water heaters, furnaces, and air conditioners. If the units are getting old, or if the units in our flips are showing signs of failing, we replace them. On the rentals, we may wait to replace older units, but we will have them inspected to make sure they are safe. It is best not to wait with hot water heaters as they can rust out and flood a house very easily. I try to keep roofs as long as possible on my rentals, but on our flips, we replace them if they are worn.

Repairing investment property can take a lot of time and money. You want to make sure you are making the right repairs for what you intend to do with the property. I know I did not cover every possible repair, but this will give you an idea of the things I do to maximize my investment.

# How much will repairing your investment property cost?

I fix up many houses: my personal residence, my rental properties, and my fix-and-flips. The most difficult part about fixing up a house is finding a great contractor and estimating how much the repairs will cost. Repair costs will vary based on the quality of products used, labor costs in your area, and the contractor you use.

## What does painting cost?

I always paint the house and replace the floor coverings, unless those items have just been completed. The cost of painting a house, both in labor and materials, has increased greatly the last few years. My interior-painting costs are about $1.50 to $2.50 per square foot. It costs about $2,500 to paint the interior walls of a 1,500-square-foot house in beige or gray with white trim.

Painting the exterior costs more because the paint is more expensive, it needs more prep work, and the weather must be nice. Painting the exterior can cost $3.00 or more per square foot depending on the complexity of the job and the condition of the house. If the paint is peeling, it will cost much more to scrape and prepare the surface for new paint. If the paint is lead-based, the costs can be much more due to the preparation and clean-up work needed to dispose of the old paint. Your contractor or painter must be certified to remove lead-based paint or they can face huge fines from the government. Lead-based paint was prohibited after 1978.

## How much does flooring replacement cost?

I usually carpet the living areas and install vinyl or tile in kitchens and bathrooms. If the floors are hardwood, I refinish them, but I do not add or replace hardwood because of the cost. Installing hardware floors costs three times as much as carpet. Replacing the carpet in a 1,500-square-foot house costs about $3,000 to $3,500. Vinyl or tile in the kitchen and baths costs another $500 to $1,000. These costs are for middle-of-the-road materials that look nice and will last but do not cost a fortune.

If a house already has hardwood, I do my best to refinish it. Refinishing hardwood is less expensive than installing new carpet. I also like the look of hardwood floors, and buyers love them. I can refinish a 1,500-square-foot house that is mostly hardwood for about $2,000.

We will use laminate flooring in some houses. We used to avoid it because it looked cheap, but many new styles look great and are affordable.

## How much does fixture replacement cost?

Another great update is new light and plumbing fixtures. Brand new matching lights, door handles, and faucets can transform a house. I like to use antique bronze, but we have also used brushed nickel. Light fixtures are as inexpensive as $10 for basic bedroom and bathroom lights. You can purchase a nice chandelier and a good ceiling fan for less than $150. Door handles are $20 or less depending on the style, and faucets run from $35 to $150. You can replace the lights, door handles, and faucets for an entire house for about $1,000 to $1,500.

## How much does appliance replacement cost?

New appliances can really spruce up a house. We put stainless steel appliances in our houses. I can get a stove for $500 to $600, a dishwasher for $300, and a microwave for $250. I usually do not buy a fridge for my flips, but I will buy a fridge for my rentals. Even with dated cabinets, appliances make a huge difference in the look of a kitchen.

## How much does cosmetically updating a house cost?

Here are the total costs for a cosmetic upgrade on a 1,500-square-foot house:

- New interior paint: $2,500
- New floor coverings: $4,500
- New fixtures: $1,200
- New appliances: $1,300
- **Total cost: $9,500**

Fixing up a house almost always costs more than you think, so be prepared to spend more than what you had planned. Spending less than $10,000 on any house that I fix up is very rare for me because there are usually many little things that need to be repaired. Drywall holes, outlet covers, landscaping, and many more things will increase the costs. I also rarely can avoid major repairs.

The repairs on my flips and rentals vary from basic cosmetics to massive remodels. Here are other common repairs and their costs:

- **Kitchens**: Replacing a kitchen isn't as expensive as you might think. The materials to replace a basic kitchen including cabinets, counter tops, and sink cost $2,500 or less. I can replace a kitchen for well under $5,000, including labor.
- **Baths**: Baths can involve gut jobs or a simple vanity replacement. For a full gut job, I can usually spend less than $3,000. I can replace a vanity, toilet, and bath for less than $1,000.
- **Roof**: I have a great roofer who will replace the roof on a 1,500-square-foot house for around $6,000. The roof can be more expensive depending on how bad of shape it is in.
- **Electrical:** Electrical repairs can vary a great deal based on what needs to be done. Minor repairs might cost a couple hundred dollars, while

major rewiring jobs can cost $5,000. Getting any electrical concerns checked out to see how serious they are is important.

- **Plumbing:** Plumbing is similar to electrical. A minor job can be very cheap, but re-plumbing an entire house can cost $5,000 or more.
- **Sewer:** Sewer line replacements can be very expensive—usually $3,000 to $10,000.
- **Foundation**: Most foundation repairs are not fun to deal with. There can be many issues such as settling, water leakage, grading issues, or structural problems. Water problems in the basement or crawl space might be due to a major foundation issue that could cost $10,000 or more, or they might be due to a simple grading issue that some dirt work will fix.
- **Windows:** We replace many windows because we buy older houses all the time. For basic vinyl windows, I usually pay my contractors about $300 per window for material and installation.
- **Doors:** We also replace many interior doors. Six-panel white doors make a house look very nice. Doors are usually $100 to $150 each, including installation.
- **Stucco and siding:** I rarely replace siding, but I have on occasion. Currently, I am paying about $8,500 to put brand new stucco on a 1,250-square-foot fix and flip. Replacing wood siding is less expensive, but you must paint it. You can usually re-side and paint a house for less than stucco in most cases.
- **Drywall/Sheetrock:** In old houses, I see a lot of plaster and bad drywall. An old house looks so much better with brand new drywall than with uneven crumbling plaster. On a recent flip, a drywall specialist charged about $3,000 to do the walls and ceilings in three rooms. The square footage was 500.
- **Furnace/hot water heater:** I had a brand new forced air furnace system installed for about $7,000 this year, including all new vents. Replacing just the furnace costs about $2,500 and a hot water heater about $800.

## How much do I spend on my remodels?

On my most recent fix-and-flip, I spent about $18,000 on the remodel. That included interior and exterior paint, new carpet, new doors, new trim, some electrical work, some new drywall, trash out, landscaping work, and many little fixes. On a flip I am about to start, I will spend over $50,000 on the repairs. That house needs new plumbing, new electric, new paint everywhere, siding work, new windows, new doors, new drywall, new baths, new kitchen, new floors, new fixtures, new trim, and more.

I shop at Home Depot for most materials, including fixtures, doors, windows, door handles, and all the little stuff. I also buy my appliances there. They offer great discounts if you spend a lot of money on materials. Ask their pro desk about becoming a member and other ways to save money. If you spend enough money at Home Depot, you can get a managed account with even more discounts and a custom representative to help you. You must spend $125,000 per year to be eligible. In the 1st quarter of 2017, we spent about $100,000 there!

Basic cosmetic repairs do not need to cost $50,000 or $100,000. I see kitchen remodels on television that cost $50,000, and I cannot believe what people pay! Even if you use high-end materials such as granite counters and custom cabinets, you should not spend $50,000 on a kitchen unless it is in a million-dollar house. Repairs can add up quickly, and I always expect about $5,000 more than planned due to unknowns. Find a great contractor, make sure the contractor does their work, and shop around for the best prices to keep your costs down. Remember, these costs are what I pay to fix up houses in my area. If you live in an expensive area, your costs may be significantly higher.

## How to find a great contractor

Finding a great contractor is difficult, but it's very important. They can be very expensive, may take a long time to finish a job, or may even quit on you. A great contractor who offers detailed bids, communicates well, and performs quality work will make your life easier. Buying an investment property takes a lot of initial money, and repairing it can cost even more. If you do not have a great contractor, costs can skyrocket due to long timelines and increased repair costs.

## What is the easiest way to find a great contractor?

My advice is to ask friends, family, and co-workers for references before you try other sources. A recommendation does not guarantee that the contractor is any good, but it does give you a place to start. Recommendations are usually better indicators than the contractor's advertising. Real estate agents, property managers, or builders may know of a good contractor. Anyone who owns a house may have used a great contractor at some point, so do not be afraid to ask your friends or family.

## Do not rely solely on recommendations

I have tried out many new contractors because I have so many rehabs going at once. I once received recommendations from my broker and a couple of other agents in my office. The contractor was a builder, seemed to know what he was talking about, and gave great detailed bids. I put him to work on two projects that were both sitting and waiting for work to be started. He told me he had a great crew and could handle as much work as I could give him. He ended up finishing one project on budget and mostly on time, but it took him two months to start the second!

I had assumed everything was going well since that was what he had told me, but the property was 40 minutes away, and I had not physically seen the work start. Failing to properly oversee and visit the job site was completely my fault. When I visited the property, which I thought was almost done, I was in for a big surprise. The work hadn't even started! I called the contractor, and he gave me a story about having too many jobs and his workers getting sick. He had been telling me everything was going great and the work was almost done. Either he had not been overseeing his workers properly or he had lied to me. That job was eventually finished about four months after it was started and three months after it was supposed to be done. I never used that contractor again, not because it took so long but because either he had not visited the site for months or he had lied to me. Even if you get great recommendations, you must still keep track of your contractors.

## How can you keep an eye on your contractor?

Keeping an eye on your contractors' work and schedule, whether you're using them for the first time or the 20th, is always best. In my experience, the more communication and oversight you provide, the better the contractor will do. I've worked with some contractors on up to 20 jobs, but if I do not keep on them, they slack off. If a contractor does a great job once, it does not mean they will always do a great job.

I had to fire a contractor this year that had worked on many properties for me and had done a great job over and over. On his last projects, he stopped visiting his work sites and started telling me jobs were done when they were not. His prices went up, and the time he took to finish jobs increased because he was never at the site and did not keep track of his workers.

Here are a few tips on how to make sure your contractor is doing a great job:

- Constantly communicate with them
- Visit the property often
- Always get a written bid first
- Get a written estimate for when the work will be finished
- Do not prepay for any work (this is not always possible. Some contractors require a deposit upfront or material cost. However, never pay for the entire job up front.).
- Help pick out materials and paint colors

I always talk to a contractor on the phone before I meet them in person. I want to make sure they know what they are talking about, and I want to get an idea of how much they charge. A contractor should tell you the hourly rate, the number of people in the crew, and how long it takes them to do an average job. I also want to know how busy they are and how many other people they are working with.

If I like what I hear on the phone, I set up a meeting at one of my properties. I go over what I want done and have them submit a bid. If you are new to real estate and to finding contractors, always get multiple bids so you know you are not being ripped off. Try to talk to the contractor as much as possible. Ask about their family and the kind of jobs they normally do. In my experience, contractors like to talk a lot, and if you get them to start talking, they may tell you some things that will help you decide. One contractor I interviewed mentioned that he had two recent DUIs, including one while he was on the job!

After I meet with a contractor, I ask them to submit a bid. This is another test to see how quickly they get it to me (and whether they get back to me at all). Two contractors I recently talked to never got me a bid, never emailed me, and never called me. Eliminating them was easy; if they cannot send me a bid, they probably cannot do the job.

Contractors' hourly rates can range from $20 to $100. If you get a bid that seems outrageous, you may have found one of the expensive contractors. There are really cheap contractors as well, but you sometimes get what you pay for. Usually, the best contractors for my strategy are not the cheapest but also not the most expensive. If I pay a contractor, and he has a few guys to help him out, I usually end up paying each person about $40 an hour. I also hire my own handyman, who is one of my employees, for $20 an hour. He is not quite as skilled as the contractors, but I can always keep him busy. Eventually, I would like to have my own crew.

## How can you find a great contractor through large box stores?

Home Depot offers a rehab program that will actually handle every job on a project, but large jobs through them are more expensive than through local contractors. I talked to Home Depot to price out their contractor program, and they were very honest and said using my own contractors would be cheaper. They even gave me the names of contractors who frequent the store often and have been around for years. This was not a recommendation from them in any way, but it gave me a lead on a contractor who I am going to try out.

Another way to meet great contractors is to visit the store early in the morning and see who is buying large amounts of supplies. Those who are buying materials are probably contractors, and they may be looking for more work. You know they currently have at least one job since they are buying materials.

## How to find a great contractor online

Many contractors advertise on Craigslist, but knowing how great they are is hard until they do some work for you. I have hired a handyman and painters through Craigslist when I was desperate. They worked out okay, but judging how good a contractor will be is difficult until they finish a job. I always ask for references and talk to those references about the any contractor's previous work.

Many contractors also advertise on the internet. Again, you must check references thoroughly when using these resources. Yelp provides contractor reviews (if they have done enough work) that can help you decide.

I am aware of a couple of other companies that offer regional or nationwide contracting services. These companies may not work with an investor who only has one small job. However, if you can offer them consistent work in one area, they may be a great choice.

Vineyard Services offers contracting services in most states. They have been around for years and do property maintenance on many REO properties.

Angie's List has provided a lot of great contractor information. They list contractors in my area, their area of expertise, and detailed reviews from people who have used them. So far, I have found multiple prospects from Angie's List that I am going to meet at my properties. You can use Angie's List for many other services besides contractors. I also use Thumbtack and

Home Advisors.

Finding a great contractor can be the most difficult part of real estate investing, but it may also be the most important part. Taking your time, interviewing multiple contractors, and keeping a close eye on any contractor you hire is vitally important. Doing the work yourself usually doesn't make sense, so hiring the right contractor is extremely important.

## How to make sure the contractor will do a good job

Once you find a contractor, you must make sure they do their job well. No matter how good the references are or how great the contractor says they are, follow these steps to make sure the contractor follows through.

Determining if a contractor is good or bad can be hard until they finish the job. Contractors can get too busy, take on too big of a job, or lose track of their workers. Any of these circumstances can cause a job to take too long or be done incorrectly. Constant communication, written agreements, and checking on a job are all keys to making sure your contractor does what he has promised to do.

However, I think walking a job with your contractor so they know what needs to be done is a good idea, even if you have worked with them before. Make sure the contractor writes things down. I've seen a few contractors fail to write things down during the walkthrough, and when I came back to the work site, they were doing things I had not asked for and had not done things I had asked for. Everything should be in writing so there is no confusion. A written bid serves multiple purposes and will save you time and money.

- A written bid ensures both the contractor and the homeowner know exactly which services and repairs are being done. You do not want any confusion regarding what was and what was not supposed to be repaired.
- A written bid lists the price the contractor charges for specific work. You do not want to be surprised with a massive bill that you did not agree to after the work is completed. A written bid helps keep the contractor honest.

- A written bid may also include timeframes for completing the work. Some investors will add incentives to contractors for getting a job done quickly. The faster they finish, the more the contractor is paid.

Most contractors require bids to be signed by both parties. The written bid not only keeps both parties honest, but it also reminds everyone of the scope of work to be done. I have many jobs going at one time, and I tend to forget what was talked about. By having a written bid, there is no confusion regarding the repairs or costs.

## Keep in constant contact with your contractor

Just because you do not hear from your contractor does not mean things are going well. I thought one job was going well because I never heard a thing from the contractor. I assumed he would have told me if there were any problems or delays. It turned out that he had not even started the job! Call your contractor to get updates on the job, and stop by the job site to see how things are progressing. You or someone you trust needs to visit the job sites at least once per week if not more.

Do not be afraid to ask your contractor if they are on schedule or on budget. Ask your contractor if there are any changes to the bid or if there is any more work to that needs to be done. If there are any changes to the work, make sure the contractor contacts you to approve the changes. Some contractors take it upon themselves to change a job or add work without asking the homeowner.

## Do not pay a contractor for work they have not done

Some contractors want partial payment before they start any work. If you have worked with a contractor before and this is their policy, paying them some money to get started may work. In some cases, I pay for materials or a small portion of the job before work is started. Often, the contractors are stretched thin from buying materials, and they need extra money before the job is done to continue working. Avoid paying large sums of money before any work is done.

If a contractor is not paid, they can place a lien on a house for completed work. It is much easier for a contractor to collect for unpaid work than it is for a homeowner to track down a contractor who takes their money and skips town before any work is done. We pay our contractors up front in some cases, but we try to limit the amount. Recently we have been paying a contractor 25% up front, another 25% halfway through, and the rest upon completion. This gives the contractor enough money to live on and also gives them incentive to finish quickly.

## Do a final walkthrough with the contractor to make sure the work has been done properly

A contractor should take pride in their work and be happy to show you what has been repaired. I always do a final walkthrough to make sure the work has been done correctly. Often, I must have the contractor go back and fix minor things or fix things we did not notice the first time we looked at the house. Do not be afraid to point out work you think was done incorrectly. If the contractor is hesitant about fixing it correctly, stand your ground. If the contractor refuses to make repairs or do things correctly, you know not to use them again.

Doing your due diligence to find a great contractor is very important. Once you hire a contractor, make sure they follow through with what they have promised. If you keep in constant contact, get everything in writing, and are clear on the scope of work, you will have much more success.

## Should you repair an investment property yourself?

At this point in my career, I use contractors to rehab all my flips and rentals. Many people try to repair a flip or rental property themselves because they think they will save money and it will be fun. In 2006, I decided to rehab a fix-and-flip myself without using a contractor. I thought I would save money on the labor a contractor would charge. Doing the work myself may have saved me money on the labor, but in the end, I lost money on the deal because of how long it took me to complete the work and because of the opportunities I missed.

I learned a lot while repairing a house myself, but I did not have much fun, and—I did not save any money. The problem with doing the work myself was that I am not a professional contractor. I had to learn how to repair the house. This particular house was about 60 years old, needed paint, carpet, new floors, new doors, new windows, a new kitchen, a wall removed, and a lot of minor repairs. I may have been qualified to paint the house, but that was about it.

## Why doing the work myself did not save as much on labor costs as I thought it would

This house needed a lot of work, and although I had done minor repairs on houses before, I had never done anything to this extent. I was sure doing the work myself would save me thousands of dollars. The problem was that it took me six months to finish. I had to learn how to do all the work on the job, and that took at least three times as long as it would have taken a professional. It may have saved me a little money on labor, but it cost me more money because it took me so long to make the repairs.

When I fix and flip a house, I use financing for most of the purchase price. I also get insurance, pay utilities and taxes, and have many other costs. All those costs add up very fast, making it important to repair the house fast. The longer it takes to make repairs, the fewer profits you will make. With rentals, the longer the repairs take, the longer you will go without collecting rent.

## What is the daily cost of owning a fix-and-flip?

Let us walk through what owning a flip will cost. I am lucky that I can finance 75% of my purchase price with a 5.25% loan because many flip loans are much more expensive. Based on this financing, this is how much it costs per day to own a $100,000 purchase with a $75,000 loan:

My costs are cheaper than most fix-and-flippers because I have great financing. The daily cost could easily double if you are using hard money.

A 10 to 15% interest rate is very typical for a hard-money loan. An interest rate of 15% on our fix-and-flip example increases financing costs to $30.82 per day. However, with hard money, you may be able to finance the entire purchase price or more (one advantage of hard money). If the loan amount is $110,000, the financing costs for a hard-money loan jump to $45.21 per day. Now your daily costs are $57.80 to own the house.

$23.28 per day equals about $708 per month in costs for me or $1,758 per month with hard money. Owning a fix-and-flip is costly, and for someone who must use hard money, holding a property too long is dangerous. It takes me about six months to sell a fix-and-flip once I factor in repair time, marketing, getting a contract, and closing.

## How much did it cost me to do the work myself on this flip?

I know repairing this house took me at least four months longer than it would have taken a contractor. It cost me at least $2,832 in extra carrying costs, which is less than a contractor would have charged me for labor. That actually is not too bad, but the truth is it cost me much more than that.

One of the most important things you can do on a fix-and-flip is sell it quickly. Not only do you save money, but you also can use your money to buy more houses and complete more flips. If all your money is tied up in one house for eight months, you may miss an incredible deal because you do not have the ability to buy another flip.

The longer you hold a house, the better chance the market will change. We are in an appreciating market now, but that could change quickly. I like to sell my flips quickly because I never know what the future holds.

## I did not save all the labor costs because my time is worth something

I may have saved money doing the work myself, but how much time did it cost me? My time is worth something. I was a real estate agent when I did the flip, and my business suffered greatly because I spent so much time working on the house. I had the worst year of my life, because I did not have time to go after business. Because of this house, I only made about $28,000 in 2006. I did not sell any houses as an agent or buy any more flips while working on this stupid house.

Since I was busy with this house and did not have time to look for new projects, it was the only fix-and-flip work we were doing at the time. Focusing on this house and not looking for others cost me tens of thousands of dollars.

Another factor I hate to think about is the quality of my work. I am not a professional contractor, yet I was doing jobs a pro should do. I was learning and definitely not doing the high-quality work my contractors do. A contractor helped me with some jobs such as taking out a wall and putting in a header because I did not want the house to fall down. Other jobs were not done as well as they should have been because I did them myself.

That flip cost me months of my life. It frustrated me; it cost me business as an agent; and it cost me flipping business. Putting a number on the figure is challenging, but I estimate this decision cost me at least $25,000, even though on the surface I may have saved a couple thousand dollars by doing the work myself. The work was not great, and that may have cost me even more money on the sale. All this assumes I paid myself no wages on that flip!

## What about doing the work on rental properties?

Obviously, this story was about a flip—not a rental property. But the same principles apply. You may lose even more money on a rental property because every day the rehab takes means lost rent. Not only are you losing rent, but must also still pay the financing and carrying costs that I had to pay on my flip. Even though, on the surface, doing the work yourself looks like a smart move, you will most likely lose money in the end. We did not even talk about the toll all this work takes on your mental health! When I was doing the work, I was miserable, I was always working, and it stressed me out. I was so happy when I was done with that house!

## Should you hire a general contractor to repair your rental or flip?

You have a couple of options when repairing rental properties, flips, or even your personal residence. You can use a general contractor who will do everything, or you can hire subcontractors who will each do a specific job. Hiring subcontractors requires more work from the homeowner but can save a lot of money. Using a general contractor can make the process easier but can also cost a lot more. I have used both options, but I like to use subcontractors for as many jobs as I can for multiple reasons.

When you use a general contractor to do the entire job, they handle almost everything that needs to be done. They determine the entire scope of work, hire subs, schedule, budget, and plan the entire project. Using general contractors, can be very expensive because scheduling and planning everything takes so much time. The other problem with using general contractors is they can be very slow if they must do all the repairs. Some contractors may be able to handle huge jobs and get them done on time, but others may struggle the more they must schedule and plan.

When you use subcontractors, you must hire out certain jobs and schedule the work. The benefit of hiring out specific jobs is that they can be done faster and less expensively. Often, subcontractors will specialize in just one thing such as:

- Electrical
- Plumbing
- Roof
- Foundation
- Sewer
- Landscaping
- Flooring
- HVAC
- Drywall
- Kitchen and baths
- Paint
- Windows

Subcontractors can save you money because that is the only job they do, and they are really good and fast. A general contractor must use their own crew or hire out a crew to complete jobs. While a general-contracting crew can usually do many jobs, they are not as fast and do not have the expertise of a sub that specializes in one thing.

With subcontractors, I can have multiple jobs done at once, which saves a lot of time. The roof, the plumbing, and the electrical can all be done simultaneously. Some of the biggest contracting problems I have had were when I gave an entire job to one contractor. The contractors got overwhelmed, took forever, and one quit on me.

Please check state laws regarding repairs. Some states have stricter guidelines for who must be licensed and how to use subs.

## How do we repair rentals and flips?

I have tried many ways to repair my flips and rentals. I have used general contractors, subs, a hired employee to run my projects, and even did the work on a flip myself. I have had some luck with general contractors, but often, they bite off more than they can chew, overpromise, and underdeliver. I think most contractors will say they can handle everything and may even believe it but are not equipped to handle large remodels on their own. I have had good luck using subs for parts of jobs and then contractors for the majority of the work. Here is an example:

Subcontractor jobs:

- Electrical
- Plumbing
- Roof
- Landscaping
- HVAC

Contractor jobs:

- Replace doors
- Replace windows
- Paint
- Kitchen
- Baths
- Fixtures

While the contractor is working on their jobs, the subcontractors can be working on their jobs. In cases like this, I do not use a general contractor because I do not need someone to schedule and hire everyone. I do the scheduling and hiring or have someone on my team do it.

A few years ago, I hired a full-time employee to handle the hiring, scheduling, and project management on my rehabs. I had high hopes for the plan but hired the wrong person! I got into more trouble than I was in before I hired them. Luckily, I did not give up and I ended up using someone who was already on my team: Nikki. She took over the management of the flips and has been awesome. Along with having a project manager, I hire as many subs out as I can. Here are the benefits of hiring subs:

- I get jobs done faster because I do not have to wait for a contractor to have time to complete a big job. I have a list of subs and can use the ones that are able to get work done the fastest.
- I save money because subs are usually cheaper due to the reasons we have already discussed.
- I'm not relying on one contractor to get everything right. If a subcontractor messes up, they will only mess up part of the rehab and other work can still be done. If the contractor messes up, it can screw up the entire project.

I will still use some contractors and still look for great new contractors to repair my houses. Someday, I might find that magical contractor who is affordable, has a huge crew, is honest, and is fast. When I am doing 10 to 20 flips at once, finding contractors that can handle that much volume without falling behind is tough. I am not holding my breath waiting for that contractor, and I also do not want to depend on one person for all my repairs.

## Is using subcontractors right away smart?

The more experience you have, the easier it will be to find subcontractors and hire out jobs. If you have no contacts and must find new subs from scratch, it can be a bit daunting. It might not hurt to try to find a general contractor and then slowly start looking for subs. If you are just starting out, try not to take on huge remodel projects that require an awesome contractor or multiple subs. As your business matures and you gain more experience, you will meet good subs and contractors. Make sure you keep track of their names and contact information!

## Conclusion

Repairing and maintaining properties is one of the toughest parts of being a real estate investor. A lot of investors try to do the work themselves, but I think that is a bad move unless you are a contractor. You need to spend your time finding the right people to repair your houses. If you are using property management, there is a good chance they will take care of the maintenance for you with their own crews. You must make sure they are charging reasonable rates.

# 10

# How to Manage Your Rental Properties

Rental properties are a great investment, but they must be managed well to generate money. Some people think of rental properties as a passive income source, but if you manage properties yourself, they are not truly passive. A property owner must take the time to screen tenants, check on the houses, take care of the property, and make sure the tenants pay on time.

Many property owners start by managing properties themselves to save money. However, you need to make sure you are cut out to be a self manager. You must be tough on your tenants, have systems in place, account for all expenses, and be quick to fix any problems that come up. Most people, including me, are not good property managers! I am not tough on my tenants; I am not always quick to jump on problems; and I believe sob stories. I managed my properties until I had seven, and then I switched the management to my team.

When I turned the management over to my team, things became so much easier, and I made more money! Even though I had to pay my team to manage the properties, they were better at choosing tenants, better at getting on them to pay rent, and were quicker to fix problems. I actually made more money by not managing my properties myself, and it removed a lot of stress from my life. Do not get stressed out thinking about how hard managing your properties will be. Remember that you can always hire a property manager, and they are usually affordable.

# Should you manage your rental properties yourself?

My rental properties are all single-family properties and are easier to manage than multifamily properties, but it still takes time. You also must pay attention to details and be firm with tenants in order to manage rental properties successfully. If you are not hands-on and tough on your tenants, you will have problems.

# What is involved in managing rental properties?

Managing a rental property involves many tasks. However, most tasks come up when first renting out a property. Once you rent it out, there is much less work involved.

- **Determine what to repair before you rent out the property**. I want to control what is repaired, whether I am the one managing the rental or I have a property manager. A property manager may help you with repairs, but they also may only help with maintenance and repairs after the house is rented out. Even before you buy a rental property, you should have a good idea of what is going to be repaired and how much it is going to cost.
- **Determine how much rent to charge**. I also like to have control of rent amounts, whether I am managing a house or using a property manager. A property manager wants to get houses rented out fast because they collect money based on rent. They may not try to get top dollar. An agent on my team recently sold a house to an investor who used a property manager. We told the investor the house would rent for $1,500 before they bought it. The property manager they hired said it would rent for $1,200! We urged the investor to rent it out for more, and they ended up asking for $1,600 per month. They rented it out at $1,600 within two days, and they were very happy they did not blindly take that property manager's advice.
- **Rent out the house**. This is the hardest part of management. If you take

time to screen and select the best tenants, you will make more money and save many future headaches. You must advertise the property, show the house, check references, check credit, create a lease, and collect money. Do not pick a tenant because they are the only ones that will pay what you are asking. Do not choose the first tenant that wants the house because you are tired of showing it. Pick the best tenant, and if you have doubts, do not convince yourself it will work out just so you can start collecting rent.

· **Collect rent**. When you rent out a house, make sure your tenants pay on time. Charge late fees if they do not. If you let late rent slide, the tenants will think it is okay, and they will keep paying late. If there are no consequences, they will pay later and later and may stop paying completely. You must be strict no matter the tenant or their story. If tenants get too far behind, do not be afraid to start the eviction process. Starting the eviction process usually gets your tenants' attention, and they start paying rent.

· **Evict a tenant**. Eviction is never fun, and I try to avoid it. An eviction could lead to your tenant trashing your house. I have had mutually agreed-upon move outs. If I can get a tenant to move out on good terms, they are more likely to take care of the house and possibly pay me what is owed. Sometimes you still must go through an eviction, which can cost a lot of money in lost rent and legal fees. A property manager will handle rent collections and evictions.

· **Check on your houses**. Just because you have a tenant who always pays on time and never causes a problem, they still may not be taking care of the property. I always write in the lease that I have the right to inspect the property with proper notice. I use this time to make sure the house is well maintained, and I change furnace filters, check smoke detectors, and make sure no other repairs are needed. Some of the biggest problems come from property owners who rent out a house and then never check on it. A tenant may be in a house for years and absolutely destroy it, but the property owner never knows because they never check on it.

· **Maintaining a house**. I have contractors inspect all my properties before

I rent them, but I still have maintenance issues. Things break, and you must repair them. I am not interested in being a slumlord that does not make repairs. I always plan for vacancies and maintenance when I determine my cash flow so when costs come up, they don't hurt my bottom line. I always fix water, roof, electrical, or any other issues. You want your house to be safe and well maintained. If you cannot afford to maintain your rental properties, you should not buy them. Problems will happen at all hours of the day and night, and if you are managing your rentals yourself, you will have to take those calls.

· **Accounting and taxes**. When you manage your own properties, you must keep track of expenses, rents, profit, loss, etc. A good property manager will give you a year-end report that contain all your profit, losses, and accounting and tax information. I always send all my information to an accountant to make sure the expenses and taxes are calculated correctly. Calculating taxes on rental properties isn't easy because you can depreciate the structure. You can also depreciate improvements and deduct some repairs, but you must be careful how it is done.

## How much does a property manager charge?

There is a lot involved in managing rental properties, but not every rental will have issues that require a lot of management. I have had rental houses that have never had a problem; the tenants maintained them well and always paid on time. I have had other rentals where the tenants are always having problems and paid late or stopped paying completely. One tenant had a heart attack and could not work anymore. We came up with a mutually agreed-upon plan where he would move out and try to pay me for back rent. He never paid, but I rented out the house right away for more than he was supposed to pay, and it worked out okay.

Many people find using a property manager is worth it, especially if they cannot handle being tough on tenants. As the owner of the house, the tenant and you both know you make all the decisions. This can make it hard to

HOW TO MANAGE YOUR RENTAL PROPERTIES

be tough on the tenants when they cause problems or get behind on rent. Property managers can be tough because they answer to the owner. If they don't do their job, they could get fired.

Property managers cut into your profits but save you time. Property management fees usually range from 8 to 12% of the monthly rent. Some property managers also charge a leasing fee, which could be one half or one month's rent. In my area, I can find property managers who charge 8% of the monthly rents with no leasing fees.

## How much time does managing rental properties take?

Managing rentals involves many tasks, but managing one property doesn't take a lot of time. The most time-consuming part of managing properties is getting them rented out. If you only have one rental property, managing it should only take a few hours each month. Many of those hours come from renting out the house and collecting rent and dealing with maintenance and other issues takes far fewer hours.

Managing two or three rental properties is not too difficult. Once you have four or more, managing them can take a significant amount of time. If you do not have the time to manage them, get help. When you do not take the time to screen tenants or check on your properties, you can have serious problems.

If you want to manage your own rentals, create systems to help you. Create a system to check your houses, to make sure rent is on time, and to make sure accounting information is logged every month. Managing my rental properties wasn't difficult for me, but I began to let things slide at the end, and that is when problems occur. If the tenants do not think you are paying attention, they will be more likely to try to take advantage of the situation. If you are looking to buy rental properties and do not think you can handle managing them, make sure to account for the cost of a property manager when calculating your cash flow.

In my experience, hiring a property manager for the peace of mind and reduction of stress is worth it. I will talk much more about finding property managers later. For now, let us focus on how to self-manage properties.

## How to rent out your property

There are many ways to rent out a house, and I will break down exactly how I advertise and pick a tenant as well as how I write a lease. I will also go over how I decide market rent, another very important piece to investing in long-term rentals.

You should determine market rent long before you are ready to rent out—or even buy—house. It is one of the first things you should do as a real estate investor.

## Why is determining how much a house will rent out for difficult?

Because I am a real estate agent, I can pull up sold comparable properties on our MLS system to help determine market value. I can see what sold, for how much, and most of the transaction details. However, in my area, the MLS is not used very often for rental properties. I must come up with a different way to determine market rent.

In Colorado and many other states, house sales are public record, but what a house rents for is not. The only way to determine market rent is to look at active listings for rentals or to talk to experts in your area. The most commonly used place to advertise rentals in my area is Craigslist or Zillow.

Before I buy a house or put one up for rent, I check Craigslist to see rents in an area. Rental listings give me an idea of what market rents are, but they are not always reliable. I have no way of knowing whether the asking prices for rent are indicative of what the house will eventually rent for. Checking Craigslist daily to see if previously listed houses are still listed is one way to track whether houses are being rented. There is a good chance that any house that has been rented will be removed from Craigslist. Make a list of houses that are similar to your rental, and save the ad, especially the contact information. If you check back and that listing has been removed, call or email the listing person to see if they rented out the house.

You can also search the Internet to find market rent. Some property management companies may not list their houses on Craigslist, but they may use their own website or another rental website. You can use those listings much like Craigslist to determine market rents. You may also find other rental websites in your area that list properties for rent. Each market advertises rental properties differently.

A property manager is a great resource for an investor. A property manager can determine rental rates in many ways and help investors determine rental rates. You can use their rental listings as a guideline for rental rates. You can probably trust a property manager's rent listings more than an individual who may or may not know how much to rent out a house for. You must be careful with property managers that charge too little rent so they can rent houses faster. Make sure you check with multiple sources to determine rents.

You can also directly ask a property manager what they think market rents are. If you are an investor looking to buy rental properties, a property manager should be happy to help you determine rental rates. If they help you out as an investor, you may use them as a property manager at some point.

Some real estate agents are experts on investment properties. Finding an investor-friendly real estate agent to help you find rental properties is important. It helps if the real estate agent can also help you determine rents. I would listen to what your real estate agent tells you and compare that to the other information you are able to gather. In areas of the country where they are a vital part of the rental market, real estate agents can be a huge help in determining market rents.

Rentrange.com can also help give you rent values, and in my experience, is one of the more accurate rental rate calculators.

# How to price a rental property

I have tried a couple of different methods to price my rentals:

- Price them at the top of market rates and try to find a renter who will pay a premium.
- Price them a little below market rates and take my pick of great renters.

My experience has been better with taking my pick of great renters. Even though the rent is lower, I usually have less worry about late rent and excessive wear and tear. Whenever I price a rental high, I am waiting for a decent to mediocre candidate to send an application in instead of picking the best tenant from multiple applications.

Once I know what a house should rent for, I place an ad on Craigslist and Zillow, put a for-rent sign in the yard, and post it on Facebook. Be sure you research what the most prominent way to advertise in your area is.

When I show rentals, I try to have an open house where every prospective tenant shows up at the same time. This saves me or my management team time and gives the tenants a sense of scarcity and urgency.

I use a rental application that I found online and altered slightly. I originally did not charge an application fee or ran a credit check, but I do now. I charge $50 for the application fee and credit check. Potential tenants have had no problem paying the application fee, and it helps make sure all applying tenants are serious. Online companies like TurboTenant, and Cozi allow you to do this as well.

A great way to judge a tenant is by talking to them as much as possible and looking at their application. I want an application to be filled out as thoroughly as possible with multiple references. If potential renters have barely filled out the application, they are not taking the process seriously, or they are trying to hide something.

When I talk to a potential renter, I want to learn as much about their previous living situation as possible. I ask about pets, employment, and who will be living in the property. The longer you talk to a tenant, the more you can learn about them. When you first talk to a tenant on the phone, take notes so you remember what they said. When you meet them in person, ask them some of the same questions to make sure they give you the same answers. If someone lies to you, it's a very bad sign.

I always call an applicant's references. I want to talk to the reference for the applicant's previous residence and their current employer. I want to know if they paid rent on time, took care of the residence, or were high maintenance. By high maintenance, I mean calling in every week for minor issues, causing plumbing problems because their children like to flush toys down the toilet, or any number of other items. I want to see if they have pets and whether that information matches up with what they are telling me on their application. Remember, some landlords want to get rid of their tenants. If they tell every other potential landlord the tenant was horrible, they will have a harder time getting the tenant to leave. You cannot always trust what previous or current landlords say.

I ask their employer how long the tenant has worked for them. I want to know if they are a good worker and how solid their position is. I will also inquire about their income to see if it lines up with what the applicant is telling me.

## Should you allow pets in your rental property?

I prefer not to rent to tenants with pets, but in some cases, I allow them. I have a dog that I love, and there is no way I would give up that dog, so I understand why tenants want to have pets. Allowing pets is tricky because they can destroy a house, but allowing them also add revenue to a rental property.

If a pet is trained well or the pet lives outside, they might not damage a house. If a pet is not trained well or is older, they can do a lot of damage. The biggest risk with pets is urination inside the house. If you have had the pleasure of being in a house that has pet damage, you know it is not pretty and smells horrible. The smell can be overwhelming, especially from cats.

Pets can destroy carpet, hardwood floors, sub floors, and even drywall. In some cases, pets will try to chew through doors and trim or destroy grass in the backyard. If you are going to allow pets, you must do your due diligence on the pet and weigh the risk of damage versus the reward of more money.

## Why would any investor allow pets in their rental property?

People with pets still need a place to live, and often, they will pay more to rent a house than non-pet owners will. Pet owners may pay more in monthly rent or pay a higher security deposit. I have rented houses to tenants with pets, but I have always charged a higher deposit or monthly pet fee. That higher rent or deposit can make the risk of allowing pets worth it if you check out the pet first.

I have never allowed a cat in my rental properties because cat odors are so much worse than dog odors and much harder to get out. I have smelled houses with cats from 50 feet away with the doors closed. If you have the pleasure of entering a house like that, the smell sticks with you once you leave. It is not fun.

The larger the pet, the better the chance they will do damage. A large dog is stronger and can do more damage than a smaller dog. A large dog also urinates more and leaves bigger messes. If I do allow a dog in a house, I prefer smaller dogs.

Many cities have ordinances against aggressive dogs such as pit bulls. If pit bulls are illegal, it should tell a property owner something about how wise it is to allow pit bulls in their rental. If an aggressive breed hurts someone and a property owner knowingly rented out a house to tenants with an aggressive breed of dog, that property owner could be held liable. This is another great reason to stick with smaller, less aggressive breeds.

The more dogs and cats the tenant owns, the better the chance damage will be done. The more pets there are the better the chance that the owners are not cleaning up or paying attention to their pets. The pets will also be more likely to play aggressively with each other and cause damage. The fewer pets a tenant has, the better off you will be.

# How do you know if a pet will do damage?

Just as you ask tenants for references, you can also ask for pet references. The best way to see how well a pet will behave is to check with previous property owners to see if the tenants had pets and if the pets did any damage. If the tenants cannot provide a pet reference, knowing how the pets behave can be difficult, unless the tenants are willing to show you their current house. Seeing how well the tenants take care of their current residence is not a bad idea...if they will allow you to see it.

I usually adjust rent or the deposit based on the individual situation. The more pets, the more I charge. For a small dog that may do little damage, I may charge $250 more for the deposit and $25 to $50 more per month. For multiple dogs, I may charge a $500 deposit and $50 more per month. All things being equal, I would rather have a tenant without any pets at all.

In my lease, I have clauses that the tenants must adhere to or they can be fined. In the lease, it says that if any pet is found on the property without permission from the property owner, the tenant can be charged $750 per occurrence. That is a hefty fine, and I hope it makes my tenants think twice about having disallowed pets. This clause does not protect against every potential problem. I think checking for pets, or any sign of them, when doing routine inspections is wise. I have a sixth sense for pets because I am allergic to them, especially cats.

I try to avoid tenants with pets, but I don't avoid them at all costs. The biggest factor I look for when renting out a house is how qualified the tenant is. If I have a choice between two equally qualified tenants and one does not have pets, I would obviously prefer the tenant without the pets. If I have one tenant with pets who I think is much more qualified than a tenant who does not have pets, I may go with the more-qualified tenant even though they have a pet. Often, a pet will behave well or badly depending on how well they are trained and how well their owner takes care of them.

# How to write a lease after you rent a property

I am lucky in that my sister is a property manager. I was able to combine her lease with one I found online and customize it for myself. Everything needs to be in writing, including rent, term, late fees, rent due dates, and things the tenant can and cannot do. I do not allow my tenants to:

- Paint without written approval.
- Hang curtain rods without written approval.
- Smoke on the property.
- Have pets on the property.
- Allow anyone not on the lease to live on the property.
- Have overnight visitors for over three consecutive nights.
- Commit illegal activities on the property.

If any of these rules are broken, the lease states that I can fine the tenants $750 per occurrence. If there are any exceptions to these policies, such as pets, I put them in writing using additional provisions.

I have a section that states which utilities the tenants pay. In my case, the tenants pay all utilities.

I have a section that says if the tenants break their lease early, they owe the remainder of the rent due for the entire lease. If I can rent out the house again, I cannot charge the previous tenants for rent as well, but I will charge a one-month rent lease-break fee.

I have many other items in the lease, but I am not an attorney, and I highly suggest you have an attorney review any lease you create.

## Lead-based paint disclosures

I must provide a lead-based paint pamphlet explaining the dangers of lead-based paint with any house built prior to 1978. I have the tenants sign a lead-based paint disclosure as well.

## Deposit on rental properties

I charge one month's rent for the deposit, and it must be paid with the first month's rent before the tenants move in. The only time I split up the rent and deposit is if the tenants want to reserve the house before they move in. They can pay the deposit first and then pay rent when they move in. When the tenant does not have enough money to pay the rent and the deposit, it never works out well. They start out behind and never seem to be able to catch up.

## Carbon monoxide detectors and smoke detectors

Each state has different laws regarding carbon monoxide detectors and smoke alarms. No matter what your state law is, I would put them in. In Colorado, we must have carbon monoxide detectors within 15 feet of every bedroom. They are very cheap for the protection they offer, and you can plug them straight into an outlet.

Colorado enacted this law after a family of five died from carbon monoxide poisoning in a short-term rental property. The furnace had a cracked heat exchange, and the leaking gas killed them while they were sleeping.

## How to find a property manager

Real estate investing is supposed to create passive income, but if you are managing your rental properties, they are not that passive. To create truly passive income, you need to hire a great property manager who can take care of the renting, repairs, accounting, and everything else that comes along with rental properties. After reading what it takes to manage properties yourself, you can see the value a property manager provides. However, you cannot hire just any property manager you find. You need to make sure you hire a manager who will do a great job.

My real estate team manages my properties for me. I pay them 8% of the gross rents, and they take care of the renting, managing, and hassles that come with rentals. It leaves me free to concentrate on buying new properties, which is much more fun.

## My experience with property managers

I helped my sister start her property management company when I was in high school in 1996. Her property management company focused on college rentals because those were her primary investments. She started investing in college rentals at a very young age and has seven college rental properties. That may not seem like many properties, but they all have multiple units (about 20 units) and a lot of cash flow. She managed 120 houses at the peak of her business but scaled down to handle just her own rentals in 2011. She has a doctorate in physics and decided she would prefer to concentrate on teaching and physics projects rather than on property management.

When I worked with my sister, I saw how a good property manager operates, but I have also seen how bad property managers operate. There is a horrible property management company in my town. I can usually spot their houses because the lawns are dead, the roofs are bad, and the houses need paint. I also have dealt with many of their property owners and have seen them rent out houses at 30% below market. You need to take your time when finding a property management company and make sure they will take care of your properties.

I bought my last rental property for $92,000 when I think market value was close to $130,000 at the time I purchased it. Part of the reason it was priced so low was the house was only rented for $700 per month. Based on that $700, the house was worth $92,000. However, when I bought it and made a few minor repairs, I was able to rent it out for $1,100. Based on that $1,100, it was worth well over $130,000. The reason the rent was so low was the previous owner used a horrible property manager who under-rented the place.

## How much does a property manager charge?

Typically, a property management company charges between 8 and 12% of the gross rents received, and some companies charge leasing fees on top of that. A typical leasing fee can run as much as one-month's rent. If you are paying 10% of gross rents and one month's rent for a leasing fee, it can eat into profits very quickly. Most investors should be able to find a decent property management company that does not charge that leasing fee. You do not want to hire a property management company based on their cost. Paying a little more—if you know they will take care of your properties—is better.

The first step is finding potential property management companies. By performing a simple web search, you should be able to find the largest property management companies, but you may also find smaller ones. My real estate office, which has about 30 agents, has three property managers, and none of them advertises except by word of mouth. My suggestion is to always ask your contacts in the area. Ask a Realtor, title company, investor, or anyone else in the area who they recommend.

## Do these things before you interview a property manager

Property managers will promise great service, but how do you know until you actually hire them and see how they perform? Here are some tips to help you find a great management company.

- Check to see how many vacant properties they have listed before you call them. They should have a website or directory that lists the properties they have for rent. When you call them, ask them how many total units they manage. You can then calculate the vacancy rate for that particular company. Check the vacancy rates in your area and see how close the company's vacancy rates are to the region's vacancy rates. A few companies in our area have 10 to 20% vacancy rates, while our regional vacancy rate is less than 2%. Red flag!

- Call the property management company as a potential renter of one of their properties. You will most likely reach someone's voicemail. See how long it takes them to call you back, how knowledgeable they are, and how soon they could show the property. When asking questions about the house, ask simple ones that the manager should know. Ask how old the house is, how many square feet it has, how many parking spaces are included, and what type of heating it has. This will give you a great idea of their knowledge and service level. People would be very surprised by the number of companies that do not call potential renters back.
- Drive by their properties and see how well they are maintained. As an investor, you will be depending on the property management company to maintain—or make sure the tenants are maintaining—the property. If there is a dead lawn in front of every house the company manages, it's not a good sign.
- Check the Better Business Bureau to see if a management company is a member or has had many complaints filed against them. This suggestion can be deceiving because almost every company that does a lot of business is liable to make a couple of people mad. Some people just like to complain, no matter how fairly or unfairly they are treated. The BBB gives companies that have complaints against them a chance to respond and give their side of the story. If a property management company cares, they should at least be responding to complaints to explain how they saw the situation. A company with an abnormally large number of complaints against them may be a bad one.

Eventually, you will need to interview property managers. You should ask many questions, and they will have their own sales pitch to give you as well. Here are some questions once you have narrowed down a few good candidates:

- How many properties/units do they manage?
- What is their specialty? College rental, single-family, multifamily,

commercial?

- How long have they been in business?
- Ask if they are a member in good standing with the BBB. You should have already checked on this, but you can see how their answers compare with your research.
- How many people work for them? This will give you an idea of how much they can handle.
- Do they have a real estate license? Many states, including Colorado, require property managers to have a license.
- What do they charge and are there leasing fees?
- Do they have any monetary agreements or affiliations with the contractors they use? Most states require property managers to disclose any kickbacks they receive from contractors. Many property managers use contractors as an extra source of income by either marking up prices or having ownership.
- Do they own rental properties? What kind? How many? If a property management company manages 100 units and owns 85 of them, whose properties do you think they are going to try to rent out first?
- What type of insurance do they carry? A property manager should have E & O insurance if licensed and general liability insurance at a minimum. The last thing you want is someone getting hurt on one of your properties and suing you because the property manager who screwed up has no insurance and no money.

Do not be surprised if many of the companies you call are not taking new clients. Managing properties takes a lot of work, and many companies do not add new clients. I know my sister would not add new clients for years unless she knew them personally.

## Conclusion

You can manage rental properties yourself, but property managers are usually very affordable. Hiring someone else to deal with the headaches and hassles is well worth it to me. I also end up getting better tenants, and they pay better because the property management companies are better at managing properties than I am.

# 11

# What Are the Different Exit Strategies with Rental Properties?

When I buy my rental properties, I plan to keep them as long as I can. I have no exit strategy and no short-term or long-term goal to cash out. What I want is long-term cash flow. I figure if I buy enough rentals to provide the cash flow that I need every month, I can retire at that point in my life. I doubt I will ever retire because I love what I do, but having the security of knowing I will have as much money as I need for the rest of my life, every month, for as long as I live would be awesome. However, not everyone has the same plan or goals as I do. Some people may want to cash out and sell their rentals at some point. There are many things to consider when selling or planning to sell. Selling a house involves many costs, and there can be some huge tax liabilities as well.

## How much does selling a house cost?

Selling a house can be a fantastic experience if you bought the house below market value, accounted for all the costs, and make a nice profit. Selling a house can also be a disappointing experience if you are forced to sell at a bad time, miscalculate the costs involved, and lose money. Knowing selling costs before you buy will make the experience much more enjoyable. You will most likely have to pay a real estate agent, title insurance, recording fees, closing fees, and possibly much more.

The rough cost to sell a house is 7 to 10% of the selling price. This assumes you don't use an agent. This figure can be quite shocking to many sellers, but if you want to get top dollar for your house, it costs money. In Colorado, where we have no transfer tax, attorneys are rarely involved, and we have minimal title insurance costs. In states like Maryland, selling costs could be thousands more because of their transfer tax and other costs. Make sure you research the costs to sell in your state before you buy.

The biggest cost, by far, is the cost to pay real estate agents. There is no set commission, but HUD pays 6% commission, with 3% going to the selling agent and 3% going to the listing agent. I will use HUD's commission structure as an example, but all real estate commissions are negotiable.

I believe paying a real estate agent to sell your house is necessary. The agent knows the market and is an expert in selling houses. If you do not use an agent, you could underprice or overprice your house, which could easily cost you the amount of money—or more—that an agent charges. An agent also knows the contract and selling process in your state. Trying to figure out pricing, contracts, marketing, showings, negotiations, and inspections on your own could be a nightmare. An agent can help with all of this and make the process easier while getting you the most money for your house.

In most states, it is customary for the seller to pay for title insurance. Title insurance is a guarantee to the buyer that a house has clear title when they buy. The title insurance makes sure all loans are paid off and all liens, judgments, and title defects are taken care of. Getting title insurance when you buy a house is always smart. In Colorado, title insurance costs between $600 and $1,200 depending in the price of the house. This cost can vary by state as some states have different laws regarding title insurance.

Many other fees are involved when you sell a house. The closing company will charge a fee to handle the closing, which can range from $200 to $800 (usually on the lower end). In some states, you must use an attorney to close. Typically, in Colorado, the closing fee is split between the buyer and seller, but that can be negotiated as well.

There are also recording fees for the deed, recording fees for any mortgages that must be released, and wiring fees for loan pay-offs. Also, many banks charge to provide pay-off figures. These fees can range from $50 to $500 depending on the amount of loans and pay-offs there are.

In most cases, when you sell, you pay the taxes and utilities up to the day you close. In Colorado, we have property taxes but usually no transfer taxes or local taxes. Even though your mortgage company may be paying your property taxes through an escrow account, there may be taxes owed at closing. These taxes must be paid at closing before the house is sold, and if the escrow account holds extra money, it will be returned to the seller after closing.

The same can happen on water bills in my area. The water account balance must be brought to zero before a sale can close. The title company will typically escrow a small amount for the water bill so they can pay the final water after closing, and any money not used will be returned to the seller.

Taxes and the water escrow can vary greatly depending on the cost of a house. Colorado property taxes are low: about .05% of the sales price in my county. A water escrow may be $100.

When you live in a neighborhood with an HOA, you must usually pay a monthly fee. The HOA also includes other costs as well as different payment structures. I just sold a house that had an HOA with no monthly HOA payments. The HOA charged .05% of the sales price of every house sold in the neighborhood, and the fee was split between buyer and seller. The sellers were unaware of this policy and were quite surprised at closing.

Most HOAs do not work this way, but many charge transfer fees or status letter fees. These fees can be $20 to $150 or more. The purchase contract determines who pays for these fees.

## What are the total direct costs when you sell a house?

Costs discussed up to this point are direct costs. On a $200,000 house, the costs may be as follows:

Real estate agent commissions: $12,000

Title insurance: $1,000
HOA transfer fees: $150
Recording fees, pay-off fees: $150
Water escrow: $100
Prorated taxes: $750
Closing fee: $200
**Total: $14,350**

Many people are surprised at how high the mortgage pay-off is on a house they are selling. The pay-off on a mortgage is figured to the day of the sale, just as the taxes are. When you receive your mortgage statement, the principal amount listed is calculated just after you made a payment on the loan. The interest increases every day after that principal amount was calculated. A $180,000 loan balance at 5% interest will accrue interest at about $25 per day. If you decide not to pay your last mortgage payment because you are closing on the fifth of the month, 30 days of interest may be included that must be paid when you sell the house. That adds up to $750 dollars and can be a shock to sellers who expected their pay-off to be the same amount as their last mortgage statement principal balance.

In some instances, buyers may need the seller to pay closing costs for them in order to get a loan. Closing costs are common and can range from 2 to 4%. It is very common for the seller to pay 3% of the closing costs for the buyer. In some cases, the price of the house is increased to account for the closing costs, and in other cases, it is not. Closing costs, like the price of a house, are negotiable. Sellers should be aware that many buyers with owner-occupied financing might ask for closing costs, which will decrease the seller's bottom line.

Selling a house costs a lot of money, but remember, the person you bought the house from paid those costs when they sold it to you. If you are planning to use the proceeds from the sale toward the purchase of another house, make sure you calculate the correct amounts so you are not shocked when you get your closing figures! If you are buying a house to flip or plan to sell a rental in a few years, make sure to account for selling costs.

# Why you should always use a real estate agent to sell a house

Real estate agents are expensive, and many sellers think selling a house themselves is a great way to save money. Sellers may save a commission by selling a house themselves, but trying to sell a house without an agent may actually cost them more than the commission they saved. I see people claim to save thousands by selling themselves. They also claim they sold within one day. There is a reason they sold it in one day: they left a lot of money on the table! A great real estate agent could have more than made up for the commission they charged by pricing a house correctly and working in the best interests of the seller.

Real estate agents are marketing and sales-process experts, and they know how to value a house. Agents are not paid just for the time they spend selling your house. They are paid for all the licensing courses and continuing education they must take. They're paid for their marketing experience and for getting the seller the most money possible.

## You may not save as much as you think when you sell a house yourself

When you try to sell a house yourself, it may appear you can save 5, 6, or even 7% of the sales price by not paying a commission (all commissions are negotiable). However, most buyers work with real estate agents when they are looking for a house (the seller pays for the buyer's agent, so using one make sense). If you are not going to pay a commission to the real estate agent representing the buyer, you have eliminated most of the buyers in your market. Eliminating most buyers will definitely decrease your selling price and cost you money. If you do agree to pay a cooperating broker, you are only saving half of a commission. Additionally, the buyer is represented by a real estate agent, and you are not. Who will have the upper hand in negotiations? The buyer's agent will have the buyer's best interest in mind...not yours.

The best opportunity to sell a house is when it first comes on the market, especially in a seller's market such as the one we have now. Buyers are waiting for the perfect home to come up for sale, and pricing a house correctly from the beginning is vital.

- FSBOs (for-sale-by-owners) accounted for 8% of house sales in 2015. The typical FSBO house sold for $185,000 compared to $240,000 for agent-assisted house sales.

That stat is from http://www.realtor.org/.

The reason FSBOs sell for so much less money is most sellers do not know what they are doing.

## Why will overpricing a house cost the seller money?

If an overpriced house comes up for sale, a buyer may not even look at it. An overpriced house may sit on the market for weeks or even months until the price is reduced. When buyers see a house has been on the market for an extended period, they start to wonder what is wrong with it. Even if the price is dropped to the right value after a few weeks, the house still may not sell for what it would have if it had been valued correctly to begin with. Houses become stigmatized the longer they sit on the market. For an investor or homeowner that no longer lives in the house, a stigmatized listing is very bad. Every month a house sits vacant costs the seller money, and if there is a loan on the house, it can cost the seller thousands of dollars per month. If the seller had priced the house correctly to begin with, they would have sold it quickly and saved thousands of dollars.

## How will underpricing a house cost a seller money?

Underpricing a house can cost just as much as overpricing one. When you underprice a house, you will most likely sell it very quickly, but there is a good chance you will sell it for less than it is worth. It is true that underpricing a house can stir up a lot of activity and produce multiple offers. You may even get offers above list price, but the problem with a low asking prices is they attract buyers who want a great deal (like me). Often, a multiple-offer situation will actually scare away some buyers. Some buyers do not want to get into a bidding war and will not make an offer on a house that has multiple offers.

If you underprice a house and get an offer above asking price, you could have gotten an even higher offer had you priced the house correctly. Most buyers will base their offer on the list price and not on what the house is actually worth. Buyers always tell me that they offered $10,000 over asking price and still did not get the house! They are basing their offer on the list price, assuming the seller is asking fair market value. They are not basing their offer on what the house may actually be worth. Another downside to an offer that is well above asking price is that it may give an appraiser a reason to come in at a low value. If an appraisal comes in low, it could cost the seller even more money! By pricing the house correctly to begin with, you will usually sell it for the most money.

If you sell to a buyer who is getting a loan, they will most likely need a completed appraisal. The bank will loan money to the buyer based on that appraisal, and if the appraisal comes in low, there is a good chance the buyer will need to reduce the price of the house. With rising house prices, we see appraisals come in low all the time, but there are ways to deal with appraisers. A real estate agent knows how to be proactive to help the appraiser and knows how to challenge an appraisal if it comes in low.

## Why is valuing a house difficult without a real estate agent?

Valuing a property is the most important aspect of selling a house. Without MLS access, getting information on recently sold properties is very hard. Recently sold properties are the most important piece of information needed to value a house. People have access to active listings through websites like Zillow, but only licensed agents have access to the MLS, which lists sold houses. Active listings can give an idea of house values, but you have no idea if houses are overpriced or for what price they will actually sell.

Every house is different because every house has different features. Plus, location affects value. A real estate agent is an expert at determining value based on these characteristics. Understanding local markets can take years, and those markets can change extremely fast. It is tough for an agent to determine value correctly; it is much more difficult for someone who is not an agent.

Many people use Zillow values since Zillow provides a Zestimate for house values. Zillow was off by as much as 40% on one of my properties! You should never value a house based solely on a Zestimate.

There is an art to marketing and pricing a house correctly. You cannot just stick a house on the MLS and wait for offers to come in. A real estate agent knows how to take the best pictures, do virtual tours, create the best brochures, which websites to use, which magazines and newspapers to advertise in, and much more. Agents also know many people. Often, an agent will have buyers waiting for a house just like yours.

## Why a seller should not use a low-fee service to enter a house in the MLS?

Many companies offer a low-fee MLS service, which allows you to pay a couple hundred dollars to get your house entered in the MLS. There are many problems with using this type of service:

- The service may never see your house and may enter incorrect information without pictures.
- The seller must still take calls and set up showings with many of these services.
- You must pay the buyer's agent and pay for the MLS listing, so are you really saving much money?
- You still have all the disadvantages of not having an agent represent you while the buyer is represented.
- You get no help with contracts, negotiations, inspections, appraisals, etc.

· Limited-service listings are not legal in all states, including Colorado.

In Colorado, the state contract is 17 pages long, which doesn't include the four addendums and disclosures that must be completed. California contracts are much longer. A real estate agent knows exactly what to look for in a state contract. They know what is customary for the seller to pay and what is customary for the buyer to pay. In Colorado, it is customary for the seller to pay for title insurance, with many other costs split between the buyer and the seller. If you do not have an agent to guide you through this, you could easily pay much more in costs than you should.

A real estate agent knows the market, and they know people in the business. They can help a seller find a title company with the lowest fees and best service. They can help the seller find the best contractor if repairs are needed before listing or after an inspection.

Using an agent to sell a house instead of selling it yourself is always better. An agent will make you more money by pricing, marketing, and negotiating correctly. The agent works for you! The money they make you will more than make up for the commissions they charge. I know many investors who have their real estate license, and they still use another real estate agent to sell their house for them. Those investors know that another agent has the time and the market expertise to sell the house. Before you try to sell a house on your own, consider whether it is worth the time it will take to understand the process—and if you will actually save any money.

## How does a 1031 exchange work?

Rental properties offer many great benefits, including favorable tax benefits. Not only can you depreciate rental properties to save on taxes, but you can also use a 1031 exchange to defer the taxes on any profit you make or on recaptured depreciation. A 1031 exchange has many rules and regulations, and you must make sure you complete the exchange correctly to avoid a large tax bill. *I am not an accountant or an attorney. Please consult your attorney or accountant for any tax or legal advice.*

A 1031 exchange is a real estate transaction that involves two like properties, one being sold and one being bought within a certain period. There are
many restrictions on a 1031 exchange, and the IRS is not perfectly clear when
describing the restrictions. Some basic principles are that the properties
must be held at least a year, must be used for business, and the replacement
property must be identified within 45 days and bought within 180 days. If
all these requirements (and a few others) are met, a rental property can be
sold without paying any taxes on the profit or recaptured depreciation.

When you sell a rental property, you must pay taxes on any profit you
make. You also may have to pay recaptured depreciation. The IRS allows
you to depreciate a rental property because the structure has a limited life
span and decreases in value every year. You can deduct that depreciated
amount from your taxes every year, which is a huge advantage. However,
if you sell a property for more than the depreciated amount, it shows that
the structure did not decrease in value, and you will have to pay back those
taxes you saved.

If you have owned a rental property for several years, the recaptured
depreciation can add up to thousands of dollars. Luckily, the 1031 exchange
allows you to move the profit and recaptured depreciation into another
similar property without paying taxes.

## What properties can be used in a 1031 exchange?

The IRS has determined that many forms of real estate can be used for
a 1031 exchange. Any property used for a business, which includes a
store, manufacturing facility, or office building, can be used. Investment
properties, including rentals, can also be used for a 1031 exchange. It has
even been determined that water rights and mineral rights qualify for a 1031
exchange.

These things cannot be used for a 1031 exchange:

- Stock in trade or other property held primarily for sale
- Stocks, bonds, or notes

- Other securities or evidence of indebtedness or interest
- Interests in a partnership
- Certificates of trust or beneficial interests
- Choses in action (a right to something, such as payment of a debt or damages for injury, that can be recovered in a lawsuit)

## Can you use fix-and-flips for a 1031 exchange?

The IRS has determined fix-and-flips cannot be used for a 1031 exchange unless you meet certain guidelines. The IRS does not want real estate investors who fix and flip constantly to be able to use a 1031 exchange to defer taxes. If you only fix and flip occasionally and meet the guidelines, you may be able to use a 1031 exchange.

- The flip must be rented out for at least one year after it is repaired.
- The house cannot be sold until after it has been rented out at least one year and should not be listed before being rented out for a year.

The problem with this strategy is the IRS does not say you must hold a flip one year to do an exchange. The IRS simply says a flip needs to be held for an acceptable amount of time, and it is up to the accountant and investor to determine if their transaction qualifies. Some people have determined that to be one year, but if the IRS thinks you are a professional house flipper trying to cheat them out of money, you still may get in trouble.

## How do you complete a 1031 exchange?

When completing a 1031 exchange, the investor must use a qualified inter-mediary to oversee the transaction. The IRS does not tell you who can be an intermediary, only that these people cannot be one:

- The TP's (the person completing the exchange) attorney
- The TP's CPA

- The TP's real estate agent
- Any relative of the TP
- Any employee of the TP
- Any business associate of the TP

The intermediary holds the funds after one property is sold in the 1031 exchange and uses that money to buy the new replacement property. When doing a 1031 exchange, the owner must identify the property being exchanged and declare it before the sale. Once the subject property is sold, the investor has 45 days to identify a new property to exchange with the old property. Once the new property is identified, the investor has 180 days to close on the new property.

To avoid paying taxes in a 1031 exchange, the investor must use all the cash from the sale of one property to buy the new property, and the new property must cost at least as much as the sales price of the old property. If the investor does not use all the cash from the sale of the old property, or if the investor buys a less-expensive property, they may have to pay taxes on the unused cash or price difference in the properties.

In a 1031 exchange, the investor must take title to the new property in the same name as used on the property being replaced.

You cannot use a 1031 exchange to sell property to someone you are related to.

You can sell one property and buy multiple new properties in an exchange.

## What is a Reverse 1031 exchange?

Most investors will sell a property they own and then purchase a replacement property. It is possible to buy the replacement property and then sell the original property. This can be a difficult maneuver because the investor will not have the cash from the sale of the original property to buy the new property.

It may make sense for an investor who is building a replacement property to do an exchange. Since it may take more than 180 days to build and buy a property, an investor might do a reverse exchange for large companies, exchanging manufacturing facilities, or other unique buildings that must be built to spec and are not available on the market.

## Can you refinance a property after doing a 1031 exchange?

One way to get the cash out of a rental property you exchange into is to refinance the replacement property. You may have $100,000 in cash proceeds from a rental property you are exchanging. That money can be used to buy a replacement property in a 1031 exchange, but that is a lot of money to have locked up. If you refinance the property after buying it, you can take out some of that cash without paying taxes on it. The government does not consider money from a refinance to be profit.

It is also possible to complete a 1031 exchange into a personal residence and then eliminate the taxes altogether. Exchange a property into a house that you would like to live in at some point. The replacement house must be rented out for at least one year after the exchange is completed. Once that year is up, move into the replacement house and live there for at least two years. Since you are using the house for your personal residence for at least two out of five years, when you sell the house, your profit could be tax free! *There are some restrictions; please talk to your accountant! I have heard that the tax law has been modified to change this rule, so you may be liable for some taxes using this strategy.*

You must adhere to many intricacies and details in the IRS tax code when completing a 1031 exchange. Talk to an accountant or attorney to make sure you are following all the guidelines.

## Should you pay off your mortgages early?

Many financial experts recommend paying off your house as quickly as possible to reduce debt, but I do not always agree with this strategy. Debt is not a bad thing if you use debt to invest and make more money than the debt costs you. Debt can allow investors and businesses to create greater returns on their investments than paying all cash.

We already talked about how leveraging your money to buy rental properties gives you higher returns than paying cash. Rental properties also generate much better returns than most consumer debt, including car loans. I feel that as long as my returns on my investments are greater than the debt used to fund those investments, it is good debt. I am a very aggressive investor, and this strategy may not work well for everyone.

## Should you pay off the mortgage on your personal residence?

Most people are able to get a very low interest rate and put little money down on their personal residence. Interest rates are currently below 5% on an owner-occupied, 30-year, fixed-rate loan. This is cheap money! If you can find an investment that gives you a better return than 5%, investing that money and not paying your mortgage off early may make sense.

Paying off my house quickly when I have such a low rate locked in for 30 years and am making so much money on my rental properties doesn't make sense. I pay the absolute minimum payment I can on my personal mortgage and save that money to buy more rental properties. If you have nowhere else to put your money besides a CD or bank account that pays less than 1% interest, paying your mortgage off early may make sense. If you are willing to work a little harder and find an investment with a better return than your mortgage, stop paying extra towards your house payments, and invest that money!

## Should you pay off car loans early or invest the extra money?

Experts will also tell you how horrible it is to have a car loan. Their reasoning is that debt on any item that will depreciate is bad, but I completely disagree with this as well. I look at it as a numbers game. Why would I care what my debt is secured against as long as the debt allows me to buy more rental properties? Rental properties give a higher rate of return than the auto loan interest rate. My current car loans are locked in for six years at less than 3%

interest. I do not pay one cent extra on them because I want as much cash as possible to buy more rental properties. I am not advocating purchasing the most expensive car you can because you still want to save as much as possible to invest with. If you have the cash available to buy a car, why not finance the car instead and invest that cash in something else?

## What about the security of paying off my mortgage early

Do not get me wrong—I am not condoning racking up debt to go on vacation or buy furniture. A lot of debt can be very, very destructive if you have no assets providing you cash flow or a return on that debt. People will still ask, "What happens if I lose my job, and I have all this debt I cannot pay off?" I think you are going to be better off with cash–producing properties than if you had paid off your primary house.

Let us assume you have a $200,000 house and owe $180,000 on the mortgage. If you put all your extra cash into the mortgage to pay it off early, you would eliminate your mortgage payment and save about $900 in principal and interest every month. We will assume you paid about $150,000 extra into your mortgage to pay it off early. I could buy five rental properties with that cash. Each property would cash flow at least $500 per month. I am making $2,500 per month off those rentals, which is a lot more than the $900 I would be saving on my mortgage.

Not only am I making more money each month with rentals, but I'm also earning an immediate return on my investment. I start making money every month as soon as the properties are rented out. If you accelerate your mortgage pay off, you will not see that $900 savings until the mortgage is completely paid off. With rental properties, I start seeing immediate cash flow as soon as I rent out the first property.

If you are choosing the accelerated mortgage payoff route and lose your income before your house is paid off, you still must make the same mortgage payment. The only way to get that money back is to sell your house or refinance. You may not be able to refinance with no income, and your only option may be to sell. If you lose your job and you have rental properties, you still have income from the rentals. You could sell a rental property to get immediate cash, and refinancing a property would be much easier because you are still showing some income from the rentals.

On the surface, it may seem like paying off your mortgage faster will offer more security, but there is actually a better chance of making it through rough times if you have income-producing rental properties. I know I would rather sell off a rental property in bad times than my personal house.

One of InvestFourMore's readers recently paid off her mortgage and decided to retire early and focus her time on investing in real estate. Saving and diverting her money towards her mortgage took a great deal of work, and it felt great when it was finally paid off. Now that she is actively investing in real estate, she wanted to tap into the huge amount of equity in her house. Since she has no job and very little income at this point, she cannot find a bank to refinance her house. Even though she did what the experts told her to do and worked hard to pay off her mortgage, she cannot access that money unless she sells her house. This is another reason to think twice before you start sinking all your extra money into your principal residence. If she had bought more rental properties with that money instead of paying off her mortgage, the bank may have been willing to loan to her because of all the rental income coming in.

Investing your money in real estate instead of paying off your debt will leave you thousands and thousands of dollars ahead. Just because the experts tell you to do it, does not mean paying your mortgage off early makes sense. Think about where you are putting your money and what kind of returns you are getting.

## Should you pay off your mortgages early on rental properties?

I used my cash flow from all my rentals to pay off the mortgage on my first rental. This is often called the snowball method and is a great way to pay off debt. The snowball method involves taking cash flow from all my rentals and paying down one mortgage at a time. When one mortgage is paid off, I apply the cash flow from all my properties to another mortgage...and so on. Using this strategy, I paid off my first rental property about three years after I bought it. Paying off that house was awesome, but for some people, it may make more sense to save the cash flow from rental properties and avoid paying off their mortgages early.

If you are just starting to buy rental properties or your cash is very tight, save your cash flow instead of paying off properties. You must consider many factors when deciding whether to pay off loans or save the cash flow. The amount of cash you have, your goals, how long you want to invest, interest rates, and returns all play a role.

## Why I previously used the snowball method to pay off my rental properties

I was using the snowball method when I first started investing because I wanted to pay off my ARMs before they had a chance to change to a higher rate. But I realized I would be ahead if I bought as many rentals as I could without paying any off. I am okay with a higher interest rate if my ARM rates go up because I can handle the higher payments, and I make much more money buying new rentals than I do by paying off debt.

Another reason I used the snowball method is I do not know if my portfolio lender will always finance as many rental properties as I want. Getting more than ten loans with a conventional lender is very difficult, and the fewer mortgages I have, the more properties I could buy if my portfolio lender changes their policies. In fact, once I hit $2.5 million in loans with them, getting loans with my portfolio lender got even tougher.

Even though I changed my strategy regarding paying rentals off early, I am still glad I did it. One key to being a successful real estate investor is having cash available for purchases or repairs. Having a paid off property allowed me to get a line of credit from a bank. I can use that money when I need it and pay it back when I do not need it. Banks like to loan to investors who have debt-free properties and are happy to give a line of credit on those properties. The more properties an investor has paid off, the more stable they look to banks.

If you are in a situation where you need more money to buy rental properties, the snowball method might not be the right strategy. It works best when you have multiple properties, have a lot of incoming cash flow, and are not aggressively buying new properties. If you cannot save enough money to buy multiple rentals, saving your cash flow instead of paying off the mortgage may be smarter.

## Why you shouldn't pay off 30-year fixed rate loans.

If you are buying your first rental property, there is a good chance you will be able to get a 30-year fixed-rate mortgage. You will not have to worry about interest rates rising in the future because the interest rate is locked in for 30 years. You can use that money to buy more properties.

If you are just beginning to invest in rental properties, you may not be concerned about financing more than ten rentals. Most likely, you are focused on buying one, two, or three properties. After you buy multiple properties and decide you like having rental properties, you can think about a larger portfolio. If you only have a few rental properties, it could be too early to decide whether paying off mortgages is the right move. I like to err on the side of caution and have plenty of cash available. If you are not sure whether paying off loans is right for you, don't pay them off. Hold the cash. You can always pay down debt later, but you cannot get money back from the bank after you pay loans down.

The biggest issue most people run into when buying rental properties is having enough cash for down payments. Saving enough money for your first rental property can take a long time. Buying another rental property will be easier if you save your cash flow for future down payments. You will also need to have extra cash for emergencies and expenses on your rental properties.

# 12

# How to Buy Rentals in an Expensive Market

Housing prices have increased in many areas of the country over the last few years. In my market, prices have increased 50 to 100% in the last five years. Buying rental properties has been much more difficult for me, but I have found good deals, even in an appreciating market. The key is always getting a great deal and making sure you can still cash flow in that market. Buying rentals in some areas may not make sense.

With housing prices rising, cash flowing on properties gets more difficult. Rents usually do not rise as high as housing prices. I bought houses costing from $80,000 to $120,000 in 2010 to 2013. Now I cannot find any decent houses for less than $150,000. I must face the reality that, if I want to keep buying rental properties in my market, I will have to pay more money for them or find different ways to buy them. Even when I find great deals, it is still tough to cash flow.

When I start, finding houses that would produce 20% cash-on-cash return was easy. Now, I am lucky to find anything that will return 15%. I have gone from buying $80,000 to $100,000 houses to buying $120,000 to $160,000 ones. Although rents have increased, they have not gone up nearly as much as housing prices have.

## How to buy rentals when housing prices are high

Sometimes, I go months without seeing a good deal in my market, especially for a rental (it is actually easier for me to find flips). If I cannot find cash-flowing rental properties in my area, I do not buy just to buy. Buying and hoping for appreciation while losing money every month is a bad idea.

I know I can still get great deals in my area. I have multiple flips going, and I purchased five rentals in 2015. Many markets are harder to cash flow in than my market, and many people are not in the business as I am. If you cannot dedicate the amount of time that I do to finding great deals, or if prices are even higher compared to rents in your area, you may have to look in another state. You could also consider buying rental properties in a slightly larger geographical area. I have looked in areas within a 45-mile radius, but my town seems to have the best rent-to-value ratios.

When prices get higher, you must look at the numbers. Are you making enough money to justify the risk versus the reward? Are you buying for cash flow and not appreciation? Are you getting a great deal? If you can satisfy all these requirements, it may make sense to keep buying, even as prices increase. If you get to a point where you cannot cash flow, it might be time to reevaluate your strategy.

## Should you sell your rentals when prices increase?

Colorado has had one of the highest appreciating markets in the country, and it is expected to keep going up. An incredibly hot real estate market is great for some, but it creates many questions for investors. My properties keep going up in value, which has been great for my net worth, but it makes it harder to cash flow. With prices increasing so much, I wonder if the market can sustain high prices. Would it be smart to sell my properties and reinvest the money?

## How much has the Colorado real estate market increased?

Five years ago, the median house price in my area was around $120,000. In 2016, the median price was $260,000, and prices continue to rise. Zillow has shown that Colorado has had the highest-appreciating market in the country for the last 13 months. Colorado has one of the fastest growing populations in the country and not enough houses for everyone.

In Northern Colorado, oil and gas have caused a huge boost in our economy, and many had predicted that our market would slow down with lower oil prices, but it has not. I cannot predict whether our market will keep increasing, stay the same, or go down, but my gut tells me it will stay strong for the immediate future. The thought has crossed my mind to sell my properties and use the cash to buy more properties, either in my area or in a different market.

## How have rent-to-value ranges changed in Colorado?

When I bought houses from $80,000 to $120,000 and made $5,000 to $15,000 in repairs, I would rent them out for $1,100 to $1,300 per month. Now, I can buy houses for $150,000, make $10,000 to $20,000 in repairs, and rent them out for $1,500 to $1,600 per month. With those numbers, I would be looking for amazing deals, not just buying whatever is available. Prices have increased much more than rents have, which makes it harder to make money as an investor. Both these price points assume I am getting a great deal on the house. I would have to work hard to find a $150,000 house that would rent out for $1,500 or $1,600, even if it needs work.

With prices increasing so much, there is also the risk that prices or rents could drop. I do not think prices will drop anytime soon, but when prices increase that much, it makes me a little nervous. I would be fine with my current rentals if prices dropped, but if I stretched my criteria to buy more rentals at even higher prices, I might be asking for trouble.

## How much have my rental houses increased in value?

I bought my first rental property in December 2010. I made money through appreciation, and I increased the value of my properties when I first bought them by buying them below market. Here is a list of my rentals showing the approximate amount I spent on repairs and how much they are currently worth.

| Rental Property | Price Paid | Repairs Made | Value in 2016 | Value at Purchase |
|---|---|---|---|---|
| 12/2010 | $97,000 | $2,000 | $215,000 | $130,000 |
| 10/2011 | $94,000 | $15,000 | $210,000 | $140,000 |
| 11/2011 | $92,000 | $14,000 | $205,000 | $135,000 |
| 01/2012 | $109,000 | $14,000 | $225,000 | $150,000 |
| 12/2012 | $88,000 | $18,000 | $200,000 | $130,000 |
| 03/2013 | $115,000 | $15,000 | $205,000 | $150,000 |
| 07/2013 | $113,000 | $9,000 | $220,000 | $140,000 |
| 11/2013 | $97,500 | $15,000 | $195,000 | $140,000 |
| 03/2014 | $133,000 | $4,000 | $185,000 | $155,000 |
| 02/2014 | $100,000 | $3,500 | $165,000 | $125,000 |
| 07/2014 | $109,000 | $16,000 | $190,000 | $145,000 |
| 03/2015 | $133,000 | $15,000 | $205,000 | $185,000 |
| 06/2015 | $120,000 | $1,000 | $185,000 | $140,000 |
| 07/2015 | $134,000 | $15,000 | $195,000 | $175,000 |
| 08/2015 | $45,000 | $0 | $45,000 | $45,000 |
| 09/2015 | $92,000 | $5,000 | $155,000 | $135,000 |
| Totals | $1,671,500 | $161,500 | $3,000,000 | $2,220,000 |

If you subtract the purchase price and repair cost from what my houses are worth now, I have gained $1,167,000. That is a lot of money to gain from buying properties over the last five or six years. That number does not quite tell the whole story if I were to decide to cash out my rentals.

## How much money would I make if I sold my rental properties?

If I sold my rentals, I would not get to keep the entire sale price. I would have to pay selling costs and taxes on the profit. The nice part about rental properties is that you only pay long-term capital gains tax when you sell them if you own them long enough (long-term capital gains is less than ordinary income.) However, I would also have to pay taxes on any depreciation I recapture when I sell the houses.

If I sell the houses, I would have to pay another agent to represent the buyer, but I could list them myself. There would be closing costs, and I would want to market the properties as vacant to get the most money from them (since they are single-family properties). I would have to wait until the leases are up, put the house up for sale after the tenants move out, and make any repairs at that time. To account for selling costs, vacancies, and repairs, I will assume it will take 8% of the selling price.

- 8% of the selling price: $240,000
- Profit: $927,000
- 20% of profit for capital gains tax: $185,400
- Estimated depreciation recapture: $100,000
- **Total profit after taxes: $641,600**

I have refinanced seven properties over the last four years, which has given me much more money to invest. Refinancing also increased the amount of money I owe on some of my properties. I paid off my first rental property, which reduced how much I owe. Right now, I owe the bank $1,383,000 on my 16 rental properties. I would actually get back about $926,600 in cash after paying taxes. The cash I would get is different from my profit because I provided down payments when I bought the properties.

That is a great deal of cash to get back from my rental properties, but that does not mean selling them all is worth it.

## How much money do my rental properties generate now?

At the time I completed these calculations, my rentals were cash flowing about $8,000 per month or $96,000 per year. Including repairs and down payments, I have spent about $495,000 on my houses. That does not include any carrying costs or closing costs, but often, I have the seller pay closing costs, and as a real estate agent, I also make a commission. I am going to assume the closing costs and commissions cancel each other out. I also refinanced seven of my properties, which gave me about $320,000 in cash back. Overall, I have spent about $175,000 of my cash to buy my rentals. The $96,000 per year I cash flow is about a 55% return on the money.

55% is an awesome return on my investment, but I need to look at the cash I would have available—not the cash I already invested—in order to make a decision about selling. $96,000 per year divided by the $926,000 in cash I could take out of the rentals would equal a return of about a 10%. I know I can make more than 10% by buying new properties below market value, fixing them up, and renting them out. However, is it worth all the hassle to sell my houses, and is it wise to do in this market?

## How many houses could I buy with $926,000?

If I sold all my properties and bought new ones, I could buy many more than 16 properties. Historically, it has cost me about $32,000 to buy a house, fix it up, and rent it out (assuming 20% down). In theory, I could buy 28 houses with that money. The problem with that theory is houses are more expensive, and finding great deals is much harder than it was three years ago. I would probably have to spend $40,000 to $50,000 per house now, which would mean I could buy only 18 houses in my market.

If I sold out, I would have a hard time finding 18 houses that would be great deals at the same time. I would also have a hard time finding properties in this market that would cash flow as well as mine do. There is the risk of the market declining, and I would be stuck with 18 houses with much higher loan amounts than I have now.

## What if I were to cash out my rental properties and buy in another market?

In 2015, I bought a turn-key rental with my self-directed IRA. I have thought about investing in other areas of the country where I may be able to buy below market value, repair, and rent the properties.

Here are the issues I have with buying out-of-state:

- I would need time to research and visit an area, in addition to finding a good agent, contractor, and property manager.
- I am only an agent in Colorado and would not be paid a commission.
- I would not know the area as well. The farther away I am, the less I would be able keep track of my properties.
- I would have to find new financing, as my portfolio lender will not loan in most states.

With all these negatives, I have previously thought buying out of state wasn't worth it. However, with our market continuing to increase, finding great rentals gets harder and harder. I am seriously thinking about buying more rentals in another state.

**If I bought out of state, I could use the cash I have now to invest, or I could exchange properties.** A 1031 exchange can be used to sell my properties and buy new proprieties tax free. This would save me $200,000 in taxes, which would let me buy five more houses. Again, I would run into the problem of finding enough great deals to replace my current houses, and I would have to find them quickly with a 1031 exchange. If I were to sell out, I think using a 1031 exchange would be the best way to reinvest my money, but I do not think it is worth all the hassle and risk.

I suppose I could sell out and use the money to buy a couple of exotic cars, but that would not be the wisest decision! I also would have a hard time reaching my goal of purchasing 100 rental proprieties.

I considered selling my rentals because our market is going so crazy. However, if I sold my rentals and bought new properties in the same area, I would have higher loans and more risk if our market declined. Selling all my properties to buy in a different location isn't worth it, but it might be worth starting to invest in a new location. Selling a couple of my properties and using that money to buy more in a new location might also make sense.

## How to buy rental properties in another market

Since prices are high in my area and there is little cash flow, I am considering buying in other states. Real estate investors have a couple of options when buying out of state. You can buy turn-key properties that are already repaired, rented, and managed, or you can buy properties that are below market value, get them repaired yourself, and find a property manager. Turn-key properties involve much less hassle and work, but the returns are not as good. When you find the great deals yourself and find a contractor and property manager, the returns are usually much greater.

One of the most important factors when investing in real estate is buying properties below market value. If you can buy a house at 20% below market value, you have built-in equity, and cash flowing is much easier. One of the disadvantages of investing in turn-key properties is that they have been purchased by investors, repaired, rented out, and property management is already in place. These features are great, but they come at a price. They are not going to be priced well below market value.

## Is investing in rental properties in another market worth it?

In the past, I have not seriously considered investing in another market because I was able to get good returns in Colorado. However, in 2015, I bought a turn-key rental in Ohio with my IRA as an experiment to see how it would work. If I were to invest out-of-state again, I would buy houses below market, repair the property, and find a property manager myself. The main reason I have not seriously considered buying out of the area is because it would take a lot of work, and I already have a lot going on. If the deals were just slightly better in other states than what I could get here, I would not invest somewhere else.

Here are some advantages of investing locally:

- I have my real estate license in Colorado. It can only be used in Colorado, and it saves me a lot of money when investing.
- I have many contractor, lender, and investor contacts in the area.
- I know my market very well, which is very important when investing.
- I can have my team manage my rentals, and I can keep a close eye on them.

Investing locally offers huge advantages, but if I am not making money on local rental properties, it does not make sense to keep buying here. I know there are other markets throughout the country that have much better rent-to-value ratios.

## How do you start looking for rental property locations?

I have a huge advantage when researching locations for rental properties. I run InvestFourMore.com, which gives me access to thousands of people investing all over the country. I talk to many investors in my podcasts and in my coaching programs. People also email me. I have a long list of areas across the country that offer better cash flow than Colorado. Florida, upstate New York, the Midwest, Milwaukee, Baltimore, and many other places have much better rent-to-price ratios.

There are steps you can take to narrow your search criteria when looking for a new place to invest:

- Before you start looking out of your own state, increase the geographical area in which you search for rentals. Driving only a couple of hours to find a good location to invest in, rather than looking three states away, is more appealing. You would probably be more familiar with the area as well.
- If you cannot find a close location, start looking in areas you're familiar

with. Did you grow up somewhere different from where you live now? Do you have friends or family in a different area of the country? The more familiar you are with an area, the easier it will be to learn the market and find good deals. If you have family or friends in an area, they can help you learn a market and keep an eye on your properties.

· If you cannot find a suitable location where you know someone, where would you like to spend time researching a market? I think you must visit any area you want to invest in, and it helps if you have a little fun while you do it (going to the beach, mountains, etc.).

· Check out publications for the best rental property locations. Many sites will show you the best rent-to-value ratios. Do not blindly accept the lists of the best places to invest. Many of these lists ignore things like cash flow, taxes, and other factors that make a good rental property. The lists only focus on economic factors, which may not be an indication of good rental property ratios.

## How do you know if an area will be good for rental properties?

Once you have found a few places to research, you need to know if you can make money in those areas. You also need to know if the economy is stable. Some areas may have great numbers but a decreasing population and a shaky economy.

· Is the population increasing or decreasing? A rising population is a good thing and is a major factor for economic growth.

· Have housing prices been increasing or decreasing? If housing prices are decreasing, it is not the end of the world. It might mean opportunity. If housing prices are decreasing and population is decreasing, the area may be in trouble. If housing prices are increasing sharply, getting a good deal that cash flows may be difficult.

· What risks are there? Is the area susceptible to floods, natural disasters, economic downturns, or wild swings in housing prices? These risks can be overcome, but make sure you know what you are getting into. Houses close to the ocean or in flood plains will have very expensive insurance.

- What are the property taxes? In Colorado, we have low property taxes. Some of my properties have taxes of less than $500 per year. Other states have taxes ten times that or more! What may look like an awesome cash-flowing property quickly becomes a bad deal once you factor in the high taxes.
- How tenant-friendly is the state? In some states, like Illinois, completing an eviction can be very tough. In other states, like Texas, evictions are extremely easy.

There are other factors to consider when deciding where to invest, such as crime rates, vacancies, and price points. To truly learn about an area, you need to visit, talk to agents and property managers, and if possible, other investors in the area.

## How do you overcome the disadvantages of investing out of state?

I mentioned the advantages of investing locally. So how do I overcome the disadvantages when investing in another area?

- I can get a real estate license in another state. It may take some time, and I might have to pass another test, but I can do it. I would have to find a broker to hang my license with, but I could find a low-cost broker to do that.
- I know many people across the country that have contacts that could help me. I also know how to find a portfolio lender, and I believe I could find one in any market.
- I could learn a new market. It would take time and effort, but I could do it. I could also use my contacts to help me learn markets faster.
- I would have to take the time to find a great property manager. However, I do not have to rely on them to watch my properties for me. I could hire a third party to take pictures of my properties, make sure they are rented

out, and even value properties for me (BPOs).

- I have a huge advantage when investing out of my area because of the people I have met and know. However, many investors on this site and on other sites are happy to share their knowledge. I also share many of my contacts and resources with people in my coaching programs.

## How to find a team for out-of-state investing

Buying, repairing, and managing houses yourself in another state is virtually impossible. In the end, using local professionals who know the market will save you money. You will need a great team to handle buying and renting a long-distance property for you.

- **Real estate agents:** A great real estate agent can help you find great deals and help you find the rest of your team. A key to getting great deals is being able to act quickly. You must be able to trust your real estate agent enough to make an offer for you sight unseen. Investors do not have time to fly out to see a good deal or plan a trip and hope that a good deal pops up while they are in town. I sometimes have to wait months to find a great deal, and if I waited three days or a week to make an offer, that deal would be gone.
- **Property managers:** You must have a property manager who will look out for your rental and rent it out for you. A bad property manager can cost thousands and thousands of dollars, while a good one will make you thousands and thousands of dollars. A great Realtor should be able to help you find a good property manager. Hopefully, this book can also help you find one.
- **Contractors:** This is probably the trickiest part of building your team. Contractors can be great or horrible and can change from great to horrible very quickly. We are constantly hiring new contractors. You must be able to depend on your team to help you find a great contractor. Agents and property managers should know local contractors to whom they can refer you. You should not have to pay in advance for work

done. Always keep in constant touch with your contractors. Always get a written bid from any contractor before they start any work.

Many different areas across the country offer great cash-flowing opportunities. If you do not happen to live in one of those places, it does not mean you cannot invest in real estate. Investing out of state may take more work, but it is possible. I think exploring new markets and finding new places to invest will be fun. If you have questions about investing out of your area or questions about which areas are good, you can always send me an email at mark@investfourmore.com.

## How to invest in turn-key rental properties

Turn-key rentals are fully repaired, rented out, and managed by a property manager. Turn-key properties allow a long-distance investor to buy a cash-flowing property with minimal work.

Some consider a turn-key property to be a house that is remodeled and needs no repairs, but it may not be rented. I consider turn-key to mean the house needs no repairs, has a tenant in place, and has property management in place. Make sure you have the same definition of turn-key properties as whomever you are talking with does! If you are investing in an out-of-state turn-key property, make sure it is already rented and has property management in place.

Here are a few advantages of buying turn-key rentals:

- **Easy to find:** You can buy a turn-key property very quickly from a turn-key provider who has many properties available for purchase. Turn-key companies can have a large inventory because the properties are providing cash flow and making them money while they own them.
- **Less work than a normal rental:** Turn-key properties are already rented, managed, and repaired. You do not have to find contractors, property managers, or real estate agents. You should still perform due diligence on the company and their team.

- **Provide cash flow from day one:** The first day you buy a turn-key, it will have a tenant in place who is paying rent. You do not have to worry about how long the repairs will take or how long it will take to get a tenant.
- **Provide a great return:** Most turn-key rentals provide returns of 10 to 15%. That return begins right away and takes little work to maintain because a property manager takes care of the house for you.
- **Provide diversification**: Buying turn-key rentals in different markets of the country gives you diversification.
- **Can be bought for cash**: Many foreign investors have trouble buying properties because they cannot get financing. Turn-key rentals can be as cheap as $30,000, making it easier to buy with cash.
- **You can invest your retirement savings:** You can invest a self-directed IRA or 401k into turn-key rentals. You can do this with regular rentals as well, but it may be easier with turn-key properties because the price points are lower.

## How can you find turn-key rental properties?

There are many turn-key rental property providers throughout the United States. Some companies are local to specific markets, such as Memphis, Ohio, Missouri, Florida, Texas, Chicago, and Wisconsin, while other companies have properties all over the country. The properties vary in price, rents, financing options, and returns, but good turn-key properties will cash flow. Even with cash flow, I would advise investors spend time researching the property manager and the area that they want to invest in before buying any turn-key property.

A Google search for turn-key rentals will give many results for property managers and houses for sale that are not rented. I have spent a lot of time researching turn-key companies and have met with turn-key companies in person. You are welcome to email me at mark@investfourmore.com about the turn-key company I used.

Every turn-key property is different and every location for turn-key properties is different. I have seen turn-key rentals that are repaired, rented out, and managed range from \$35,000 to \$150,000. I do not usually see turn-key properties in higher price ranges because it is much harder to cash flow on a higher priced property.

I usually do not buy rental properties that are turn-key ready because getting a great deal on them is hard. This is the same reason I rarely buy properties that are fully repaired. My ninth rental property was the closest thing I have purchase to a fully repaired property. It needed a bit of paint, but that was about it. In a perfect world, I would love for all the rentals I buy to be repaired and rented before I buy them, which is one advantage of turn-keys.

When I buy my rentals, they usually need work, and I get a discount for the money and time I put into repairing the houses. It is harder to have built-in equity on a turn-key rental, but you do not have to spend time repairing the house, renting it out, or finding a property manager.

## When would investing in a long-distance turn-key property be a good idea?

Many people reach out to me asking about investing in rental properties, but they do not know how to start because their market is too expensive. When starter houses are \$300,000 or more in an area, cash flowing on a rental property is almost impossible, unless you pay cash. When you pay cash, your return is not nearly as good as if you can get a loan (as long as the property cash flows). Rents are almost never high enough on a \$300,000 house to cash flow no matter where you live (unless you are buying multifamily).

The down payments on a \$300,000 property are going to be at least \$60,000 unless you use a technique to buy with less money down. Then you must add closing costs, reserves, repairs, and other costs associated with buying a rental property. I can buy two or three rental properties in my market, where someone in a more expensive area could only buy one rental property that may not cash flow at all.

## What are the possible downfalls to investing in turn-key properties?

Just because a house is rented out, repaired, and managed by a property manager does not mean you may not run into problems. You must do your homework and make sure the person or company you are buying the property from follows through on their promises. There can be problems with renters, property managers, maintenance, and repairs.

Here are some proactive things you can do to prevent a disaster with a turn-key property:

- Always get references for any company with which you are going to do business. Ask the company for references from current customers, and search online for any reviews of that particular company.
- Always check the value on the properties you are looking to buy. Find a local real estate agent who can tell you what a house is worth in the area. Even if a house cash flows well, you should shy away from houses that are priced 10 or 20% above market value.
- Always check out the property manager that is managing your rental property.
- Check the history and record of accomplishment of a company. Check the BBB, see how long they have been in business, and ask how many deals they have done.
- Ask for the details on any house you want to buy. How old is the furnace, hot water heater, wiring, plumbing, etc.? You want to make sure the major components are good and the company did not put lipstick on a pig to cover up faults. Don't be afraid to hire your own inspector to check out the property.
- How realistic are the company's projections and cash-flow estimates? Even with a turn-key property, you may still have some maintenance and vacancies, unless the turn-key company guarantees those. Some turn-key companies will not list any expenses for vacancies or maintenance, which is a huge red flag to me.

276

Turn-key rental properties are a great way to invest for cash flow when cash flow is hard to find in your market. Turn-key rental properties are also a way to invest in rental properties without having to repair a house, rent out a house, or find a property manager. However, getting a great deal on turn-key rentals is hard because the turn-key provider wants compensation for all the work they do.

## Can foreigners invest in United States real estate?

There are no restrictions on foreigners (including Canadians) buying real estate in the United States. However, that does not mean investing in property in the U.S. is easy for foreigners. I have had many inquiries on my blog from foreigners wondering how they can invest in the U.S. housing market because their market is very hard to invest in.

There are many things a foreigner needs to consider, such as financing, U.S. taxes, taxes in their home country, and the cost to buy a house in the United States. Just because it is possible for foreigners to buy a house in the United States does not mean it will be worthwhile. They must really do their homework. I love investing in the United States because I live here, and the U.S. has one of the best markets in which to invest.

## Why is the United States one of the best places in the world to invest in real estate?

I have talked to many foreign investors through coaching, comments on the blog, and on my podcast. The United States has a unique system for buying real estate. In most areas of the world, you cannot get a 30-year mortgage. A 25-year mortgage is about the most you can get, but that is not available everywhere either. Many parts of the country also have great rent-to-value ratios. Getting monthly rent of $1,000 on a $100,000 house is common. Some markets are different from others, but those numbers are almost impossible to find when you look at other parts of the world such as England, Australia, Canada, and many other countries. With the U.S. real estate system, buying a house is also safe and easy. Many countries have much different systems that are not as clear-cut as the U.S. system. Because the United States has such an incredible housing market with incredible lending options, many investors look here to buy.

That does not mean it is easy to get a loan or find a lender that will loan to a foreigner. Most of the information I have found on this subject is regarding Canadian policies since Canadian citizens make up the highest number of foreigners trying to buy real estate in the U.S. Most U.S. banks do not want to loan money to someone who has never paid taxes in the U.S., has no permanent address in the U.S., and has no ties to the country. There is obviously going to be a lot more risk to lenders when they loan to a foreigner who lives outside the country. It is also difficult for a Canadian or any other foreigner to get a loan in their home country on a property in another country. Most lenders do not want to loan outside their home country or may not even be able to depending on that country's laws and regulations.

The good news is that it is possible for a foreigner to get a loan on a property in the U.S. Some banks will loan to Canadians who can prove income and work history, much like a U.S. citizen would have to do. The problem may be finding a bank that will do it. Usually, you need to find a local bank that will lend to a foreigner. There could also be some national rental property lender who lend to foreigners. Please reference chapter 6 for information on financing.

## What does a loan for Canadian citizens cost in the U.S.?

The loan process in Canada is much different from in the U.S. In the U.S., the loan costs include an origination fee, appraisal fee, flood certifications, recording fees, closing fees, prepaid interest, and insurance. These can easily reach 2 to 3% of the mortgage amount for a U.S. citizen, but the costs may be higher for a Canadian citizen due to the increased work and risk the bank is taking on. The interest rates and closing costs will most likely be higher as well.

Rental properties offer great tax advantages for U.S. citizens, but taxes are the tricky part for any foreigner. The U.S. requires foreigners to pay taxes in the U.S. on real estate gains. Foreigners may be required to pay taxes in their home country as well. The United States and Canada have an agreement that meets some of these concerns regarding income taxes for Canadian citizens. I would talk to a tax professional in both countries before buying any property as I am not an accountant nor am I offering legal advice.

You must include the cost of travel in any investment you make unless you never plan to see the property. One thing Canadians need to consider is their health insurance may not cover them when they travel to the U.S. You must also factor in airfare, hotel costs, and other travel costs when looking at property in the U.S.

## Can you get a great deal on U.S. houses when buying from Canada?

I think the biggest issue for any foreign investor is being able to act quickly to get a great deal. I get great deals on my rentals because I can act very quickly. Acting quickly means a foreigner may not be able to personally view the house unless they are already in the country, and if you are in the country, a great deal may not pop up while you are here. Great deals can take me months to find. The best option may be to find a real estate agent you can trust to find a great deal for you.

Because of the unique housing market in the U.S., it may be worth it for many foreign investors to buy houses here. It will not be easy to do, and it is hard for me to say whether it is worth all the trouble. One thing I have learned is becoming and investor who successfully invests outside their own country takes work, research, and trust.

For those looking to buy out of state, it can be a daunting process. If you would like more information on the process, I did a webinar on the subject. It's on my YouTube Channel: https://www.youtube.com/watch?v=CmRHSJkG59w

## Conclusion

My market is getting more and more expensive, which makes investing in rentals that make sense more difficult. It would be awesome if you could invest in rental properties that had cash flow in any market. We must adapt to what our markets are doing and possibly invest in other markets. Like I have said many times, if investing in real estate were easy, everyone would do it!

# 13

# How Do You Build a Rental Property Empire?

In this book, you may have seen many references to my plan to purchase 100 rentals. I made that a public goal back in 2013. I made it public to help motivate myself and keep me accountable. You can read about that goal and my updates at: https://investfourmore.com/100-rentals-by-2023/.

That plan has helped me buy more properties, be more creative, stay focused, and build wealth. I think creating a plan is the first step toward success. You can read this book, get motivated, learn how to buy properties, learn how to finance properties, learn how to manage properties, yet never actually buy a property. Education does you no good unless you take action and implement what you have learned. If you are not sure where to start or how to build an empire, start writing!

I had no formal training in making plans or setting goals—I just started writing. I tweaked the plan as I reviewed it, and things changed. The act of writing things down makes them stick in your brain. You also have a plan that you can read over and over. We all think we can remember our plan or will always think about it, but as time passes, our memory fades, and we forget.

This book has a lot of information on rental properties, but I give no specific plan for others to use. That is because we are all in different places financially and geographically. What works for me may not work for you. I cannot create your plan—you must do it yourself.

## What should you include in your plan and goals?

Plans and goals work best when they are specific and detailed. If you say you want to be successful, what does that mean? Some people may see success as someday buying a house of their own, while others may see success as making $100 million. The more specific you make your plan, the easier it will be to achieve

Here are some basics that I would include in a plan to build a rental property empire:

- When do you want to buy your first property?
- What type of property will you buy?
- What type of financing will you use?
- How much money will you need?
- How much money will the property generate?

To answer these questions, you will have to research the market you want to invest in. Knowing your market is one of the most important things you can do. After you have answered those questions, you need to expand on your plan:

- How will you find the property?
- How will you manage the property?
- How will you repair the property?
- How will you save the money you need?

You will most likely need a lot of help to successfully invest in rental properties. You will need a great team, so who will be on that team?

- A real estate agent

- A lender or bank
- A contractor or handyman
- A property manager

Once you have this basic plan written down, you can start working on it right away. You may not be able to buy a house yet, but you can start building your team. You can start researching your market; you can talk to banks; you can research market rents; you can go see properties and learn what a good deal is. The more action you take, the more specific you can make your plan:

- How much will you pay for your rental?
- How much will your property rent for?
- How much equity will you gain once you buy a property?
- How much cash flow will you make?
- How much taxes will you save?

Now you have a plan for one rental. That is where many people get stuck. You must expand your plan to build your empire. Sometimes it helps to work backwards:

- How much money do you want to make every month from rentals?
- How many rentals would you need to make that money?
- How long will it take you to buy those rentals?
- How can you buy them faster using refinances, house flipping, or partnering?

Now you have the start of your plan. Read it; tweak it; change it; take action; and tweak it again. Write out the full plan so that it makes the most sense to you. Maybe you use bullet points or write out a story about how your perfect life looks thanks to all the properties you bought.

Do not forget to add some motivation for why buying these properties will make your life awesome.

## What was one of my motivating factors?

Another public goal I set was purchasing a Lamborghini, which I did in 2014. Owning a Lamborghini has been a goal of mine since I was a little kid. Thanks to my real estate business, I was able to buy one in May 2014. It was delivered to me one month later...on Father's Day. I was not planning to buy one so soon, but circumstances lined up, and I could not pass this car up. My real estate business and blog took off, and this car was the perfect color as well as a great deal.

One of the most important keys to wealth is saving money. Saving money gives you options that allow you to make much more money, such as investing in rental properties and buying fix and flips. Saving money also allows you to be more flexible with your career or even start a business. If you never save any money, getting ahead in life is very hard, no matter what you do. I would never have bought a car like this if I was not in a very good financial position and if it was not extremely important to me.

I also do not believe in being cheap and skimping out on the things that make you happy. I have worked very hard to be in the position I am in now, and I believe people need to do things that make them happy. Not everything that makes us happy takes money, but some things do. Do not refuse or be afraid to spend money on things that truly make you happy when you have saved enough money to afford them.

Many people will question the wisdom of buying a $100,000 car, but I think it was a great decision. Wanting this car motivated me every day and allowed to me to improve my business, take chances, and be more successful. I am a car nut, and buying a car like this may not motivate others as it has me. Pick something that you really want, and use it to motivate you and push you further.

## How setting goals helped me buy a Lamborghini

I also believe that setting big goals that motivate you will make you more successful. Setting big goals that are exciting and easily visualized, such as buying a Lamborghini, can really motivate you. Some might say setting goals such as providing for your family or retiring early are more important, but how easy is it to picture providing for your family or retiring early? Obviously, these are important big-picture goals, but these goals are very vague, and picturing them is difficult. A 1999 blue Lamborghini Diablo is specific and easy to picture!

I have set many bigger and smaller goals, including my plan to purchase 100 rental properties. Goals have helped me tremendously. They've helped me make more money, buy more investments, save money, and improve my personal life. I am less stressed now than I have ever been, and I spend more time with my family than I ever have.

## Why was this car important to me?

I have loved exotic cars since I was a young child. I had many car books, hot wheels, and model cars that I always played with. I loved Ferraris, Lamborghinis, Maseratis, Aston Martins, and many other makes. Over the years, Lamborghinis grew on me more and more. They are extremely rare, very fast, unique, and outrageous.

I have always wanted a Lamborghini, and when I was a kid, I believed I would have one. Then, after college, I entered the real world. Everyone tells you if you do your job, make a decent living, and save for retirement, you will be happy. It was hammered into my head that I shouldn't want expensive cars or houses because chances were I would never have those things. After a few years of taking the traditional route, I decided I wanted more.

In my late 20s, I decided I could have an exotic car, and I could do it in the next decade or two. I started setting goals, making plans, and visualizing my future. I became an REO agent (an agent who sells bank foreclosures); my real estate career took off; and I started saving a lot of money. I began investing in rental properties and doing more fix and flips. I started InvestFourMore.com and took over the real estate business from my father.

Suddenly, I was reaching goals more quickly than I ever thought possible. I had to constantly change and create new goals because I was reaching them so quickly.

On a side note, I believe in very aggressive goals because they will push you harder than easy goals will. If you achieve all your goals quickly, you may not be motivated to keep working hard. If you do not reach your goals, it is not a big deal because you will be better off for having chased that huge goal than not having any goals or reaching an easy goal.

After all this change and success, I decided to set a huge goal to buy a Diablo in 2014.

Spending so much time talking about a car in a rental property book may seem very out of place. I wanted to tell that story so you could see my passion for cars and how that passion helped motivate me in my real estate career. You do not need to have a passion for cars, but everyone has a passion for something...something they love to do or would love to have. I am not talking about buying the newest SUV because the neighbors just bought one but something you personally love without outside influence. Too many people hide their passions because they are worried what others will think or they want to fit in with societal norms. Find your passion and use it to your advantage. Set goals for how your investing or career will help you achieve your passions in life, and remind yourself of them constantly!

I hope you have enjoyed this book and that you have found many tips, techniques, and methods for buying your own rental properties. Rentals have been awesome to me and have given me many choices. They have given me time, which has allowed me to pursue what I love in life.

One of the things I love to do is help others succeed. I have many articles on my website and many resources for those of you looking for more help. I have coaching programs as well. These are not the $30,000 plus coaching programs that many real estate gurus promote and then have someone else you have never heard of teach them. I created these affordable programs, and I'm personally involved in them. Many of the programs include coaching calls directly with me. I love helping people solve problems, analyze deals, and get started investing in real estate. However, I am not a hand holder, and I won't do any of the work for you. I am still an active investor and only have time for those who are super motivated and work hard. My goal is to teach others how to analyze deals and build their own business so they don't have to rely on anyone else. Please check out my blog, InvestFourMore.com, for more information, or send an email to Mark@InvestFourMore.com. Yes, that is my personal email as well. I, and not a hired minion, answer my emails (I have five-year-old twins, and I am very familiar with minions!).

I wish you personal and financial success! -Mark

# 14

# Commercial Real Estate

I wrote *Build a Rental Property Empire* when I was buying residential rental properties in Northern Colorado. I was getting great deals on houses that cash flowed very well. However, I bought my last residential rental property in 2015. The market in Colorado has been going nuts, and I could no longer make the money I wanted to with rentals in this area. The prices have risen too much compared to the rents. You will find cash flowing on residential rental properties is tough when housing prices are high. You might also find this happening in your market.

I did not give up my goal to buy 100 rental properties. I also did not keep blindly buying properties that made no sense to buy. I did change my strategy. My first idea was to buy rental properties in another market. I searched all over the United States looking for decent markets to invest in. I wanted a market that had low prices...but not too low. I wanted a market with a growing population. I wanted a market that had the potential for appreciation. I wanted a market with low property taxes. I wanted a market that had laws that were not too tenant friendly.

After talking to many people, I decided to investigate Florida more. I found several decent markets in Florida and even took a trip there to check them out. I was able to find houses that were fairly priced and had great rent-to-value ratios, and there was a booming demand for rentals in the area. I was working on finding a local bank who would fund my deals when my house flipping business took off. I decided that I would invest my money into the flipping business for a little while longer until I figured out what I really wanted to do with rentals.

The house flipping business did take off. I went from flipping 8 to 13 to 18 to 26 houses per year. I was making great money flipping houses, but I still loved rentals. As soon as you sell a flip, the house will not generate more money. Rental properties will keep making you money as long as you own them. I love flipping houses, but I still needed to find a way to buy more rentals.

In 2017, I saw a cheap property come up for sale on the MLS. It was a commercial building with a retail side and a workshop. A furniture repair company had owned the property for decades, but they wanted to sell it. I made an offer on it and ended up buying it 10 months later! They had some IRS issues that needed to be worked out before they could sell. Getting that property under contract opened my eyes to the world of commercial real estate. I bought a couple of other commercial properties before I closed on the furniture repair shop.

I talk about the difference between commercial real estate and residential real estate in this book. I wrote that chapter before I bought any commercial real estate, but I feel the same way about most of the concepts now that I own commercial properties. Commercial real estate is complicated! I do not recommend jumping into commercial real estate without a lot of education and possibly experience in other areas of the business. Here are some of the major differences:

- Commercial agents tend to be very different than residential. There are pocket listings everywhere, and speed seems to be frowned upon.
- Commercial property values have huge differences based on the location, the lease, the condition, the type of property and so much more. I bought a 68,000-square-foot building for $2,100,000 in 2018, and a few months later, a 35,000-square-foot similar building sold for $5,500,000 a few blocks away.
- Leasing commercial real estate is completely different from residential

real estate. Some places will have a ton of demand and lease out right way while others can be vacant for years.

· Financing commercial real estate is much different from financing residential real estate.

If you find the right commercial property, it can make you a ton of money, but the wrong property can cost you a ton of money. You must be very careful in the commercial real estate world, but once I got into it, I loved it!

## What kind of commercial properties have I purchased?

I have purchased a small commercial shop for $72,000 and a huge commercial strip mall for $2,100,000. In total, I have purchased six commercial properties in the last two years. Finding these properties has not been easy, just like finding the residential rental properties that I bought wasn't easy. Finding them took a lot of time, and buying them took a lot of hard work. I don't want to give the impression that switching from commercial to residential was easy. Just like with residential rentals, you cannot simply look on the MLS or Loopnet (a commercial listing site) one day and expect to find an amazing commercial rental that would generate a ton of money.

I purchased small commercial rentals for $100,000 that rent out for about $1,500 after minimal repairs. I purchased a larger office building (7,500 sq. ft.) for $292,000 that I spent $50,000 on for repairs, and it rents for $4,500 per month. I bought the big one that has a grocery store, restaurant, coffee shop, and office space for $2.1 million, and it brings in about $22,000 per month. I also bought a small restaurant that we are currently renovating for $110,000 that we could possibly get $2,000 to $3,000 in rent from. We may be able to turn it into a 2-unit property! I have a 4-unit mixed-use property under contract to buy with 1 commercial unit and 3 residential units. It is possible to make money with all kinds of different commercial rentals.

You can see a list of all my rentals at https://investfourmore.com/rentals/

# Why are commercial rentals so different from residential rentals?

I mentioned in another part of this book about the difficulty in buying commercial rentals because they are so complicated. I stand by those points, even after buying them and making money with them. Commercial real estate is tough, and it is easy to lose a lot of money in the business. I have looked at properties that were owned by commercial brokers who have been in the business for decades, and they were selling at a huge loss because they grossly miscalculated the investment.

One of the trickiest things to figure out is the value of commercial real estate. Yes, the CAP rate will give you an idea of what a property is worth. However, the CAP rates vary in different markets on different types of properties, based on the vacancies, leases, and the property's condition. Not only do the CAP rates differ based on these factors, but the CAP rate can also be easily manipulated. The CAP rate is supposed to be the net income divided by the value or purchase price of the property.

**Capitalization Rate = Net Operating Income / Current Market Value**

That seems like a simple equation, but the net operating income number can be grossly miscalculated on purpose or on accident. Many people also may like to use the gross income instead of the net income to calculate the CAP rate. The listing agent who is trying to get the most money they can for their seller may list that the property is selling at a 9% CAP (the higher the CAP number the better the return), but the buyer may find the real CAP number is only a 5%. The listing agent could be counting potential rent income instead of what the actual rents are. They could be leaving out the management fees and may not be including any maintenance costs or vacancies. There are many ways to manipulate the CAP rate, and part of being a good investor is figuring out what the real return will be on your own.

Once you figure out the CAP rate, you must figure out what the going CAP rate is for that type of property in that market. Colorado properties tend to sell with CAP rates as low as 5% or 6% for some properties, while other markets may see CAP rates of 10% or more! The cool thing about commercial properties is there can be a ton of room to add value with the right property.

I mentioned the going CAP rates in Colorado can be as low as 5% or 6%, but I would never pay that as an investor. I always get loans on my rentals, and it is almost impossible to make money with that low of a CAP rate and a loan.

To relate the commercial CAP rate to a rental property, consider this: a property that costs $200,000 but makes $1,000 per month or $12,000 per year would have a CAP rate of 6%. That is without a loan, as the CAP rate does not consider financing. $12,000 / $200,000 = .06. If you were to get a loan on that property, it would basically wipe out almost all the profit.

If the property made $1,333 per month or $16,000 per year and cost $200,000, it would have a CAP rate of 8%. This is getting to be a much better investment as you can get a loan and have cash flow left over. Remember, this is net income that we are talking about. The actual rents would be much higher than $1,333 per month.

Why in the world would I be investing in commercial real estate in Colorado if the CAP rates are so low? Just like with residential rental properties, I am not about to pay market value for anything. I want to buy my commercial properties at a 9% CAP, and I have.

## How can you get a great deal on commercial real estate?

I go over many ways to get a great deal on residential rentals in this book, but commercial real estate is also a different beast in this department. The difference in the way things worked in the commercial world drove me crazy. Everything is slower, less transparent, and more about who you know than what you know.

While commercial real estate is a different beast, some of the techniques used to buy residential rentals work with commercial rentals as well. I bought some of my commercial rentals from the MLS by being fast, an agent, and making my offers hard to resist. One of the first commercial offers I ever made was on the furniture restoration store. It was listed on the MLS for $110,000. I made an offer on it without even seeing the inside of the property. I asked for an inspection on the property, which I rarely do now, just because I wanted to make sure the inside was not a fire-bombed shell. On a side note, the commercial restaurant I recently bought involved a site-unseen offer without an inspection clause because I knew it was such a good deal.

The agent for the furniture restoration store called me and asked if the offer was correct. He could not believe he got a full-price offer so fast (it was not even the first day it was listed). I said yes it was right, and I would remove my inspection contingency as soon as I saw the inside and it was halfway decent. He agreed to meet me that day at the property. It was halfway decent, and I removed my contingency. That deal worked out exactly as a residential deal purchased from the MLS would work out.

Not every commercial real estate property is on the MLS or easy to find. In fact, over the last two years, there have only been a few properties that seem like good deals on the MLS. I think I bought most of them. In my experience, there has been less competition for commercial properties on the MLS, which is so nice. Although, after writing this additional chapter, that may change...

I bought one commercial property from Facebook marketplace. It was priced at $79,900, which was a steal! The seller had a lot of offers, and I decided to go up to $101,000 or so. I ended up getting it, and it has been an amazing rental for me. I bought the big commercial property because I made friends with a commercial real estate agent. When I first got started in commercial real estate, I was looking at some really big properties, and I knew I should not be going at it alone. I talked to a local commercial agent who had helped me learn the business and find a few deals. He had the listing on this property and told me about it first. I jumped on it and never looked back.

After being in the commercial real estate world for a while, you start to realize that not every property that can be bought is for sale. That is true in the residential world as well—but even more so in commercial. A lot of properties are for sale but are not listed publicly. I had a giant

280,000-square-foot property under contract for a while that was not listed anywhere. The reason I was able to get it under contract was my agent knew it was sort of on the market. The seller even had their own agent representing them. That deal fell through for many reasons, but it was a huge eye opener for me.

There is another big commercial property for sale in my area now that has a giant for sale sign. The only reason I know it is for sale is the giant sign on the building! It is not in the MLS or LoopNet, but it is on the commercial agent's website. I hate to talk bad about an industry, but many commercial properties are not marketed well. A lot of commercial agents do not use MLS, as they consider it only for residential properties, and there is no one-stop commercial MLS system. There seems to be a misconception that commercial real estate investors are all well known and will know about the properties for sale because they have connections as well.

If you want to know about the larger commercial real estate deals in your area, you need to be part of the commercial network in some way. There is a monthly commercial broker meeting in our area every month that is a great way to network.

## What is a great deal on a commercial property?

Something else that took me a while to figure out in the commercial real estate world was what made a good deal. When I first started in residential real estate, it took me a little while to figure out what a good rental property was. But once I figured it out, finding more great deals was a simple process. However, commercial properties are all so different! The cost per square foot on one property in my area might be $40, while on another property that doesn't seem that different it might be $150. The $40 property is most likely vacant, needs some work, or has some other major issue. The $150-dollar-per-square-foot property has a 5-year NNN lease in place and is in great shape.

If you are wondering, I am way more interested in that $40 property than I am the $150 one! I don't like to pay premium prices for anything, but other investors do. That is something that I learned with commercial real estate. Premium properties that are set up very well command very high prices. Not a lot of commercial real estate investors are looking to take on projects. They are often big institutional players who want solid steady returns with low risk. That is not my style. The difference in styles can create opportunity in the commercial real estate world.

If you can take a low-performing commercial property with issues and turn it into a steady earning property, you can make a lot of money. If you happen to find that property off market or through networking, you can make even more money because of the deal you get on it. That is how I can buy 9% CAP or higher properties when the going rate is 6% or lower.

I will use the big property as an example. If you have not figured it out yet, the big property is the 68,000-square-foot one I bought for $2.1 million. It will be known as the big property until I buy something larger. When we bought this property, the total rents were about $20,000 per month. The rents were actually very low for this size property and the location. The grocery store occupies a huge chunk of the property, and they have a very low lease rate because they have been there 30 years and are a stable tenant. All the leases on the property were NNN (triple net), which means the tenants pay for everything, including maintenance, utilities, insurance, property taxes, and even property management.

NNN is great if the entire property is rented, but if there are vacant units, the landlords are not only missing out on rent, but they are also paying those NNN costs for the vacant space. On this building, there was about 8,000 square feet of vacant office space. That vacant space added to the expenses because the landlord had to pay NNN costs on that space, but it also presented opportunity. If you could lease that space, you could greatly increase the returns and the CAP rate.

After considering the rent and the expenses, the property was advertised to us as a 9% CAP. This was an amazing deal, and I was skeptical. It generated about $20,000 per month, and the asking price was $2,250,000. If you were to get a loan, the payment would be about $10,000 per month, leaving $10,000 in net income, which meant the CAP rate was actually 5%. $120,000

/ $2,250,000 = 5.3. What?

That was my test to see if you were paying attention to anything I have said. We don't factor the loan in the CAP rate! There are also more expenses, so the actual CAP rate was about 9% or more. $17,000 per month in income or $204,000 a year divided by $2,250,000 = .0906. It was a true 9% CAP with room to grow!

I used a partner to buy this deal because I was not sure I could pull it off on my own. My partner is a real estate investor as well and constantly loans me private money on my house flips. He had done much more commercial investing than me, which helped as well. He thought it was a great deal. We decided to do something stupid. We did not offer full price. I offered $2,000,000, and the agent who helped me was visibly annoyed. He thought this was a smoking deal as well and could not believe we were trying to negotiate. Looking back on the deal now, I cannot say that I disagree with the agent! However, we ended up getting the property under contract for $2,100,000. We had a few hiccups but closed on it, and it was awesome.

Part of my grand plan in buying a giant commercial property was to open my own real estate brokerage, which I did. I opened it in one of the vacant spaces of the big building we bought. That increased our rent by $2,300 per month, and I had to pay NNN costs as well. Instead of the landlords paying utilities, taxes, insurance, maintenance, etc. on the vacant space, I paid it. I was okay with paying those costs since I was paying half of them to myself. By renting that unit, we had greatly increased the CAP rate. We still had 4,000 square feet of vacant space yet reduced the landlord expenses and increase the rents. Now the property brings in $22,500 in rents plus more NNN costs. It is pretty close to an 11% CAP now, and there is still room to grow!

If you look at market CAP rates, which are around 6% for this type of property, the property is now worth close to $4,000,000, when we bought for $2,100,000 less than a year ago. In fact, a property down the street sold for $5,450,000 right before we bought this property. That property had 37,000 square feet and less land. However, it was set up better for more retail spaces and most likely had higher rents, but it still shows the deal we got.

That is the great thing about commercial real estate. If you know the value of properties, can add value through rent increases or other factors, or have great connections, you can make a killing in the business. I must warn you: we have been looking for similar deals for months and have not found one. These deals do not come along often.

A great commercial deal does not have to cost millions. I have bought great deals for $70,000. To know what a great deal is, you must know what it will make you monthly, what it will be worth, and how easy the deal will be. Renting out or adding value to commercial properties is not always easy.

## How hard is it to lease a commercial property?

When we bought the big commercial property, it had two vacant units. They had been vacant for years. The marketing was not amazing on these units, but they were some of the cheapest office spaces in the area. Why were they not being leased when they were so cheap? Leasing out commercial real estate is still something I am learning to this day. I cannot seem to figure out why some places lease easily and others do not.

One of the biggest risks I ever took was buying the 7,500-square-foot commercial property for $292,000. It was an office building that had been used as a dentist office, a doctor's office, and who knows what else. When I bought it, it was completely vacant. I probably would not have bought it except for a mistake by one of my team members. I made an offer on the property when it was listed for $325,000. This was the first office building I had ever made an offer on, and I sent an email to my team member saying to include an inspection and loan conditions deadline. I usually do not include these items on my flips or rentals as you know. However, the team member wrote the contract with no inspection and no loan conditions deadline.

I must take responsibility for this happening as I did not review the offer thoroughly before signing it. I should have looked at these items, but I did not. In the end, I had decided that I wanted to cancel the deal, but I had paid $10,000 in earnest money. I did not realize I had no way to get out of the contract until that time when I wanted out. It was Nikki, my project manager, who convinced me this was a good deal and to just buy the property. I bought the property, we started to renovate it, and a broker called me. He said he had a company that wanted to rent it and wondered if it was for lease. We ended up leasing it before it was finished, and it was an awesome deal.

My other commercial properties have not had any trouble being leased either, but for some reason, we still have this vacant unit in the big commercial property. It is not easy to know which property will be easy to lease out and which property will be tough.

One of the biggest risks of commercial real estate is leasing out vacant units, especially in large properties. If you have one large tenant, you run a huge risk of losing your tenant and not making any money. Even long-term leases can go bad. Large companies, like Sports Authority, can and do go bankrupt. The tenant may owe you money for the rest of the lease, but good luck collecting it!

Commercial properties are also leased differently than residential rentals. Most properties are rented by the square foot. You might see a commercial office listed for $8 per square foot. That means if the office had 2,000 square feet, the rent would be $16,000 per year (8 x 2,000). You will also see different terms like NNN or gross for the lease. An NNN lease means the tenants pay for everything—all the repairs, the utilities, the maintenance, and even property management. A gross lease means the landlord pays for everything. A modified gross lease means the landlord pays for some things and the tenants pay for other things. How much rent you charge will be based on what kind of terms you offer. If you have an NNN lease, you must charge CAM every month on top of the base lease amount. CAM stands for common area maintenance but covers much more than just common areas. On our big property, the tenants pay CAM on top of their base rent to cover all the expenses since it is an NNN lease. The CAM can change from year to year based on the expenses and how well the property is managed.

There is also something called TI on commercial rental properties. I remember sitting in a meeting with my commercial real estate brokers talking about the big building and a few others we were going to look at. They kept talking about TI. I thought maybe it meant taxes and insurance, but I had no idea. I nodded my head and pretended to know what they were talking about. Once the meeting was over, I looked up what TI meant. It stands for tenant improvements. On many commercial properties, the landlord will pay for the tenants to complete TI, or the landlords will complete the work themselves. There was significant TI done for some of the tenants in our big building before we bought it. TI can be a few thousand dollars or hundreds of thousands of dollars. The oil company that leased my other office building wanted a few custom features, and we added those for them at no cost.

The other hard part about leasing out a commercial property is marketing it. There is LoopNet and other commercial websites that list commercial properties for lease. There are also some commercial properties for lease in the MLS. Some properties that are available for lease have only a sign in front of them or are on the broker's website. You can use a real estate agent or broker to lease the property for you, or you can try to do it yourself. The agent who represented the oil company wanted a commission for bringing the oil company to me, which made sense. I paid him 3% of the total amount of the lease. Often, commercial leases are three to 10 years long...or sometimes longer. The commission can be huge on a long-term lease.

When I prepared the lease for new tenants, I learned the commercial lease is much different from the residential lease. Our residential lease, or the one my property managers use, is a couple of pages. The lease for a commercial tenant can be 30 pages or longer! There are so many more things that need to be covered. Luckily, there are many commercial leases online that cover most anything.

## How hard is managing a commercial rental property?

Another aspect of owning commercial real estate is managing it. I have property managers for all my residential rental properties, but I have been managing the commercial properties on my own with help from my brokerage. Commercial tenants tend to be much easier to manage than residential tenants. They pay rent on time, often make minor repairs themselves, and tend to have fewer problems. Managing commercial properties the last two years has been very easy. I have a bookkeeper and plenty of help. I am not doing it all on my own.

The big property we bought had a property manager, but they did not handle any of the leasing or rent collection. All they did was maintain the building and take care of the parking lot and landscaping. They charge $400 per month for those services plus whatever the maintenance and repairs cost. I took over that part of the management as well and can charge it back to the building.

When you are dealing with commercial real estate, you run into maintenance and repair items that you do not have with residential properties. The heating systems are often different; you must maintain parking lots; there may be fire sprinkler systems that need maintenance; building codes are different; and construction is different. I had to find many new people to help maintain the building.

I have also done work on commercial buildings and was planning to do a lot of work on the 280,000-square-foot building that I did not end up buying. I obtained bids from two large commercial contractors to renovate the property, and the bids were both in the millions of dollars. I have talked to other commercial property owners and have seen receipts for work done on commercial properties. I am blown away by how much working on commercial properties costs! Many companies have huge upcharges because owners do not know any better or are not bothered by the huge bills. Everything tends to cost more on commercial properties, regardless of whether it should cost more or not. I have been able to use my own crews to fix up my commercial properties since no major work was involved. I am sure I saved tens of thousands of dollars using my crews instead of a commercial contractor. Even thought my plumber, HVAC company, and electrician usually work on residential jobs, they all knew how to work on commercial properties.

A different set of skills is needed to manage commercial rentals versus residential, but I like the management better. You are dealing with businesses when renting commercial rentals, and they are less emotional than residential tenants. There can still be problems like evictions, late rent, and businesses failing. However, most people in a position to rent a commercial property have had some level of success in their life, and you have a better chance of them being a better tenant.

## How does financing differ on commercial real estate?

One of the biggest differences between residential real estate and commercial real estate is the financing options that are available to investors. I have used big banks, local banks, hard money, and private money when financing my investment properties. With every lender, they tend to treat commercial different than residential. Most lenders feel that commercial real estate is riskier than residential. Everyone needs a place to live, even in bad times, but not everyone needs a place to run a business. When the economy is down, commercial properties can suffer, while residential rentals may not.

I have an awesome lender for my residential rentals. They are local and will give me loans with 30-year amortization schedules with no balloon payments. A balloon payment means they can call the loan due at any time after the balloon date. The loans are ARMs, as I talked about earlier in the book, but still great loans. That same lender is not as great with commercial loans. They will not do a 30-year amortization. In fact, they only want to lend on a 15-year fixed loan for my commercial rentals. Honestly, a 15-year fixed loan is not bad for commercial as you will find that many lenders want very short balloon periods.

One of the biggest scares shortly after the housing market crash in the mid to late 2000s was commercial real estate. The media talked about all the people who lost their homes, as they should have, but many people in the industry were worried our economy would completely collapse because of commercial loans. During the collapse, commercial lending almost came to a complete stop. No banks wanted to give out commercial loans. The issue with commercial loans was that many have a balloon payment date of 5 years from the time the loan was taken out. That means after five years, the bank can call a commercial loan due in full. The borrower must pay the bank the full amount of the loan, or they can lose it to foreclosure.

In the past, refinancing a commercial loan every five years was a pretty simple process. But during the housing crash, most lenders did not want to touch any commercial loans. There was so much worry that tens of thousands (or more) commercial loans would come due, the lenders would call them, and the business owners would not be able to pay off the loans. Why would the lenders call loans due when they knew they would have to foreclose? The banks had no choice. They were too thin on cash and too heavy on loans. Government regulations said they had to reduce the amount of loans they had and increase their cash. Foreclosing on and selling properties was one way to do that.

So why didn't the commercial-lending industry implode? This may be an unpopular opinion with many people, but the government bailout of big banks may have saved the commercial-lending industry. When the government bailed out the big banks, they did not have to call all those loans due. Many people feel the bailout was to save the residential loans, but it was to save the commercial loans. No one was offering refinancing of commercial loans, and a disaster was imminent. The housing crash could have been so much worse and known as the business crash instead.

As you can see, the balloon payment on most loans is a big deal. When I am getting financing on my properties, I try to have as long of a secured loan period as I can. On the big property I bought, we have a fixed interest rate period of 5 years but a balloon period of ten years. That means our loan cannot be called due for at least ten years if we are making payments. But there are so many different commercial loans out there.

I bought my BRRRR commercial property thinking I would get a loan from the same lender who loaned on the big property. I repaired the property, rented it, and was ready for the appraisal. This was after the lender had told me that they would do a similar loan as what they had done on the big property. We got the appraisal, and it came in really close to the value I was hoping for. Then, the lender said that they could only do a three-year balloon because my lease was only three years long. What?! I could not believe what they were saying. I told them to stop everything and I would shop around.

I talked to another lender, and he said he could do a ten-year balloon with a 25-year amortization. This was another local bank, and they were so easy to work with. They even had to complete another internal appraisal to confirm value but did not charge me for it. These stories may seem to be random, and that is my point. With commercial rentals, you will see so many different terms and conditions. It pays to talk to and meet as many lenders as you can. Do not be afraid to shop around for the best loan option. I was very honest with all my lenders and mentioned I was looking at multiple banks for the best loan.

Something else that you will find with commercial loans is experience is key. Sellers, agents, and lenders do not like working with people who are not in the commercial real estate industry. I bought a couple of small commercial properties, which showed I had some experience in the business. It may sound crazy, but those small commercial-property purchases meant a lot to sellers and lenders. You may hear that you need to be in the network to buy multifamily properties, and the same is true for commercial real estate. People do not believe you are a real investor until you have actually invested.

While small deals may not seem like a big deal, they can be the difference between someone taking you seriously and not taking you seriously. I would not go around bragging that you did a small deal here or there, but saying you are a commercial real estate investor doesn't hurt.

When investing in commercial real estate, the deal also matters. Commercial real estate lenders do not want to foreclose on people. Foreclosing on someone can take a lot of money, time, and resources. Selling a vacant, broken down, foreclosed commercial property can also take a lot of time. Commercial lenders want to know that they are lending on a good investment. They want to know:

- The cash flow.
- The leases.
- The long-term potential.
- The tenant quality.

· The quality of the owner.

You cannot half-ass your way through a commercial deal. You need to know your numbers and your market. The more prepared you are, the better chance you have of getting the loan. If you have a track record of fantastic commercial rental property purchases, great. If you do not, you need to have an entire presentation put together on why you should be getting this loan and why it is a solid investment for the banker.

## Repairing and maintaining commercial properties

Something I learned right away when investing in commercial real estate was that the contractors are much different from residential contractors. They are very professional, do good work, and are extremely expensive! I do not mind good work, but I don't see how some commercial investors make any money using contractors that charge so much. I also found that bigger contractors do not have any in-house people doing the work—they are outsourcing everything to subcontractors. They have entire management teams to manage the subs. Again, that is great, but the property owner is paying for that entire office.

While I would love to use very expensive contractors because of the work they do, I would rather find less-expensive ways to get the same work done. It takes more work and more management, but it saves a lot of money. On my commercial properties, I have not had to use a commercial contractor. I used the same guys I use for my rentals and flips. I was surprised at how many of them already knew a lot about commercial. They just didn't work on commercial jobs while working for me. Many of my subs knew all about commercial properties as well.

My HVAC, electrician, plumber, and roofer all had experience with commercial. I did not tell them that all they had to do was add commercial somewhere on their truck and they could be charging twice to three times as much. I think the higher rates come from very wealthy investors in the commercial world who are not as concerned about maximizing their investment as they are preserving it. They are willing to pay high prices for the peace of mind that it is done right with no involvement from them. I prefer to maximize my investment.

If I had bought the huge 250,000-square-foot building and completely remodeled it, I would have had to use one of the big commercial contractors. It was a huge job, and I would have needed their help and experience. For almost all the other commercial properties I have bought, I have been able to get away with using my residential guys. I still must be careful with what we do and what we spend. Some of my subs want to go crazy with fancy heating systems or suddenly charge a ton more for electrical work just because it is commercial.

## Conclusion

Commercial real estate is a completely different animal than residential. The properties are different; the lending is different; the tenants are different; and the market is different. You can make a lot of money with commercial real estate, but you can also lose a lot. Do not tread into this business lightly.

# What is the next step?

I wrote this book a couple of years ago and things have changed for me. I no longer buy residential rentals because our market has changed so much in Colorado. Prices have tripled since I first bought a rental in 2010. I stopped buying residential rentals in 2015 in Colorado. I was planning to buy properties in Florida, but caught the commercial bug instead. I ended up buying 4 commercial properties in 2017 and a 68,000 square foot strip mall in 2018. The same techniques apply to commercial as they do to residential, but figuring out values is a much more complicated process. My goals and plans have changed, but I still buy as many rentals as I can as I adapt to different markets. I talk about all of this in my coaching.

This book talks about how rental properties can be an awesome investment and business. I am a current investor and Realtor working in today's market (at least at the time of the first edition of this book in 2016). If you want to get involved in real estate, I would love to help you learn the ins and outs. It is not as easy as they make it look on television.

If you invest the right way, rental properties and flips can change your life. They changed my life by giving me a better way to invest, a better way to make money, and a better way to retire. I am 37 years old and am in a better position to retire right now than most people will ever be. I am by no means done!

There is a lot going on at my blog: Investfourmore.com. I have a podcast, a forum, the blog, eBooks, paperback books, coaching programs, and many videos. I encourage you to sign up for my email list if you have not already done so. The emails I send you will help you navigate through the site, will give you the most valuable resources, and will help you decide how much or little you want to be involved in real estate.

- You can sign up for my email list here: https://investfourmore.com/
- If you are interested in becoming an agent, I have a separate email list with more resources here: https://investfourmore.com/agents/
- If you want to become a real estate agent, I just came out with How to Make It Big as a Real Estate Agent, which is a 200+ page book on how I sold over 200 houses in one year and how I created my team. I am still an agent but rarely talk with sellers or buyers. My team does it all. http://www.amazon.com/How-Make-Real-Estate-Agent/dp/153366160X/
- If you want to learn about how mindset and attitude can determine your success, check out my book How to Change your Mindset to Achieve Huge Success: https://www.amazon.com/Change-Your-Mindset-Achieve-Success-ebook/dp/B01HT1470G/
- I have a fix-and-flip video training course here that has over 3 hours of videos and more resources for learning how to successfully flip houses. https://learn.investfourmore.com/p/the-fix-and-flip-system
- I have a quick-start video training program that shows exactly how I get awesome deals, including videos of me touring potential deals and how I search the MLS. You can find my coaching products on my blog here: https://investfourmore.com/resources/

I have made my books and coaching products as affordable as possible. I know people who are starting out in a new business do not have a lot of extra money. For those of you who know you need a little extra push and accountability, I created more in-depth training courses. These come with conference calls and email training with me personally. The Complete Blueprint for Successful Real Estate Investing is a rental property program that I created and comes with personal coaching from me as well as audio CDs/MP3s, videos, a huge how-to guide, and much more. If you are interested, email me, and I may have a special coupon for those who read this book all the way through! Mark@investfourmore.com.

If you want to connect with me on social media, find me on:

- Facebook

- LinkedIn
- Twitter
- Instagram
- Google +

# Real Estate Terms and Glossary

- **1% Rule:** A rule of thumb used to determine if the monthly rent earned from a piece of investment property will exceed that property's monthly mortgage payment.
- **2% Rule:** A general guideline many investors use to determine if a rental property is a good deal. The basics say the monthly rent from a rental property should be 2% or more of the cost of a rental property.
- **50% Rule:** The 50% rule is one way to estimate what the expenses will be on rental properties. It states that the expenses on a rental property will be 50% of the rents. This rule does not account for any mortgage expenses.
- **70% Rule:** A common term used among many real estate investors when flipping houses. The 70% rule is a way to determine what price to pay for a fix-and-flip to make money. The rule states that an investor should pay 70% of the ARV (after repair value) of a property minus the repairs needed.
- **1031 Exchange:** A section of the U.S. Internal Revenue Service Code that allows investors to defer capital gains taxes on any exchange of like-kind properties for business or investment purposes.
- **Active Status:** Most MLS systems use specific status to show if a house is available. Active means the house is available and has no accepted offers on it. Active/backup means the house has an accepted offer, but the seller is accepting backup offers. Pending means the house has an accepted offer and the seller is not accepting backup offers. The status meaning can vary by MLS.
- **Active/backup status:** See above

- **Acre:** A unit of land area used in the imperial and U.S. customary systems. It is defined as the area of 1 chain by 1 furlong (66 by 660 feet), which is exactly equal to 43,560 square feet.
- **Adjustable Rate Mortgage:** A type of mortgage in which the interest rate applied on the outstanding balance varies throughout the life of the loan.
- **Amortization:** A method of equalizing the monthly mortgage payment over the life of the loan by adjusting the proportion of principal to interest over time. At first, the interest payment is high and the principal payment is low.
- **Appraisal:** Most lenders require an appraisal on houses to confirm they are worth what the buyer is paying. A licensed appraiser conducts the appraisal.
- **ARV:** After repaired value. This is the value of a property once it has been remodeled and marketed.
- **Asbestos:** A natural material made up of tiny fibers that is used as thermal insulation. Inhalation of asbestos fibers can lead to asbestosis and mesothelioma.
- **Assignment:** A term used with similar meanings in the law of contracts and in the law of real estate. In both instances, it encompasses the transfer of rights held by one party (the assignor) to another party (the assignee).
- **Attached home:** Any property that is attached to another property. This could be half of a duplex, a condo, or townhome, which is attached to another unit.
- **Backup Offer:** A backup offer can be accepted by the seller but will not go into effect unless the current offer terminates.
- **Bird Dog:** A real estate investing term that refers to someone who spends their time trying to locate properties with substantial investment potential. Usually, the intent is to find properties that are distressed and selling at a discount that can be repaired or remodeled and sold for a sizable profit.
- **Broker:** A real estate broker has different definitions in different states.

Usually, a broker has more experience and education than an agent, which allows them to work independently or manage an office of agents. In most states, real estate agents who are not brokers must work under a broker.

- **BRRRR:** A real estate investment strategy: buy, rehab, rent, refinance, repeat.
- **Building Codes:** See Code violations
- **Buyer's Agent:** A real estate agent who is contractually obligated to help a buyer find a house. Agents also work with buyers without a contract but do not have as much responsibility towards helping that buyer find a house.
- **Carport:** A shelter for a car consisting of a roof supported on posts.
- **Crawlspace:** An area of limited height under a floor, giving access to wiring and plumbing.
- **Central Air Conditioning:** Circulates cool air through a system of supply and return ducts.
- **Cistern:** A reservoir, tank, or container for storing or holding water or other liquid.
- **Close in Escrow:** Means essentially that a real estate transaction has been completed and that the sale is final. An 'escrow' is a common feature of standard real estate transactions. They function as an independent third party that holds all monetary funds and documents until the close of the sale.
- **Closing:** When a house is sold. This usually occurs at a title company or attorney's office.
- **Closing Costs:** Expenses over and above the price of the property in a real estate transaction. Costs incurred include loan origination fees, discount points, appraisal fees, title searches, title insurance, surveys, taxes, deed-recording fees, and credit report charges.
- **Closing Fee:** A fee charged by the Title Company to close a real estate transaction.
- **Code Violations:** Each city, county or state creates or adopts municipal codes. There are codes for building, landscaping, and more. If a property

violates these codes, it could be in violation, which allows the city to fine the property owner until the violation is fixed. If the property was once in adherence to the codes but the codes changed, a property may be grandfathered in. When a property is grandfathered in, they may not be in violation of codes as long as the use of the property does not change.

- **Commercial Real Estate**: Properties that are used for commercial purposes: stores, offices, etc.
- **Commission:** A fee paid to a broker/salesperson in exchange for services in facilitating or completing a sale transaction.
- **Condo:** A condo is like an apartment, but you own the space. A condo may have neighbors above, below, or beside it. The space in the building is owned but not the land in most cases. Condos will have association dues that cover exterior maintenance, landscaping, and common amenities.
- **Contingency:** A clause in the contract that allows the buyer or seller to back out based on certain conditions (inspection, appraisal, etc.).
- **Consignor:** If a buyer cannot qualify for a loan, they may be able to use a consignor. If a consignor signs for a loan, they are responsible for that loan and it can count against their debt-to-income ratio.
- **Conventional:** Refers to a loan that is not insured or guaranteed by the federal government. A conventional, or conforming, mortgage adheres to the guidelines set by Fannie Mae and Freddie Mac. It may have either a fixed or adjustable rate.
- **Counter Offer:** The seller can accept, reject, or counter an offer. When they counter an offer, the seller can change the price, dates, contingencies, or many other terms. Any changes the seller wants must be listed in the counter.
- **Covenants:** Most HOAs have covenants which are rules the properties within the HOAs must follow. They could cover parking, size of the house, outbuildings and much more.
- **Credit:** Credit is how lenders, banks, and other financiers judge a person's ability to pay back a loan. The better your credit, the better chance you have of getting a loan. Late payments, judgments, foreclosures, and

short sales all hurt credit scores. If you never have loan payments, it can also hurt your credit score.

- **Debt-to-Income Ratio:** This is the ratio a lender looks at when qualifying a buyer. The lender looks at the buyers' monthly income versus their monthly debts. The ratio allowed varies based on the type of loan the buyers are getting.
- **Deed in Lieu:** A potential option taken by a mortgagor (a borrower) to avoid foreclosure under which the mortgagor deeds the collateral property (the house) back to the mortgagee (the lender) in exchange for the release of all obligations under the mortgage.
- **Disclosure:** What a seller must tell the buyer of a house. They must disclose any material facts that are known.
- **Double Closing:** The simultaneous purchase and sale of a real estate property involving three parties: the original seller, an investor (middleman), and the final buyer.
- **Due on Sale Clause:** A clause in most mortgages that states when the owner of the house sells the property, the mortgage must be paid off.
- **Earnest Money Deposit:** The money needed for a deposit to buy a property. This can be refundable under certain circumstances based on inspection, loan approvals, appraisal, and other contingencies.
- **Easement:** A right to cross or otherwise use someone else's land for a specified purpose.
- **Eminent domain:** The right of a government or its agent to expropriate private property for public use with payment of compensation.
- **Escrow (held in escrow):** Funds pertaining to a real estate transaction can be held in Escrow. That means the title company, a real estate office, or another party can collect funds and hold them until they are ready to be released. Earnest money, money to repair a house after closing, and much more can be held in escrow.
- **Escrow (house in escrow):** Some states call a house "in escrow" when someone has a contract to buy and the seller accepts the price. This is similar to a house going "under contract." Once the buyer and seller have signed a contract, the seller cannot accept another contract from a new

buyer (except a backup offer) unless the current contract terminates.

- **Fee simple:** A way that real estate may be owned in common law countries and is the highest possible ownership interest that can be held in real property.
- **FHA:** The Federal Housing Administration (FHA) is a U.S. agency that offers mortgage insurance to lenders that are FHA-approved and meet specified qualifications. If a borrower defaults on a loan, the FHA pays the lender a specified claim amount.
- **FHA Loan:** An FHA loan is a mortgage issued by federally qualified lenders and insured by the Federal Housing Administration (FHA). FHA loans are designed for low- to moderate-income borrowers who are unable to make a large down payment.
- **Fix-and-Flip:** A type of real estate investment strategy in which an investor purchases properties with the goal of reselling them for a profit. Profit is generated either through the price appreciation that occurs as a result of a hot housing market and/or from renovations and capital improvements.
- **Fixed-Rate Loan:** A loan with an interest rate that remains the same for the entire term of the loan.
- **Flood Zone:** Geographic areas that FEMA has defined according to varying levels of flood risk. These zones are depicted on a community's Flood Insurance Rate Map (FIRM) or Flood Hazard Boundary Map. Each zone reflects the severity or type of flooding in the area.
- **Forced-Air Heat:** System that uses air as its heat transfer medium. These systems rely on ductwork, vents, and plenums as means of air distribution separate from the actual heating and air conditioning systems.
- **Foreclosure:** If a homeowner stops making payments on their loan, the bank can take the house back. The foreclosure process is different in every state regarding how the bank takes possession of a house.
- **Habitable:** Suitable or good enough to live in.
- **Hard Money:** A short loan typically used for fix-and-flips (usually 6 to 18 months). Hard-money loans normally have interest rates from 10 to

16%.

- **HOA:** Home Owners Association. HOAs are present in most newer subdivisions and regulate neighborhood ordinances or covenants. They may also take care of yard maintenance, common utilities, trash service, and other services for a monthly, quarterly, or yearly fee.
- **Hold Harmless Agreement:** An agreement or contract in which one party agrees to hold the other free from the responsibility for any liability or damage that might arise out of the transaction involved.
- **Homeowner's Insurance:** This protects against damage to a house. Lenders require that homeowners have homeowner's insurance to protect their investment. If your house burns down, homeowner's insurance will cover the cost of rebuilding your house. It also protects against roof damage from storms, water damage from plumbing leaks, wind damage, and vandalism. However, it may not protect against actual floods unless you have separate flood insurance.
- **Hot Water Heat:** Central heating by means of hot water circulated through pipes or radiators.
- **House Hacking:** When you live in one of the multiple units of your investment property as your primary residence and have renters from the other units pay your mortgage and expenses.
- **HUD Home:** When a government-insured loan (FHA) gets foreclosed and the Federal Housing and Urban Development pays the defaulted loan off and then puts the house on the market.
- **ILC:** Improvement Location Certificate (ILC) An ILC is not a survey but a certificate used in order for mortgage and/or title companies to have some assurance that the improvements to a property are not encroaching into an easement or beyond the deed lines.
- **Industrial Real Estate:** Properties that are used for storage, manufacturing, and possibly commercial as well.
- **Inspection:** Most contracts allow a buyer to conduct an inspection on a house, which allows the buyers to look for problems or code violations.
- **Interest Rate:** A rate which is charged or paid for the use of money. An interest rate is often expressed as an annual percentage of the principal.

- **Leach Field:** Subsurface wastewater disposal facilities used to remove contaminants and impurities from the liquid that emerges after anaerobic digestion in a septic tank.
- **Lead-Based Paint:** The U.S. government defines "lead-based paint" as any "paint, surface coating that contains lead equal to or exceeding one milligram per square centimeter (1.0 mg/cm2) or 0.5% by weight."
- **Lease:** A contract outlining the terms under which one party agrees to rent property owned by another party. It guarantees the lessee, the tenant, use of an asset and guarantees the lessor, the property owner or landlord, regular payments from the lessee for a specified number of months or years.
- **Leasehold:** The holding of property by lease.
- **Landlord:** Someone who owns a property that they rent out to a tenant.
- **Legal Description:** The geographical description of a real estate property for the purpose of identifying the property for legal transactions. A legal description of the property unambiguously identifies the location, boundaries, and any existing easements on the property.
- **Lender:** A lender is someone who works for a bank or mortgage company and is the direct contact for the buyer of a house.
- **Listing:** A house that is up for sale.
- **Loan Payoff:** A statement prepared by a lender showing the remaining terms on a mortgage or other loan. The payoff statement shows the remaining loan balance, number of payments, and the interest rate.
- **Loan Term:** Period over which a loan agreement is in force and before or at the end of which the loan should either be repaid or renegotiated for another term.
- **Lot:** A parcel of land that a house, duplex, or multi-unit property is located on.
- **Material Fact:** A fact that, if known, might have caused a buyer or seller of real estate to make a different decision regarding remaining in a contract or to the price paid or received.
- **Mixed-Use Real Estate:** Properties that are used for a variety of uses, usually residential and commercial.

- **MLS:** The Multiple Listing Service (MLS) is a marketing database set up by a group of cooperating real estate brokers. It also is a mechanism for listing brokers to offer compensation to buyer brokers who bring a buyer for their listed property.
- **Mortgage:** A type of loan used to buy houses with a portion of the payment going towards interest and principal each month. Money may also be collected every month for property taxes and homeowner's insurance.
- **Mortgage Broker:** A mortgage broker is a lender who can shop loans from multiple banks. Sometimes, a mortgage broker can get a better deal for buyers by checking with different banks. In other cases, a lender can get a better deal because they work directly for the bank and there is no middle man.
- **Multifamily:** A multifamily or multi-unit property has more than one unit on the same property. An apartment complex or a duplex could be multifamily if they are on the same lot.
- **New Construction:** Refers to site preparation for, and construction of, entirely new structures, whether or not the site was previously occupied.
- **Offer to buy:** A buyer makes an offer to buy a house with a contract. The contract lists all the terms, financing, and contingencies. The offer means nothing unless the seller accepts it by signing the contract.
- **Origination Fee:** A fee charged by a lender on entering into a loan agreement to cover the cost of processing the loan.
- **Owner Occupant:** A resident of a property who also holds the title to that property.
- **Patio Home:** A patio home is usually a free-standing house, but the landscaping and exterior is maintained by an association.
- **Pending status:** When a house goes under contract and the seller does not want to accept a backup offer.
- **Pre-qualification:** Most sellers require a buyer be pre-qualified before they will accept an offer. A buyer must get pre-qualified with a lender who checks credit income and other financial information.
- **Prepayment Penalty:** A clause in a mortgage contract stating that a

penalty will be assessed if the mortgage is prepaid within a certain timeframe. The penalty is based on a percentage of the remaining mortgage balance or a certain number of months' worth of interest.

· **Principal:** The portion of a mortgage payment that goes toward paying off the balance of a loan. Part of your payment will also go toward interest.

· **Private Money:** Money borrowed from private individuals. Example: A loan from a parent to buy a house.

· **Pro-rated:** To divide or distribute a sum of money proportionately.

· **Property Disclosure:** A disclosure the seller completes describing all material facts they know about a house.

· **Property Management:** When a landlord uses a company to manage their rental property instead of doing it themselves.

· **Property Taxes:** A levy on the value of a property. The tax is levied by the governing authority of the jurisdiction in which the property is located.

· **PUD:** A planned-unit development (PUD) is a type of building development and a regulatory process. As a building development, it is a designed grouping of both varied and compatible land uses, such as housing, recreation, commercial centers, and industrial parks, all within one contained development or subdivision.

· **Radon:** A colorless, odorless, radioactive element in the noble gas group. It is produced by the radioactive decay of radium and occurs in minute amounts in soil, rocks, and the air near the ground.

· **Realtor:** A Realtor belongs to the National Association of Realtors (NAR) and is also a licensed real estate agent. NAR is a trade association for agents.

· **Recording Fees:** The fee charged by a government agency for registering or recording a real estate purchase or sale so that it becomes a matter of public record. Recording fees are generally charged by the county.

· **REIT:** Real estate investment trust (REIT) is a company that owns, and in most cases operates, income-producing real estate. REITs own many types of commercial real estate, ranging from office and apartment buildings to warehouses, hospitals, shopping centers, hotels, and timberlands.

- **Rent to Own:** An alternative way to buy a house: a rent-to-own agreement, also called lease option. When buyers sign this kind of contract, they agree to rent the house for a set amount of time before exercising an option to purchase the property when or before the lease expires.
- **REO:** Real estate owned, or REO, is a term used in the United States to describe a class of property owned by a lender.
- **Residential Real Estate:** Properties that are zoned for residential use. You may not be able to legally run a business out of them.
- **REI:** Real Estate Investors
- **Senior Living:** Some subdivisions are designated for seniors only (usually 65 or older). Only seniors can buy or rent properties in those areas.
- **Septic System:** A septic system is a type of OWTS (Onsite wastewater treatment system).
- **Settlement Statement:** An itemized document of services and charges relating to the closing of a property.
- **SFR:** Single Family Residence. This is a house that is zoned for one family to live in (zoning may allow more unrelated people to live in the property). The house can be detached (standalone) or attached (a neighbor connected), but the property comes with land ownership rights.
- **Short Sale:** A short sale occurs when the mortgage company allows a homeowner to sell a house but pay less to the mortgage company than what they are owed. Mortgage companies allow this in some cases when the homeowners are behind on payments because it is faster and cheaper than a foreclosure.
- **Space Heater:** A self contained appliance, usually electric, for heating an enclosed room.
- **Staging:** The act of preparing a private residence for sale in the real estate marketplace. The goal of staging is to make a house appealing to the highest number of potential buyers.

- **Survey:** A process carried out to determine property lines and define true property corners of a parcel of land described in a deed. It also indicates the extent of any easements or encroachments and may show the limitations imposed on the property by state or local regulations.
- **Tax exempt:** Some organizations, like churches and non-profits, are exempt from paying property taxes. In some areas, seniors pay fewer property taxes. In some areas locals pay less taxes than those who live out-of-state.
- **Tax Lien:** When homeowners stop paying property taxes, the state can place a tax lien against the house or even sell it at a tax sale. If you have a mortgage, the mortgage company will usually pay the taxes if the homeowner does not.
- **Tenant:** Anyone who leases a property instead of purchasing it.
- **Title Company:** A company that provides title insurance and many times provides closing services for real estate transactions.
- **Title Insurance:** Insurance that guarantees a property has no debts or liens against it when sold.
- **Townhouse**: A townhouse is like a condo, but there aren't any neighbors above or below the unit.
- **Transactional Funding:** A form of short-term, hard-money lending which allows a wholesaler the opportunity to purchase a property with none of his/her funds, provided that there is already an end buyer in place to purchase the property from the wholesaler within a short time frame, usually 2-5 days.
- **Turn-key Rental Property:** A fully renovated house or apartment building that an investor can purchase and immediately rent out.
- **Under Contract:** A house goes under contract when a buyer and seller accept the contract terms. A new buyer cannot buy a house that is under contract unless the accepted offer terminates.
- **USDA:** A USDA home loan from the USDA loan program, also known as the USDA Rural Development Guaranteed Housing Loan Program, is a mortgage loan offered to rural property owners by the United States Department of Agriculture.

- **VA:** A mortgage loan in the United States guaranteed by the U.S. Department of Veterans Affairs (VA). The loan may be issued by qualified lenders. The VA loan was designed to offer long-term financing to eligible American veterans or their surviving spouses (provided they do not remarry).
- **Water Rights:** The right to make use of the water from a stream, lake, or irrigation canal.
- **Well Water:** An excavation or structure created in the ground by digging, driving, boring, or drilling to access groundwater in underground aquifers.
- **Wholesaling:** A real estate wholesaler contracts with a house seller, markets the house to potential buyers, and then assigns the contract to the buyer.
- **Zoning:** How the city, state or county classifies the use of land.

# About Mark Ferguson

I created InvestFourMore to help people become real estate investors, either as rental property owners, flippers, wholesalers, real estate agents, or even note owners. You may see pictures of me with my Lamborghini. It is a 1999 Lamborghini Diablo, which I bought in 2014. I had dreamed of owning a Lamborghini since I was a kid, and one of my public goals I wrote about was buying one in 2014. Accomplishing that goal and being held accountable by my readers was an awesome experience. I even make sure I buy my cars below market value. I bought this car for $126,000, and it is worth about double that two years later.

The car is not a flashy marketing ploy but a reward for hard work and to signify that we really can have what we want if we put our mind to it.

# How did I get started?

I have been a licensed real estate agent since 2001. My father has been a Realtor since 1978, and I was surrounded by real estate in my youth. I remember sleeping under my dad's desk when I was three while he worked tirelessly in the office. Surprisingly—or maybe not—I never wanted anything to do with real estate. I graduated from the University of Colorado with a degree in business finance in 2001. I could not find a job that was appealing to me, so I reluctantly decided to work with my father part-time in real estate. Fifteen years later, I am sure glad I got into the real estate business!

Even though I had help getting started in real estate, I did not find success until I was in the business for five years. I tried to follow my father's path, which did not mesh well with me. I found my own path as an REO agent, and my career took off. Many people think I had a huge advantage working with my father, and he was a great help, but I think that I actually would have been more successful sooner if I had been working on my own, forced to find my own path.

Now I own a real estate brokerage. I fix and flip 20-30 houses per year, and I own 20 long-term rentals. I love real estate and investing because of the money you can make and the freedom running your own business brings. I also love big goals, and one of those goals is my plan to purchase 100 rental properties by January 2023.

I started InvestFourMore in March 2013 with the primary objective of providing information about investing in long-term rentals. I was not a writer at any time in my life until I started this blog. In fact, I had not written anything besides a basic letter since college. Readers who have been with me from the beginning may remember how tough it was to read my first articles, with all the typos and poor grammar (I know it still isn't perfect!). My goal has always been to provide incredible information, not to provide perfect articles with perfect grammar.

The name "InvestFourMore" is a play on words, indicating that it is possible to finance more than four properties. The blog provides articles on financing, finding, buying, rehabbing, and renting out rental properties. The blog also discusses mortgage pay down strategies, fix and flips, advice for real estate agents, and many other real estate related topics.

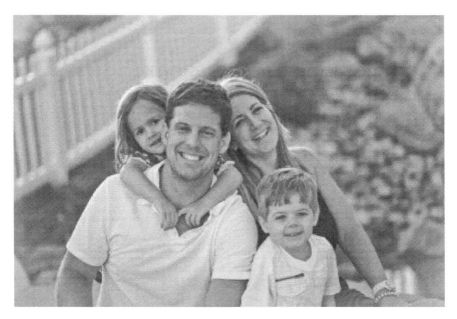

I live in Greeley Colorado, which is about 50 miles North of Denver. I married my beautiful wife Jeni in 2008, and we have twins who turned seven in June of 2018. Jeni was a Realtor when we met in 2005 but has since put her license on ice while she takes care of the twins. Jeni loves to sew and makes children's dresses under the label Kaiya Papaya.

Outside of work, I love to travel, play golf, and work/play with my cars.

# Acknowledgements

I could not be where I am at without a lot of help from many people. I tried to go at it alone when I first started in the real estate business. I thought I was smart and could figure it out without anyone else telling me how to do things. I let my ego make some very bad decisions for me. Here are a few people I must thank.

My dad, Jim Ferguson, who has been an entrepreneur most of his life. He taught me a lot about flipping houses and being a real estate agent. He was very patient with me when I was not patient with myself.

My wife Jeni, who has been incredibly supportive through the good times and the bad. The year I met her, I made $28,000 (2006). Things were not easy in the beginning, and breaking out of the grind and finding my way in real estate was a struggle for me. She was there for me when I started to find success and was working 80 or more hours per week to get everything done. She put up with me working on vacations and never really taking time off in the beginning. Luckily, I was able to create a business where we can now take real vacations without me working. I now rarely work more than 40 hours per week (if that), and we have a wonderful family. Most importantly, she supported my car addiction!

Justin Gesso is my team manager and keeps our team together. He works with our agents, helps with the blog, helps with my coaching programs, helps with my books, and keeps me sane. Thank you, Justin!

Nikki True has been my assistant/project manager for 9 years. She was the person who helped me stop working 80 hours per week and take control of my life. She has always been extremely proactive, has an incredible work ethic, and has been willing to work on any project. She is now helping me with my flipping business and is doing an amazing job.

Jack Canfield Coaching is a program I took a few years ago. It gave me the confidence to buy my father's business, take the blog to new levels, hire more staff, and take more chances. Not only that, but I gained more freedom, reduced my stress, and am a happier person because of it.

Josh Elledge with Upend PR has helped me be featured on numerous major media sites, like the Washington Post, Yahoo, Zillow, The Street, Forbes and many more.